BALLAD

★ ★ ★ ★ ★ OF THE ★ ★ ★ ★ ★

GREEN BERET

THE LIFE AND WARS OF STAFF SERGEANT BARRY SADLER

FROM THE VIETNAM WAR AND POP STARDOM TO MURDER

AND AN UNSOLVED, VIOLENT DEATH

MARC LEEPSON

STACKPOLE
BOOKS

GUILFORD, CONNECTICUT

Published by Stackpole Books
An imprint of Globe Pequot
Trade Division of The Rowman & Littlefield Publishing Group, Inc.
4501 Forbes Boulevard, Suite 200, Lanham, Maryland 20706
www.rowman.com

Distributed by
NATIONAL BOOK NETWORK
800-462-6420

British Library Cataloguing in Publication Information Available

Library of Congress Cataloging-in-Publication Data Available

ISBN 978-0-8117-1749-6 (hardcover)
ISBN 978-0-8117-6568-8 (e-book)

♾️™ The paper used in this publication meets the minimum requirements of American National Standard for Information Sciences—Permanence of Paper for Printed Library Materials, ANSI/ NISO Z39.48-1992

To my fellow Vietnam War veterans and in memory of those who made the ultimate sacrifice in that war

CONTENTS

PROLOGUE

A SOLDIER AT HEART

"Barry was one of the nicest guys you ever met in your life and had one of the biggest hearts you'd ever seen. Made the best friend you could possibly ask for—and the worst enemy that you didn't want."
—EARL OWENS[1]

When the telephone rings at 6:20 in the morning, the news rarely is good. The news wasn't very good at all when the bedside phone at Nashville literary agent Robbie Robison's suburban home bolted him awake before dawn on Saturday morning, December 2, 1978. His client and friend Barry Sadler—the former Green Beret staff sergeant whose song "The Ballad of the Green Berets" was the No. 1 hit single of the year 1966—was on the other end of the line.

Sadler, age thirty-eight, was nursing a mug of coffee in a Shoney's restaurant in Hendersonville, a Nashville suburb. It had been a long, violent, memorable night.

"Robbie, it went down last night," Sadler told his half-awake manager.

"What went down?"

"I shot him. I shot that dude. Would you come out here and let's talk?"[2]

Sometime between 10:30 and 10:50 the night before, on Friday, December 1, 1978, after an evening of drinking that started in a bar called the Natchez Trace Lounge, Barry Sadler shot and killed a washed-up country music singer/songwriter named Lee Emerson Bellamy. Barry gunned him down in the parking lot of the Knollwood Apartments in one of Nashville's quiet suburbs. Bellamy, a fifty-six-year-old World War II veteran whose police record was almost as long as his recording credits, had made the mistake of trying to barge in on Barry Sadler and his female companion, Darlene Sharpe, Bellamy's former girlfriend. For weeks Bellamy had been harassing and threatening the twenty-five-year-old waitress and would-be country music singer, as well as her famous former Green Beret friend.

On this night, though, Lee Bellamy was not up to no good. He was looking for some recording equipment he'd left in the apartment. When Barry Sadler realized it was Bellamy ringing the apartment's doorbell, he bolted out the sliding patio doors—armed with a .38-caliber Smith & Wesson revolver and a nightstick given to him by the Chicago Police Department in 1966. When Bellamy saw the former Special Forces soldier, he hotfooted it back to his dilapidated, white 1970 Ford cargo van, jumped in the driver's seat, and grabbed his keys. Sadler then ran up to the van.

That's when Lee Bellamy made a literally fatal mistake. He dropped his car keys at his feet near the gas pedal. Then Bellamy looked up and turned to his left. The last thing he ever saw was Barry Sadler firing a shot with his .38 through the driver's-side window. The bullet hit Lee Bellamy directly between the eyes. The shot propelled him backward and he landed between the van's two front seats—the only ones in the vehicle. Barry then walked around to the other side of the van, pulled the sliding door open, climbed inside, and tossed the .38 on the floor at the bleeding Bellamy's feet. Then he commenced to beat Bellamy with the nightstick.

Minutes after the shot rang out, eyewitnesses saw Darlene Sharpe run out of the apartment into the parking lot, huddle with Barry on the passenger side of the van, and then walk back inside. She came back out a few minutes later and handed Barry another gun, a .32-caliber Mauser automatic pistol. He ejected a round from the Mauser's chamber and jacked a new one in, making it appear as if the gun had recently been fired.

At 11:14 p.m. Darlene Sharpe went back inside her one-bedroom apartment and called 911 to report a shooting. When K-9 Officer Johnny Lucas arrived on the scene a few minutes later, he found Barry and Darlene in the parking lot. Lucas asked Barry to take a seat in the back of his cruiser. Barry told Lucas that he confronted Lee Bellamy after he had threatened Darlene, and that he thought Bellamy was going for a gun, so he pulled out his .32 and shot—to miss. If he had aimed to kill, Barry told the police officer, he would have done just that. Somehow, Barry said, Bellamy's gun (actually, Barry's .38) went off in the car and a bullet from that weapon wound up between his eyes.

"I saw him get into the passenger side of the van," Barry said. "I was coming up on him and I said, 'Stop.' Then he came up with what looked like a piece. I got mine out and I again said, 'Stop.' Then he began to turn. I'm an expert marksman but I aimed in front of him so as to hit the glass. I shot one time and the glass exploded and he lurched backwards. I went over and climbed inside with him and I saw blood but I thought it was where the glass had hit him."

Barry neglected to mention whaling Bellamy with the nightstick or throwing down the .38.[3]

Two more patrol cars arrived, as did Nashville homicide detective Jim Sledge, who was in the area working the midnight shift. A blunt-talking, solidly built, stocky former Marine, Sledge had been on the homicide squad for about two years. In that relatively short time, he'd investigated nearly two dozen murders. He was about to get involved in the biggest murder case of his career.

An ambulance came screaming into the parking lot and quickly sped Bellamy, who was still breathing, off to nearby St. Thomas Hospital. He was pronounced dead at 6:55 a.m. the next day, about a half hour after Barry Sadler had called Robbie Robison from Shoney's.

The police took Barry and Darlene to St. Thomas, where they sat down with Jim Sledge in the hospital's quiet room. It was around midnight. Darlene was "very upset," Sledge reported. She told him that she didn't know anything about the shooting. Barry was more forthcoming, giving Sledge his version of the events. At 2:30 a.m. Barry made a formal statement and signed it at the Criminal Investigations Division headquarters in downtown Nashville.

After he fired his weapon, Barry said in the statement, "I went over and climbed inside with him and I saw blood but I thought it was where the glass had hit him. I told Miss Sharpe to call the police, which she did." He tried to "assist" Bellamy, Barry said, since "his breathing was raspy." When Barry got in the van, he said, "I saw a piece on the floor which I left there until the police arrived."

Jim Sledge did not arrest Barry Sadler or Darlene Sharpe that night. He spent the next six months investigating the physical evidence and interviewing witnesses. The detective work paid off. Sledge took Barry into custody on June 1, 1979, at the bar in the Commodore Lounge at the Vanderbilt Holiday Inn. The charge: second-degree murder. Sledge arrested Darlene the same day and charged her with accessory to murder.

Barry Sadler hired the top criminal defense attorney in Nashville, Joe Binkley Sr., to defend him. There never was a trial. On May 8, 1980, Barry pleaded guilty to voluntary manslaughter and Darlene to being an accessary after the fact. The judge gave the former Green Beret four to five years and his companion a year in jail. On September 26, 1980, Barry Sadler's sentence was reduced to two years' probation and thirty days in the county workhouse, and Darlene Sharp's to one year probation. Barry served twenty-eight days at the minimum-security workhouse and then walked out a free man.

That sordid episode—Barry Sadler called it "the worst experience of [his] life"—came at the lowest point in the life of the formerly unknown thirty-nine-year-old former Green Beret staff sergeant. Barry was a high school dropout from a broken family who became a media sensation in February 1966 when his old-fashioned, pro-military "The Ballad of the Green Berets" became the best-selling record in the country. The single would go on to sell some nine million copies; the song's album sold more than two million. The records earned Barry fame—and about half a million dollars in royalties in 1966 alone.

But the fame was fleeting. The army took Barry off regular duties and sent him around the country as a human recruiting poster. Barry hated it. He got out of the U.S. Army as soon as the term of his enlistment ended, in May of 1967, and moved to Tucson with his wife and two young sons. The plan: to make a living as a musician and an actor. But Barry never had another record even approaching a hit song. His acting career went nowhere. He opened a bar that leaked money. He tried running a battery store. That venture fizzled.

The family moved to Nashville in 1973, where Barry tried to jump-start his musical career. He couldn't. By 1978 with the royalty money long gone, Barry carried on open love affairs and drank to excess.

Barry Sadler's second act—as the author of a slew of pulp fiction novels—began soon after the Lee Bellamy episode. But the drinking and womanizing continued. Before long Sadler's wife, Lavona, decided they could no longer live together, and he moved out of their modest suburban home. In January 1984 Barry went into a kind of exile, moving to Guatemala and settling into a small ranch outside Guatemala City. Rumors flew that he was running a mercenary operation, training anti-communist Nicaraguan guerrilla fighters (the Contras), and conducting international arms deals. But he was mainly churning out books and drinking and carousing in his four-bedroom country villa and in the bars of Guatemala City.

On September 7, 1988, Barry Sadler took a bullet to the head in a taxi cab in Guatemala City after a day and night of drinking. Details of the shooting are murky. The authorities said he shot himself in a drunken accident. Others claimed it was a robbery or an attempted assassination by communist guerrillas or personal enemies.

He was brought back to the United States and spent the next sixteen months as a brain-damaged quadriplegic in three VA hospitals. Barry Sadler died on November 5, 1989, four days after his forty-ninth birthday.

The startling but short-lived success Barry Sadler had in 1966 turned out to be a very sharp double-edged sword. After overcoming a difficult childhood, serving honorably for four years in the U. S. Air Force and five more in the army—and after surviving a five-month tour of duty in the Vietnam War—Barry Sadler was on the road to an honorable, if under-the-radar, military career. But "The Ballad of the Green Berets" uprooted him from the military life that he had envisioned.

Soon, he was broke, unhappy, and stumbling along life's path. He ran with a rough crowd. He also read voraciously and wrote twenty-nine pulp fiction books. His dry wit charmed many a man—and many women.

"Nobody could tell a joke like Barry did, often in dialect," a friend from the 1980s, Jay Diamond, said. "He was the best storyteller I ever knew, and one of the funniest."[4]

Barry's marriage, though, was dysfunctional at best. He killed Lee Bellamy and all but got away with it. He fled the country to live a wild life in Central America. He wound up with a bullet in his head in the middle of the night and died after more than a year confined to hospital beds barely able to speak and unable to walk or feed himself.

The man who in 1966 was the Audie Murphy of the Vietnam War—a handsome, famous, charismatic war hero made into a showbiz celebrity—had been undone because he couldn't handle the fame that his creation unleashed.

"The Ballad of the Green Berets" is very much alive today, more than fifty years after its sensational birth. "It became the song of the century as far as Special Forces is concerned," said Steve Bruno, who went through Green Beret medic training with Barry.[5]

"The Ballad," the theme song for the U.S. Army Special Forces, is played for Special Forces trainees at Fort Bragg, and is heard at every Special Forces reunion and at more than one Green Beret's funeral. "The "Ballad" also was the only notable and popular pro-military song to come out of the entire Vietnam War. And Barry became arguably the most famous American who served in that controversial war.

And yet "The Ballad of the Green Berets" all but destroyed the man who created it.

"In many ways the success of that song was the worst thing that ever happened to him," said Jim Morris, a writer and a former Green Beret who edited Barry's last two books. "Without that, I have the feeling that he would have stayed in the army. He would have been happier."[6]

Barry "looked at that song as a curse in a lot of ways," Sadler's onetime Nashville drinking buddy Bill Parrish said. "He said all he ever wanted to do was be a soldier."[7]

"He's a born soldier, a dedicated soldier," Barry's mother, Bebe, said in 1988. "He told me, 'That's what I'm good at. Let me be one. I'm a soldier at heart.'"[8]

The song "kept him forever from doing what he liked doing—soldiering," Lavona Sadler said. "He wasn't a happy man."[9]

"Barry never had a carefree life," his Nashville friend Gary Sizemore said. "Like people with a remarkable mind who aren't using it in a way that pleases them, he was never happy. He would have been happier if he'd never written that song."[10]

"I wish," Barry told his friend Robert M. Powers in 1971, "that I'd never, ever written that stupid song."[11]

CHAPTER 1
TOUGH GUY

"Sometimes they had nothing to eat except ketchup and bread."
—LAVONA SADLER

Barry Allen Sadler was born on November 1, 1940, in the southeastern New Mexico city of Carlsbad. In his 1967 autobiography, *I'm A Lucky One*, Barry briefly speculated about his ancestry, saying that he had an idea that the Sadlers were "of German descent," with "a touch of Black Irish."

A genealogical chart indicates that Barry's oldest Sadler relative, William Sharp Sadler, was born in 1778 in South Carolina. The chart also shows his mother's and father's forbearers were born in France, Canada, and England, but not Germany. The most common of his ancestors' surnames are French and English in origin: Bonin, Borel, DeRouen, Hayes, Littlefield, Stanley, and Taliaferro.

One of the Littlefields, Barry's maternal grandmother, Ethel Bell Littlefield, came to an untimely end. On April 14, 1928, at age thirty, she was shot to death by a man named S. J. King at a filling station she operated in the tiny North Texas town of Memphis. King then committed suicide with the same pistol he used to shoot Ethel Littlefield to death.[1]

In his book Sadler painted an idyllic picture of his earliest days growing up in the high-desert oasis town on the Pecos River best known for the nearby Carlsbad Caverns. He wrote that he and his family—his father, John Bright Sadler, who was twenty-nine when Barry came along; mother, Blanche Handsford "Bebe" Littlefield Sadler, age twenty-two; and four-year-old brother, Bob—enjoyed the good life on a twenty-one-acre farm called Happy Valley just outside town. His father, who had studied at Arizona State University, Barry wrote, was from Phoenix,[2] as was his mother, whom he believed took the name "Bebe" because she admired the popular, and Texas-born, Hollywood silent film actress Bebe Daniels.

John Sadler "developed a successful plumbing and electrical business in Carlsbad," his son wrote.[3] With that success Sadler senior bought several farms in and around the city, where the Sadler boys spent their earliest years. "My brother and I did some of the farm work," Barry said. "Dad worked hard himself and believed that everybody else should work."

Dad also was a former boxer and a "very strong man." His sons would inherit that physical strength—in spades. Bob Sadler spent many years working as a miner in New Mexico and Colorado. His younger brother, at around five foot eight and 200 pounds, "was, pound for pound, one of the strongest men I've ever known," Bill Parrish said. When he first met Barry in the late seventies, Parrish said, "he could get in the squat position and pick up a 200-pound man by the ankles and stand up with him with his arms extended straight."[4]

In 1945, when Barry was five years old, his parents divorced. On January 11, 1948, John B. Sadler died of cancer at his home in Carlsbad at age thirty-six. The Sadler boys, aged seven and twelve, fell into what Barry called "a wandering life with our mother." They banged around the Southwest, stopping in a slew of places in New Mexico, Arizona, California, and Colorado. "They moved around a lot," John Buchan, another friend from Sadler's days in Nashville, said. "Barry said it was a pretty chaotic life."[5]

Bebe Sadler, Barry wrote, "had few skills but plenty of courage and determination." She managed restaurants and bars, he said, some of them in "gambling casinos."

His mother managing restaurants and bars—sometimes in the occasional gambling establishment—and his father running a big plumbing and electrical business was the story Barry Sadler chose to tell for the record. But he gave different versions to friends and newspaper reporters.

He told a *Time* magazine reporter in 1966, for example, that his father was an "itinerant plumber" and his mother a "barmaid."[6] And, in fact, the 1940 U.S. Census lists John Sadler's occupation as "plumber's helper" and his place of employment as a "plumbers shop." The census also has the family living—not on a ranch—but in the Silver Dollar Apartments on West Bronson Street in the city of Carlsbad.[7]

Then there is the matter of his mother's occupation. At different times later in life, Barry Sadler told friends that his mother was an itinerant gambler, a poker shill, and a sometimes prostitute. In April of 1966, for example, when a young woman asked him how he learned to play the guitar, he replied: "in a whorehouse in New Mexico where my mother was working."[8]

Barry "told me on one occasion—and I don't know whether it was under the influence or it just came out—that his mother was a prostitute," Jimmy Walker, who served with Barry in Vietnam, said. "It seems to me that he [said] he sort of had multiple 'mothers' who were sisters in prostitution and they took good care of him."[9]

Bebe Sadler "was a prostitute," a woman who knew Barry and his family as a teenager in Leadville, Colorado, said. "You would see her at two in the morning in Clyde's Café after the bars closed. She [and other prostitutes] would be in there with men. The guys would have a cup of coffee and buy steaks for the women. That was the fifties in Leadville."[10]

Barry told his old Nashville friend Bill Parrish that his mother "was a shill in poker games and a prostitute growing up around mining areas in New Mexico and Leadville, Colorado," Parrish said in 2015. "He said he never really had a mother."[11]

It's all but certain, then, that Bebe Sadler plied the world's oldest profession. She "probably" was, her daughter-in-law Lavona said, "but I don't know. I do know she was a gambler and hung in the bars and she was married quite a few times."[12]

Bebe, Barry, and Bob settled in the two-mile-high Colorado Front Range Mineral Belt city of Leadville in the heart of the Rocky Mountains when Barry was about ten years old. The onetime booming gold-mining, and then silver-mining, town of the 1870s hardly resembled its former self in the early 1950s. Its population had dwindled from more than 40,000 at its peak to some 5,000 hearty souls. It was a gritty, mostly blue-collar lead-mining town that happened to be the highest incorporated city in the country. Perched at just over 10,000 feet amid the Rocky Mountains' highest peaks on the Continental Divide, Leadville is surrounded by high alpine forests and glacial lakes and the ski resorts of Vail, Copper Mountain, Breckenridge, and Aspen. Snowfall averages more than ten feet a year.

Leadville "still had the rough edge that had earned it a reputation as the 'wickedest town in the West'" when the Sadlers lived there, Gillian Klucas wrote in her history of Leadville. "Transient miners could choose from a number of raucous bars. It was said that distributors sold more alcohol to Leadville's liquor stores and bars than to any other Colorado small town."[13]

"When I grew up in Leadville" in the 1950s, "it was a rowdy town," Thomas Gomez, a younger brother of Barry's best friend, Delfino ("Del") Gomez, said. "Harrison Avenue had bars on every corner. When we'd go out for Halloween, my parents would always tell us to say away from the bars."[14]

It appears that Bebe and her two boys lived in an apartment in the building that housed one of Leadville's oldest and most famous drinking establishments, the Pioneer Club Bar and Cafe on West Second Street, which had been built in 1882. The Pioneer—which was nothing much to look at on the outside, but retained its two ornate bars (complete with bullet holes), glassware cabinets, and other trappings inside—featured a dance floor on the ground level. The Pioneer also housed a brothel on the second floor with private rooms that men patronized using a separate entrance.[15]

The colorful Hazel Gillette "Ma" Brown ran the place until her death in 1970. "Everybody in town knew of Ma Brown," said Howard Tritz, who was born in 1936 in Leadville and grew up there. "The Pioneer was a brothel for years. By the sixties it had dwindled down to one or two working ladies."[16]

Ma Brown, who sported cat's-eye glasses studded with diamonds, had a reputation as a madam with a soft spot for wayward boys. "She still had a brothel in the 1960s and had girls at the bar," according to Janice Fox, the local history coordinator at the Lake County Library in

Leadville. "And Barry's brother was the manager of the bar" in the mid-1960s. Ma Brown "must have taken [Barry] under her wing as well. She was wonderful to the boys she raised."[17]

"There were no luxuries" growing up in Leadville, Barry said in his book. "But we didn't miss any meals." That was the *I'm A Lucky One* version of life with Bebe as a single mother. But, again, Barry told a different story about his childhood to friends and family. "He told me they didn't have anything," Lavona said. "I thought he was making it up." There were times, she said, when Barry told her that "they had nothing to eat except ketchup and bread."

Barry wrote that he loved the outdoors, especially hunting. "My brother says the first gun I fired was a shotgun," he said. "When I was nine or ten, I was shooting rabbits and trying for bobcats in the cliffs around Leadville. I shot grouse on the wing with a .22-caliber pistol. In fact, I was a better shot with a pistol at fifty yards that most men are with a rifle."[18] Weapons would play an integral part in his life until the day Barry Sadler died in November 1989 after taking a gunshot wound to the head in September 1988.

Music, too, was always part of Barry's life. His earliest memories included listening to Cowboy, Western, and Mexican music on the radio. As a boy, he played the flute, harmonica, drums, and guitar—although he never took a lesson and could not read music. He told a reporter that he learned to play the drums in honky-tonks where his mother worked. "I wasn't no [Gene] Krupa, but I could get by," Barry said of his drumming ability.[19] Barry's favorite tunes growing up included "Cielito Lindo" ("Ai, Yi, Yi, Yi"), "La Cucaracha," "Deep in the Heart of Texas," "Home on the Range," and "Oh, Bury Me Not on the Lone Prairie."

When life with Bebe was too much—as it often was—Barry sought refuge in several ways. One was reading. "Barry told me he started reading at age three as an escape," Bill Parrish said, and that he became a lifelong voracious reader.[20] Barry also sought refuge with Ma Brown. In fact, Barry listed Hazel Brown of 118 W. 2nd St. in Leadville as one of his credit references on a military security form he filled out in 1963.[21]

Barry also spent a good deal of time in the welcoming home of Del Gomez, who became his best friend. Barry spent many hours and days in the Gomez house with Delfino's father, Eppie, his mother, Cidelia, and their ten children—five boys and five girls. He called Cidelia Gomez "Mama" and loved her cooking, including his favorite meal, chili and beans.

"They were extremely close; they were like brothers," said Delfino's daughter Loretta Sparkman. "Barry would spend the night at my grandma's. She said it was because his mom wasn't really all that great of a mom. Sometimes it would be for a couple of days. Sometimes it would be for overnight or he'd come after school and hang out." Barry and Delfino "would go downtown and hang out with all the girls. And go out on double dates."[22]

Barry—whom the Gomez family called "Bear"—"spent a lot of time at my home," Tommy Gomez said. "He didn't have what I would call a real home. He was at my home at least four to five days a week. He would eat with us. He spent many holidays with us: Christmas, Thanksgiving, and Easter. He was very, very close to my mom and dad. They became more or less surrogate parents to Bear. He would share everything with them."[23]

He and Delfino "were both from the wrong side of the tracks," Barry wrote in his book, "had been in all sorts of scrapes together and liked each other a lot." Barry, who had a lifelong affinity for foreign languages, learned to speak Spanish during the countless hours he spent in the Gomez home.

"He learned that from Delfino," Lavona Sadler said of her husband's proficiency in Spanish. "Barry was always over at his house where he learned to speak fluent Spanish."

Barry and Del often hung out with a handful of other Leadville teenagers. "Bear was always wearing Levi's and he'd always have a leather jacket and engineer boots and he wore his hair in a pompadour," Tommy Gomez said. "At that time he had almost white, blond hair. Bear was a tough guy and nobody messed with him."

Barry, Del, and the boys got into their share of mischief and trouble with the law. But were they juvenile delinquents? Howard Tritz, for one, didn't think so. "They looked like ordinary kids," he said of Barry and Delfino. "Maybe all the kids looked like that in Leadville. They didn't look that bad. I'd call 'em rascals."

Still, there were joyrides, hubcap stealing, lots of other mischief, and petty theft. Blowing up the occasional phone booth with a string of M60 firecrackers. Drinking. Smoking cigarettes. Getting into fights in Leadville and in the nearby town of Buena Vista.

"Bear was always the tough guy," a high school friend said. "Nobody messed with Bear and nobody messed with Bear's friends. If you were one of Bear's friends, nobody messed with you."[24]

Tommy Gomez said he never saw Barry hit anyone. But, he said, "if they came looking for it, I'm sure he'd take care of it."

On occasion someone did mess with Barry, who—he admitted in his autobiography—was quick to anger and quicker with his fists. "Somebody would say something that I thought reflected on my family, and before I knew it I'd be hitting him," Barry wrote. "I couldn't pick unimportant people. I'd always have to tangle with the son of the head of the Chamber of Commerce or the brother of the Mayor, people like that, and I was soon very unpopular with the big people in town and known as a 'rotten' kid."

Barry started at Leadville Senior High School as a tenth grader in the fall of 1955. He completed tenth and eleventh grade there, but did not exactly excel academically. His report cards were dotted with C's, D's, and F's. Barry did not return to Leadville High for his senior year, which started in September of 1957.

Sometime that summer he left town and started "hitchhiking across the country," he wrote. But life on the road offered nothing but misery for the troublemaking, uneducated teenager. So, in the spring of 1958, Barry went back to Leadville and decided to join the U.S. Air Force. He raised his hand and promised to support and defend the Constitution of the United States against all enemies, foreign and domestic, on June 2, 1958. On his enlistment form Sadler wrote his home address as 118 W. 2nd Street in Leadville, the same address as the Pioneer.

The Gomez family believes that Eppie Gomez played an important role in Barry's decision to get out of Leadville and into the military. "My dad was a very well-spoken man; he was well respected in Leadville," Tommy Gomez said. "Bear knew this. And he always wanted to emulate something that was good, not the negativity he grew up with. He would spend a lot of time talking with my dad. Bear would ask him for advice.

One of the things my dad always told him was, 'You need to get beyond the way you grew up, the things you were exposed to, and you need to be a good person.' He told Bear numerous times, 'You have the potential to become something if you just put it to use.'

"I remember Bear having respect enough for my dad that whenever he would tell him something, Bear would listen. And I truly believe that's part of the reason Bear turned his life around and decided to do what he did after he went into the military." Eppie Gomez, his son Tommy said, "had a major, major influence on [Barry's] life."

In his book Barry wrote that he joined the military because he felt the air force could "do things for me." But again, he told friends a different story.

"He said he was a big boy for his age; at fifteen he was bouncing in a bar," Bill Parrish said. "Some guy was in there having trouble and Barry kinda sucker punched him. He said the guy bounced right back up and Barry said it was time for him to get out of Leadville, and go in the air force."

"At 17, Sadler was a bar bouncer in Leadville, Colorado," R. Kent Burton wrote in a profile of Barry in the *Tucson Daily Citizen* in 1972. "He was knifed seven times and shot once before he turned 18."[25]

That most likely is an exaggeration. But it's all but certain that Barry realized he needed to change his life drastically in 1958. He told a *Chicago Sun-Times* reporter that he was "getting into a lot of trouble—trouble and fights and going nowhere so I figured if I didn't join up—well, I'd wind up a bum."[26]

Barry told another interviewer the same thing. "I knew I'd wind up in jail the way I was going," he said. "All I knew how to do was fight, so I enlisted in the Air Force and they took me."[27]

Another important factor motived the seventeen-year-old to join the military—something Barry Sadler didn't mention in his autobiography or speak of to many friends.

"Why the hell did you quit school and go in the service?" Sadler's literary agent and friend Rob Robison asked him one day.

"Dammit, Robbie," Sadler replied. "I was hungry."

"That," Robison said, "tells you a lot."[28]

CHAPTER 2
AN EXTREME BEGINNER

"I showed Barry some chords and we would sit around the barracks plunking our guitars."

—PAUL ALFORD

Barry Sadler served in the U. S. Air Force for four years. The onetime rotten kid received his honorable discharge on September 26, 1962, having, indeed, served his country honorably beginning with Basic Training at Lackland Air Force Base in San Antonio, Texas. His service included a year in Japan and three stateside assignments.

As it has been for untold numbers of American young people, serving in the military served as Barry Sadler's rite of passage into young adulthood. He stayed out of official trouble, worked conscientiously as a radar technician, picked up his high school diploma, learned Japanese, and became a martial arts expert.

Sadler's service began at Lackland—then, as now, the air force's only basic training center for enlisted personnel—where he found plenty to eat and plenty of ways to excel. "I did feel a little proud when I saw 'SADLER' in block letters on my blouse" for the first time, Barry wrote in his autobiography. "I had no problems—I liked the Air Force. Thanks to my mountain-developed marksmanship, I had the highest score on our first day at the rifle range."[1]

Barry wanted to be an armament maintenance specialist primarily because of his "interest in and success with guns." But after he took the military aptitude test, the military decided Airman Sadler would best suit the service's needs by becoming a radar technician. So Barry and about twenty other recruits piled into a bus in July of 1958 and went off to Keesler Air Force Base in the Gulf Coast city of Biloxi, Mississippi, for radar training.[2]

He may have had an aptitude for it, but when Barry arrived at Keesler, he had never so much as even seen a piece of radar equipment. That did not deter the teenaged recruit. He sailed through radar school. After a twenty-day leave back in Leadville, Barry shipped out to his first permanent duty station: a radar installation in Japan.

Late in September of 1958, Barry climbed aboard a chartered Flying Tiger Line C-121 transport plane and flew across the Pacific. After stopping in Hawaii and Wake Island to refuel, the four-prop C-121 landed at the U.S. military air base at Tachikawa, just outside Tokyo. The air force assigned Barry to an Aircraft Control and Warning Service air defense radar station on Mount Mineokayama on a peninsula across Tokyo Bay from Yokohama. Airman Sadler spent the next thirteen months in Japan. It proved to be a rewarding experience.

"I liked Japan from the start," Barry said. The people were friendly, the duty (tracking planes coming into Japanese airspace) was not difficult, and there was plenty of leisure time. In his off-duty hours Barry read voraciously. He also went eel fishing, swimming, and skin diving in Tokyo Bay. And he played tourist in small towns and large cities near the base. But he didn't exactly keep in touch with his family back home.

"Barry wasn't much of a letter writer," said fellow airman Harold ("H. D.") Graham, who met Sadler at Travis Air Force Base in California in 1962. "I think he told me that all the time he was in Japan he maybe wrote his family five or six times." Barry and H. D. Graham corresponded for about twenty years, but "for every two letters I wrote [to him], he probably wrote one back."[3]

On November 1, 1958, his eighteenth birthday, Barry visited Tokyo for the first time. He went to "the usual tourist attractions," sampled Tokyo's shops, and then spent most of the night in a bar. Barry and a buddy "bought" the bar, he said, "chased everybody out except some girls, and spent the night sampling everything." On a subsequent trip to Tokyo, Barry underwent another young serviceman's rite of passage: He had a small blue panther tattooed on his right arm just below the shoulder.

Barry had arrived in Japan as an airman, the second-lowest enlisted rank in the air force. Within a few weeks he received a promotion to airman second class, the equivalent of the army's private first class. He studied for and passed the GED test, receiving his high school diploma. He acquired a Japanese girlfriend—"Yoko, a five-foot-two-inch living doll," as he put it, who worked at a bar near the radar base.

He apprenticed himself to a judo and karate teacher, Aikawa Kaiichi, a carpenter at the radar station, who was in his seventies. "He took me into his home and made me a member of his seaside village," Sadler wrote. "Thanks to Kaiichi's interest and friendship, I saw more of Japanese family life than do most Americans who go to Japan."

Barry "really enjoyed Japan and the Japanese families he met," H. D. Graham said. "They treated him very well—more or less took him as their own son." Before long Barry had mastered rudimentary Japanese, his third language.

Barry said he took judo lessons for four hours a day four or five days a week at his mentor's home and at the judo hut on the radar base. The intense training paid off. Barry gained about 35 pounds of mostly muscle, putting close to 200 pounds on his five-foot-nine frame. He claimed he "developed" a seventeen-inch neck and seventeen-inch biceps. And he sparred against "the toughest professionals in the neighborhood." Barry thrived in judo tournaments, including, by his account, winning nine straight fights in one afternoon—a feat that earned him a black belt.

Barry "told me he 'almost went Oriental' because of all the training," Bill Parrish said. "It was the whole Samurai aspect of it, the mental aspect. In fighting, if you're injured, as an example, the Samurai developed the mental ability to put a tourniquet on an extremity to stop the bleeding. I've seen Sadler demonstrate many times being able to stop the blood flow to an arm and have you check for a pulse. And he said he could do it with his legs or arms. I'd try both arms and [there was] no pulse rate."[4]

Although Barry never practiced as intently as he had in Japan, he continued to keep his hand in with karate, judo, and other martial arts for decades. "Barry knew many styles of martial arts, Shotokan, Isshinru, and a little bit of everything else," Parrish said. In the 1980s "his right hand looked like a shillelagh from his breaking techniques—breaking boards, breaking block, brick. The two knuckles of the index finger and middle finger were more like weapon, I'll put it that way."[5]

Barry's tour of duty in Japan ended in October of 1959. His next assignment: the General Surveillance Radar station at Madera Air Force Station in Central California.[6] He plied his radar trade—still on the lookout for attacking aircraft from the Soviet Union—with the 774th Aircraft Control and Warning Squadron at Madera until July of 1960 when he received orders to go to Richards-Gebaur AFB near Kansas City, Missouri. He learned the ins and outs of the newly developed automated SAGE radar system for three months there. Barry ended his air force career at Beale AFB in the small Central California town of Marysville, about 125 miles northeast of San Francisco.

He did not have a guitar during his air force days—until he got to Beale. "I sold him a guitar, a Harmony Monterey, that I bought in Kansas City, for twenty-five dollars, I think it was," Paul Alford, one of Barry's best air force buddies, said in 2016. "I showed Barry some chords and we would sit around the barracks plunking our guitars."

What kind of a musician was the twenty-year-old Barry Sadler? "He was an extreme beginner" on the guitar, Alford said. "He knew the basics. He could make a C chord and a G chord." As a singer, "he was certainly no Vic Damone or Frank Sinatra. He could sing really simple stuff. He was kind of an average guy who could carry a tune."[7]

Barry received his second promotion at Beale, to airman first class. He also gave the occasional judo lesson at March Air Force Base in Southern California and at the sheriff's department in Marysville. Barry also took part in the activities that most young servicemen indulged in at the time: drinking and partying hard in the barracks and in off-base bars, along with the occasional wild road trip.

"It was just normal stuff, nothing out of the ordinary," Paul Alford said. "We'd drink beer or tequila in the barracks" during off-duty hours. "Once in a while we'd go down to a bar, usually Eddie's Lounge, in Marysville. Barry's favorite drink was [straight] tequila with a little lime and salt."

After one solo trip to Marysville, Barry wound up spending a night in jail, although he was not charged with any crime. After getting a ride to town, he hitchhiked back to the base. "The police stopped the car that picked me up," he later said, "and took everybody in. [They] released me with no charges."[8]

The road trips included jaunts to Sacramento, San Francisco, and even Los Angeles, about 500 miles away. One time Barry, Alford, and two buddies crammed into a tiny Triumph sports car and sped off to San Francisco. "After driving around Frisco all day, we parked at a remote beach area to try and get a few hours shut-eye," Alford said. The other guys "slept in the front seats and I tried to sleep in the jump seat. Barry had found an old blanket in the back of the car and rolled himself up in it on the beach sand. He probably got a better night's sleep than any of us."

One weekend the group took off for L.A. on the spur of the moment. "'Let's go,' we said, and we did, just like that," Alford said, "with only the clothes we had on and less than ten dollars apiece. We stayed at a buddy's parent's house and just about drove them crazy at night and hit the beach all day."

Some of his fellow airmen thought Barry was "kind of strange," Alford said. One of his eccentricities was Barry's ability to hypnotize people. "He would entertain us in the barracks some evenings, hypnotizing guys who volunteered," Alford said. "He said he learned it from a psychiatrist in reform school in Leadville."

Barry occasionally, Alford said, slipped into "somber" moods at Beale. "You didn't want to mess with him when he was in that mood," he said. "I never saw him get into a confrontation where he needed to use his [martial arts skills], but he was not a guy I'd mess with if I was going to mess with somebody."

And then there was Barry's penchant for talking about how much he admired Nazi Germany. "If you didn't know him, you would have gotten the impression that he was an extreme kind of Nazi and anti-Jew," Alford said. "He was fascinated with military regimentation and command strategy and admired the German solider mystique and Hitler's use of discipline. Because he expressed this, I think he felt a need to seem anti-Jewish."

Barry would joke with the two Jewish guys in his squadron, Alford said. "He liked them and kidded with them and made jokes that were extremely distasteful and repulsive under normal circumstances—like saying 'I'm gonna turn you into a lampshade'—but he made them in a joking, teasing manner. If they had asked him for five bucks he'd lend it to them. It's not like he was out to get them or anything like that."

Barry found little to like at Beale AFB. For one thing the base wasn't exactly a garden spot. "It was a rambling dusty place in the early stages of being reclaimed from long disuse," Alford said. For another, Barry was growing tired of staring at radar screens day and night.

"Barry never seemed particularly happy there," Alford said. "We were in radar. It was essential, but rather boring. The air force was easy and not particularly military in the same sense the army was. The character of the air force didn't seem to fit [Barry's] character."

H. D. Graham agreed. Barry "was an outdoors person, rough and ready," he said. "It seemed to me like he was not displeased with the air force, but was not really happy because it wasn't exactly like he thought it would be."

Learning where his next assignment would be convinced Barry to end his commitment to the air force when his four-year enlistment ended. "He was told he was going to be shipped to the Aleutians," Graham said. "He didn't want that. He didn't like cold weather."

So Barry took his honorable discharge on June 1, 1962. He hung around the farming community of Marysville for a short time and then went home to Leadville. When he couldn't find a job, Barry said that he and a buddy named Walter Lane "tossed my guitar and his drums into a 1953 Chevrolet and we hit the road in an effort to make a living playing in bars, honky-tonks, shopping centers, and any place else that would have us." It was the first time, Barry said, that he sang in public.

He liked it—and contemplated for the first time what it might be like to make a life (and living) as a singer. "I was sitting out on the patio of a Nuevo Laredo whorehouse and all the girls came out to listen to me sing instead of staying inside to hustle," Barry said in 1966. "I decided I might someday have a future as a singer."[9]

With "a Negro piano player" named Elmo from Marysville, the trio wandered through Colorado, Wyoming, Montana, Washington, Oregon, California, and Texas in that 1953 Chevy looking for gigs. When they couldn't find them, the budding musicians took temporary jobs working in orchards, including DeGiorgio's Fruit Company in Marysville. They also loaded crates of fruit onto railroad cars for $1.10 an hour.

"It was backbreaking, and by August I was tired of it," Barry said. "I was getting nowhere."

He also realized, he said, that he was "becoming a hood."[10] So, on August 8, 1962, a little more than two months after he left the air force, Barry drove to Oakland, California, and walked into a military recruiting office. He intended, Barry would later tell people, to re-join the air force. But the air force recruiter was away from his desk, so Barry went next door to the army recruiter's office and enlisted for three years.[11]

He listed his permanent mailing address again as 118 West Second Street in Leadville (the Pioneer Bar), his height at five feet eight inches, and his weight at 175 pounds. As for family, Barry wrote that both his mother Bebe and his brother Robert's addresses were "unknown."

"Have not seen or heard from any of my relatives since 1961," he wrote on the form.

Because of his former service, the army let Barry Sadler begin serving as a private first class, two pay grades up from Private E-1, the standard rank for new enlistees. Barry spent the next two months at Fort Ord in California.

"I arrived there with just $3 in my pocket, the clothes on my back," he said, "and a little carry bag in which I had one pair of Levi's and a shirt."

CHAPTER 3

WHY DON'T YOU WRITE A SONG ABOUT US?

One hundred men will test today. But only three win the Green Beret.
—"THE BALLAD OF THE GREEN BERETS"

When Barry Sadler joined the U.S. Army, he chose the most rigorous and difficult military occupational specialty: Special Forces (SF). The military had informal units that took on unconventional, dangerous, and sometimes covert missions going back to the French and Indian War. The nation's first organized Special Forces, the famed Office of Strategic Services (OSS)—the predecessor of the CIA—and the army's 1st Special Service Force (nicknamed "The Devil's Brigade"), were not formed until World War II.[1]

On June 20, 1952, the army formally started its first SF unit, the 10th Special Forces Group at Fort Bragg, North Carolina. The following year some Special Forces outfits began wearing green berets. Within a few years all Special Forces troops sported the distinctive headgear. Even though the men wore them, though, the beret was not an official part of the uniform.

That didn't happen until 1961. The catalysts were President John F. Kennedy and U.S Army major general William "The Big Y" Yarborough, the commander of the Army Special Warfare Center at Fort Bragg. The young, dynamic president and the battle-hardened general both strongly believed in the unconventional, counterinsurgency SF concept—and both knew very well the value of symbols to sell the public on what was then a largely untested and potentially controversial idea.

On October 12, 1961, nine months after taking office, Kennedy paid a highly publicized visit to the Special Warfare Center at Fort Bragg. General Yarborough—a West Point graduate and World War II paratrooper who had fought in North Africa, Sicily, and Italy—greeted JFK wearing a green beret. What came next is part of Special Forces lore.

"Those are nice," JFK told Yarborough. "How do you like the green beret?"

To which the general replied: "They're fine, sir. We've wanted them a long time."

A few days later the commander in chief sent Yarborough a message. "The challenge of this old but new form of operations is a real one and I know that you and the members of your Command will carry on for us and the free world in a manner which is both worthy and inspiring," JFK wrote. "I am sure that the Green Beret will be a mark of distinction in the trying times ahead."[2]

The green beret, the president later wrote in a White House memorandum, "is again becoming a symbol of excellence, a badge of courage, a mark of distinction in the fight for freedom."[3]

Within a month the green beret became the official Special Forces headgear, creating a distinctive symbol of a new, innovative kind of modern, cold war warfare. Not long after that people began referring to the Special Forces as "The Green Berets." But that moniker never became the official name of the outfit, despite its even more widespread colloquial use after Barry Sadler's song became a national sensation in 1966.

In November 1961 the public-relations-savvy General Yarborough made sure word got out that SF troops would soon be wearing the distinctive green berets. The PR effort worked. Soon, print and broadcast news media reporters were speaking glowingly of the highly trained, innovative fighting men sporting the distinctive green headgear.

At first the beret itself was a bit of a mystery to most Americans. One newspaper in California reporting on the new uniform change felt the need to explain to readers: "A beret is a round, flat cap. They are presently worn by soldiers of Belgium, Canada, Netherlands, and the United Kingdom. British Gen. Bernard L. Montgomery of World War II African campaign is one of history's more famous beret wearers."[4]

A wire service article around the same time went into more detail: "Made of dark green felt, the beret is worn across the forehead about an inch above the eyebrow. The top is draped over the right ear. The insignia [two silver arrows crossed with a dagger] is positioned above the left eye."[5] The insignia also contains the SF's Latin motto, *De Oppresso Liber*, which usually is translated as "To Liberate from Oppression" or "To Free the Oppressed."

The army told Barry that he didn't have to take Basic Training, as he had done so in the air force. But, Barry said, he volunteered to take basic one more time. "I wanted to learn soldiering from the grass roots," he wrote in his autobiography. Barry had basic at the huge training center at Fort Ord in California. He thrived and was sent to a special three-week leadership course at Ord, and then he had mandatory Infantry AIT (Advanced Individual Training) at Ord.

On December 29, 1962, Barry began Basic Airborne Training at Fort Benning in Georgia. He learned to jump out of perfectly good airplanes and, when the training ended three weeks later, earned his Basic Parachutist Badge, a silver-colored representation of an opened parachute with stylized wings on either side—often called "jump wings."[6]

Receiving his jump wings, Barry Sadler said, "gave me my happiest days since winning the black belt in Japan. I began to think about writing a song involving the airborne. I had no idea what it would be, but I wanted it to include the line 'silver wings upon their chests.'"

Barry decided to volunteer for Special Forces during jump school. In his telling, the decision to join the outfit that he later would call "America's best" was not exactly motivated by patriotism or by a burning desire to be part of an experimental, elite unit to free the oppressed.

"We were told we would get the afternoon off" one day during jump school if we took the Special Forces examination," Barry told *Soldier of Fortune* magazine in 1988. "Hell, I didn't know what Special Forces was, but an afternoon off seemed like a good idea at the time."[7]

He told friends a slightly different, but equally flip, version about why he went SF. To wit: One day during jump school, "this guy came up to me in a faggoty-looking hat. He said, 'You look like a big strong boy. Do you want to be in the Green Berets?'"[8]

Whether or not he was joking about the reasons—Sadler had a sly sense of humor—Barry did choose Special Forces and he opted for medical training, one of the four Green Beret specialties in 1963. The others were engineer and demolition; communications; and operations and intelligence. Although Barry did not explain in his autobiography or in newspaper interviews exactly why he chose to be a medic, one of his fellow SF trainees, Al Weed, shed some light on the subject. It had to do with women.

"A bunch of us who were scheduled to go to Special Forces were going to Fort Bragg from jump school on the same bus," Weed said. "One of the guys already had gone through medical training at Fort Sam Houston. He had nothing but wonderful things to say about Fort Sam primarily because there were women there—and there weren't anywhere else in the army almost."

After the bus carrying Weed, Sadler, and the other trainees "pulled up in front of the Special Forces training group in-take place," Weed said, "the sergeant in charge of filling up the class of medics gave this pitch about how valuable medical training was. He was prepared to do whatever he had to fill up the class. He got five minutes into it and somebody said, 'Isn't there some way we can volunteer for medical training?' And he said, 'Well, sure.' Damn near everybody in the room put their hand up."[9] That included Barry Sadler, who at age twenty-three was a few years older than most of his fellow SF recruits.

Weed, Sadler, and the rest of the volunteers reported to Fort Sam Houston's Brooke Army Medical Center (where the women were) in San Antonio, Texas, on February 2, 1963, to start Special Forces medic training. It was a long, challenging course of study. First came five months of basic medic training at Fort Sam. Then two months of on-the-job training (for Barry, at Fort Jackson, South Carolina), then nearly four months of SF Advanced Medical Training School back at Fort Bragg. All the men who qualified for Special Forces medic training—including Barry Sadler—had scored highly on the military intelligence test, known as the GT.

"I had two years of college," Weed said. "There were more than a couple of guys with bachelor's degrees. At least one with a master's degree.

All but two, including Barry Sadler, didn't even have high school. But their GT scores were sufficiently high that they made the cut. And both of them got through the training quite fine."

The training "was long and arduous," said Doug Peacock, a former SF medic who served two tours in Vietnam and took the training at Brooke in 1965. "It was harder than any college class I took. If you were in Special Forces, you were smart. It was too much for older NCOs who hadn't gone to college."[10]

"Barry was a real serious student and he took the course seriously," said Larry Emons, who trained with Sadler at Brooke. "You had to. If you didn't take it seriously, you didn't make it through. They threw stuff at you so fast it was unbelievable."[11]

The first eight weeks—the basic aide man's course—however, consisted primarily of classes on fairly simple, mundane medical tasks. "It was basic, like how to change a bed with somebody in it and how to carry a litter over a bridge and over a fence," said Steve Bruno, who trained with Sadler at jump school and at medic school at Brooke. "We had to start from the beginning."[12]

Much of what was taught during those first eight weeks, Bruno added, "was bullshit. That's when we got drunk all the time. We all drank a lot and we all partied a lot. It was just that kind of mentality. We came from Fort Bragg, which is a really strict military place—paratroopers, 82nd Airborne, Special Forces—to [what was practically a] country club there in Texas." Doug Peacock called Brooke "a kind of social place. There were civilian nurses, places to drink beer."

Barry Sadler "was a partier," Bruno said. "He had a lot of fun. He took his training seriously; he took his partying seriously. We drank until we fell down. I picked him up off the floor more than you would pick up a normal man. That's just the way it was."

Sadler alluded to the drinking and partying—in more sanitized words—in his autobiography. "It was not all hard work at Brooke," he wrote. "We had a lot of fun." Without going into detail Barry mentioned "weekend trips to Nuevo Laredo, across the Mexican border," and drinking at bars in San Antonio. He didn't say anything about a memorable fracas he got into one night.[13]

Barry "was in a bar drinking by himself," Al Weed remembered. Two of his buddies were sitting at the other end of the bar. "And all of a sudden a fight breaks out," Weed said. "And Sadler is right in the middle of the damn fight. They think they'll need to help him. So these two guys from our class decide they better jump in and help him."

But Barry, Weed said, "was so busy flinging people, he didn't pay attention to who he was flinging. Both of those guys got flung on their asses and out the door. They came back to Fort Sam, and said, 'Man, we got into a fight, but he beat us up more than the other guys.'"

After the first eight weeks, "hardly anybody dropped out," Weed said. "We started, I think, with sixty-five in that group. We might have lost one or two because of family pressures or disciplinary stuff. The big thing was, if you screwed up, it was BTB, back to Bragg. Nobody wanted to go back to Bragg. So they tried not to screw up."

The next part of the training, which included a heavy dose of classroom work, was much more difficult. "They really started to put the pressure on in terms of academics," Weed said. "People were dropping like flies. Barry was academically not all that experienced compared to the college guys in our group, but he buckled down. When we took tests on Fridays, we would fill up eight or ten pages of material. You had to write clearly and explain what it was you were writing. He struggled with that, although he managed to do it quite well."

"That training was very difficult and it was long, and the dropout rate was huge," Steve Bruno added. "Barry made it through. My memory of him—as far as test taking—was that he was very good. He always managed to come out on top like the rest of us without really putting a lot of effort into it. But he was a good medic and was serious about that."

Barry had a guitar with him at Fort Sam. During his medic training there, he began writing the song that would become "The Ballad of the Green

Berets." In later years Barry gave several versions about how the song came to be. Sometimes he said that he wrote it while drinking and carousing in a Mexican brothel just over the border. "Few people realize," Barry told *Soldier of Fortune* magazine in 1988, "that 'The Ballad of the Green Berets' was written in a whorehouse in Nuevo Laredo, Mexico, while I was on leave from SF medical training in Fort Sam Houston, Texas."[14]

Sometimes he said he came up with the song during off-hours in the barracks at Fort Sam. "I'd been sitting on the steps of my barracks" in 1963, Barry told a reporter in 1966, "when one of my friends said, 'Sadler, why don't you write a song about the Special Forces?' I felt that it was a good idea and I felt we needed one. It was probably about an hour later that I had the rough form of the song done."[15]

Barry "wrote songs for friends in the barracks—just for fun," he told another reporter around that same time. "The guys would throw bottles at me, and that's fun."[16]

He told *Life* magazine at just about that same time that he was "at Fort Sam Houston drinking tequila when a friend said, 'Why don't you write a song about us?' So I sat down with my guitar and my bottle of tequila and between the three of us, we came up with the ballad."[17]

Sometimes he said the idea came to him in a bar in San Antonio. That's how Barry told it in his autobiography in 1967. In his spare time at Fort Sam, Barry wrote, I "played and sang and worked on songs of my own." Then, one night in May, when he was drinking tequila in "a San Antonio night spot," a fellow trainee named Robert Macdonald asked: "Why don't you write a song about us?" So Barry picked up his guitar, he said, "and in a quarter of an hour or so came up with the original version of 'The Ballad of the Green Berets.'

"I started the chorus with the line about which I had been thinking, 'Silver wings upon their chests,' and continued with 'these are men, America's best. One hundred men we'll test today, but only three win the green beret.' These survived unchanged."

Macdonald, Barry said, suggested he copyright the song, so Barry "sent my lines with four dollars to the Library of Congress." He also performed the song "on leave in some Mexican-border and San Antonio night spots," he wrote, and "earned considerable applause."

Which version is true? It helps to keep in mind that "Barry liked to put people on," the journalist and author Robert M. Powers, a friend from the early 1970s, said. "He'd tell them what he thought they wanted to hear. He had a habit of stretching the truth. He told a good story."[18]

Barry told Powers that he did just that in the *Life* magazine interview. "I said I composed the 'Ballad' outside a Nuevo Laredo whorehouse," Barry told his friend. "But that's not exactly the truth. Hell, I didn't want to come off as some Boy Scout who accidentally wrote a song. I was a veteran airborne medic and I wanted people to know it. Actually, I revised the song in several places, including Vietnam."

The guys Barry trained with all agree that Barry did, in fact, revise the song many times. They say that Barry spent hours and hours working on the song inside the barracks, on the front steps of the barracks, and even in the barracks latrine. As he refined the words, Barry constantly asked his fellow trainees for suggestions.

"He'd sit in the barracks and play his guitar," Larry Emons said. "I always kid people, saying I helped write that song, because he'd do verses and ask us what we thought. We'd say, 'That sounds good,' or 'No, the other one was better.' He worked on it quite a while."

Barry went through the song "many times trying to get the words together," another one of his fellow trainees said. "He'd grab his guitar and he'd sit out on the back steps, or even the front steps. I remember him even discussing 'back at home a young wife waits.' Once in a while he would say, 'What do you think, guys?'"[19]

Barry wrote "The Ballad," Steve Bruno said, "in bits and pieces. It was a collaboration. It wasn't him alone. I don't want to take anything away from the man, but we were all putting words in. Everybody added their two cents: 'Wouldn't this sound a little better?' or 'Wouldn't that sound better?' But he did the actual putting it together and singing it."

Barry "was the fellow in the barracks constantly playing this guitar late at night and pissing off the folks trying to sleep or study," another fellow Fort Sam medic trainee, Joe Hannon, said.[20]

That's where the latrine came in.

Barry would escape there on occasion when the guys got tired of hearing him working on the lyrics sitting on his bunk. The "advantage of the latrine," Weed said, "was it was all tiled, sort of an upscale military barracks latrine. The acoustics were very interesting. It was like playing with an amplified guitar.

"So when the guys in the barracks said, 'C'mon, Sadler, just stop that shit,' he would go into the latrine to work on it. For some reason, I had the patience to sit there with him. I was a friendly audience. [I'd say], 'Yeah, that sounds pretty good' or whatever you'd say to somebody just to encourage them."

Aside from beginning the song that would change his life, Barry experienced another life-changing event at Brooke Army Medical Center. It began one afternoon in the middle of June when he walked into the mess hall for lunch.

"I noticed a slender WAC with a high hairdo under her chef's hat dishing out mashed potatoes," Barry wrote. "She handed me mine with a smile. On her [name] tag, I read 'Edelman,' a name that could be German. 'Spechen Sie Deutsch?' I asked.

"'Nein,' she replied."

The slender Women's Army Corps trainee working in the mess hall that afternoon was Lavona Edelman, a nineteen-year-old from Lehighton, Pennsylvania, near Allentown, studying to be an operating room technician. "After a little salesmanship on my part," Barry wrote, Lavona "agreed to go on a double date" that night. Barry brought his guitar along and sang several songs for her, including "The Ballad."

After that night, Lavona said, Barry "kept calling and we'd go out. And then he asked me to marry him. I wasn't looking for that, but after three weeks I married him anyway. I had to ask permission from my [commanding officer]. We only knew each other for three or four weeks. I didn't want to be married. But he gave me an ultimatum: 'Marry me or I'll go away.'"[21]

Barry Sadler and Lavona Edelman married on July 18, 1963. A justice of the peace in San Antonio performed the ceremony. "I gave her my silver parachutist's ring as a wedding ring," Barry said.

"Marrying Barry," Lavona said, "completely changed my life."[22]

Within days the newlyweds went their separate ways. Lavona had to report to Fort Gordon in Georgia for more medical schooling. Barry went to Fort Jackson in South Carolina for the next phase of his SF medic training, two months of on-the-job work at the U.S. Army hospital there. Al Weed and Steve Bruno also wound up at Jackson for on-the-job training (OJT). The medics in training worked for the most part with Basic Training recruits who landed in the hospital suffering from illnesses or with injuries.

"Barry did very well when his shift came during the on-the-job training in the hospital in the ER and elsewhere," Bruno said. "The main thing was the ER. We wanted to see trauma. We didn't give a shit about old men dying or whatever. We wanted to see people stabbed, shot, blown up, in car accidents, crushed heads, that kind of thing. That's what we were training for and it wound up that we all saw it for real."

Barry, Bruno said, "was almost the top of the class" at OJT. "And he never did any studying whatsoever. He was one of those guys who was gifted with a high IQ."

During Barry's time at Fort Jackson, the army held a huge training exercise called Operation Swift Strike III, during which thousands of troops, including paratroopers from the 101st Airborne Division, took part in simulated battlefield action. Even though the fighting wasn't real, more than a few soldiers wound up in the hospital. Barry and six of his OJT buddies—including Al Weed—volunteered for extra duty at the hospital to help.

"You showed initiative, interest and gave outstanding care to each patient that was assigned to you," an official Army Letter of Appreciation from the head of the Fort Jackson Army Hospital's Nursing Service noted. "My staff has nothing but praise for your outstanding efforts that enable us to maintain optimum patient care."[23]

PFC Barry Sadler began the last phase of his SF medic training, Advanced Medical Training School, on September 2, 1963, back at the Special Forces Training Center at Fort Bragg. The men called it "Dog Lab" because they did a lot of work on man's best friend. "There was the surgery, plus all the book learning," John Gissell said. "That course was without a doubt the toughest thing mentally or educationally that I had ever done in my life. It was unbelievably hard."

The training "really got serious," in Dog Lab, said Al Weed, who wound up finishing first in his (and Barry's) advanced training class of twenty-five. "That's when we started getting our animals, shooting them and taking care of the gunshot wounds and that kind of thing—operating on the dogs, stitching them up. A guy who got through that training—and I include [Sadler]—could do as much as a country doctor could fifty years or sixty years earlier. We were well trained. We were stitching. We were writing prescriptions."

Although he does not mention it in his autobiography, Barry was not among the twenty-five who graduated from Dog Lab on November 23, 1963—the day after President Kennedy was shot and killed in Dallas. Because he didn't complete all the course work, Barry was, in military parlance, "recycled." He finished the course several weeks later, earning his green beret.

Lavona managed to visit Barry at Fort Bragg on November 1, his twenty-third birthday. She then requested an early discharge, which she received. The newlyweds began their married life crammed into a small trailer in Fayetteville.

Money was short, and at the end of the year, Barry went on a road trip with John Gissell, Larry Emons, and another newly minted SF medic, John Argue. They drove to Texas, where Barry played "The Ballad of the Green Berets" at Argue's parents' house. "It was a complete song by then," Gissell said. "Sadler went on to Colorado to play in the honky-tonks to make some money."

Barry Sadler was promoted to specialist 4 (spec 4), the equivalent of corporal, on March 3, 1964. Soon thereafter he and Lavona drove to Pennsylvania for a belated wedding celebration. "My mother had a wedding cake," Lavona said. "I didn't know how Barry would react. But he was pleased and happy."[24]

Barry took what is known as a "short discharge" on May 7, and re-enlisted for a three-year hitch the following day.

"On my own time, I continued to play my guitar and work on my songs," he wrote in his autobiography. "I earned a $600 reenlistment bonus by signing up for three more years and spent part of it for a recorder of my own and began to play my songs into it. This tape recorder—which cost only $98, as I recall—proved to be the best investment of my life."[25]

CHAPTER 4
BY AN UNKNOWN SOLDIER

"I feel the ballad might be a potential seller to the general public."
—GERALD GITELL, JUNE 17, 1964

"With no previous experience in the music business, I recognized the financial potential and public relations value of a ballad by an unknown soldier. I coordinated, through military chain of command, Army acceptance of the ballad. [I] researched public reaction to the ballad, polished the initial product and marketed the song 'The Ballad of the Green Berets,' and the writer, Barry Sadler, to a contract with a music publisher and R.C.A. Victor. This eventually proved to be a several million dollar business venture."[1]

That's how Gerald Gitell, a twenty-three-year-old second lieutenant serving as the head of the Third Special Forces Group's Public Information Office at Fort Bragg, later explained the unlikely story of how he came to help Barry Sadler sign a songwriters contract in the summer of 1964. And how he would come to share in the six-figure royalties from the sales of "The Ballad of the Green Berets."

How unlikely was it that Gerry Gitell and Barry Sadler would get together and pave the groundwork for what would become 1966's number one hit record? Aside from the fact that the two men served in Special Forces, Gitell and Sadler had precious little in common. Gerry was a Boston-born Easterner who graduated from high school (in Newton) at eighteen and from Boston University four years later with a B.S. in public relations. Barry grew up in the West, never made it past his junior year of high school, and earned his GED in the air force.

Gerry—unlike Barry—was not at all physically hungry when he joined the army to go Special Forces in 1963. He had taken ROTC at

Boston University and chose to be an army officer; Barry was an enlisted man. Gerry completed Officer Candidate School (in armor) and then earned his green beret as a second lieutenant. With his PR degree Gerry Gitell talked the Third Special Forces Group into forming its first Public Information Office (PIO), which he was running in the spring of 1964 when he met Barry Sadler at Fort Bragg.

According to his son Seth, Gerry Gitell—who died at age sixty-nine in 2010—told two different stories about how he and Barry Sadler came to join forces. "The first one is that Sadler approached him and said, 'Gerry, I hear you went to B.U., you have a communications background, and also you're Jewish and you might know people in the music business,'" Seth Gitell said. "I don't know if that's what was explicitly said, but that was the idea."[2]

In the second version Gerry Gitell sought out Barry Sadler. "I've heard a lot about the song," he said. "Why don't you play it for me?"

In his autobiography Barry Sadler is vague about how the two men got together. Gerry "took a professional and also a personal interest in my songs," Barry wrote. "He sent them to a lot of people and took me with him to New York and Boston in an effort to sell them."[3]

Gerry Gitell did a lot more than that. He scrounged up recording equipment on the base, found a room at the Special Warfare Center that would be suitable for recording, and had Barry made a rough demo of the song, then titled "The Ballad of the Green Beret."

Lieutenant Gitell had a willing accomplice in the PR-savvy General Yarborough, his commanding officer. Yarbrough had recently given his official blessing to a song called "The Green Beret March," written by Phyllis Fairbanks. So Yarborough had his official SF march; Gitell walked into the general's office and made a case that Barry's "Ballad" should be the official SF song. Yarborough immediately agreed.

The young lieutenant wrote letters to record companies and music publishers pitching the song. And he somehow talked the SF brass into approving a road trip for him and Barry to go to New York City and Boston to promote the song.

"They saw a local Boston deejay and played the song for him," Seth Gitell said. "The deejay did not see any value in the song whatsoever."

He told Gerry and Barry that "The Ballad" was little more than a novelty song, comparing it derisively to "Domininque," a hugely popular 1963 folk-like tune sung in French by a Belgian woman who recorded it using the name, "The Singing Nun."[4]

On June 17, 1964, 2nd Lt. Gerry Gitell mailed copies of two demo tapes to Chester Gierlach, a longtime songwriter and record producer in New York City. Gierlach had worked with Phyllis Fairbanks, among other songwriters. One tape had Barry doing "The Ballad"; the other contained Barry's song "Trooper's Fall," about an airborne ranger whose parachute fails to open.

"The ballad," Gerry Gitell wrote in the cover letter he sent to Gierlach, "is a Folk Song and is entitled appropriately 'The Ballad of the Green Beret.' Since it is about Special Forces, we had the Commander of the Special Warfare Center approve" the song. "We also have approval to sell the song at the book store." Gerry went on to say that Special Forces troopers at Bragg liked the song, as did people "outside the military."

In light "of recent publicity about Special Forces and the popularity of Folk Songs, I feel the ballad might be a potential seller to the general public. I know people associated with Special Forces would also buy the song." In the letter Gerry did not mention Barry Sadler by name. "The singer," he wrote, "is a Special Forces medic who wrote the songs."

Chet Gierlach was intrigued. "I wasn't impressed with the quality of his voice on the demonstration tape, but I wanted to hear more songs," he told a reporter after "The Ballad" became a big hit.[5] Gierlach "was interested," Barry wrote. His company—Music Music Music—"would do what it could with the tapes, and I assigned my copyright on 'The Ballad' to the company." Barry (and Gerry) signed a Uniform Popular Songwriters Contract with Music Music Music on July 15, 1964.

"I was greatly encouraged," Barry wrote. He was so grateful to Gerry Gitell for his help that Barry gave him 25 percent of the royalties.

My father "thought Sadler was very generous with him," Seth Gitell said. "He didn't write the song; he recorded it and acted as a de facto manager even though he was a lieutenant in the Third Special Forces Group. It was an ad hoc thing that Barry did for him, and he was always grateful."

There wasn't exactly a big demand for "The Ballad" in the summer of 1964. There would, in fact, be no recording contract until late 1965 after Barry had served his truncated, five-month tour of duty in the Vietnam War. In December of 1965, just before Barry signed with R.C.A. Records, Gerry Gitell had come home from his assignment in Vietnam. He had spent a large part of an action-filled tour of duty leading a group of South Vietnamese local militia forces in combat operations against the Viet Cong in the Mekong Delta along the border with Cambodia.

"He led a hundred local fighters. His job also involved winning the hearts and minds of the civilian population," Seth Gitell said of his father. "Dad and his colleagues thought of themselves as 'a Peace Corps with guns.'"[6]

When Barry and Gerry signed that music publishing contract in July 1964, some 20,000 American troops were in South Vietnam. Nearly all were advisers to the South Vietnamese military in its fight against the local insurgents known as the Viet Cong, who were being supported by the communist government of North Vietnam. The number of American personnel in South Vietnam had increased greatly after President Kennedy took office in February of 1961—from around 900 at the end of 1960 to 16,300 by the end of 1963.[7]

Despite the large and increasing number of American troops, in the summer of 1964, not one U.S. combat unit was fighting in South Vietnam. That would soon change.

In July of 1964 the U.S. Navy began a covert operation known as DeSoto in the North Vietnamese coastal waters of the Tonkin Gulf. One of the DeSoto vessels sailing along the coast, the destroyer USS *Maddox*, was equipped with electronic listening devices. Its job: monitoring North Vietnamese military transmissions, gathering intelligence on coastal radar stations, and keeping an eye on communist ships in the area.

On August 2, 1964, the *Maddox* reported that it came under fire from North Vietnamese torpedo boats in international waters. Two days later the *Maddox* and a second DeSoto destroyer, the USS *C. Turner Joy*, reported a second attack. Even though the ships' commanders said that they couldn't absolutely confirm the second attacks, President Lyndon B. Johnson ordered retaliatory air strikes against North Vietnamese torpedo boat bases and oil storage depots.

Johnson immediately authorized American forces to retaliate, and then asked Congress for permission to widen the American military mission in Vietnam. On August 7, 1964, Congress overwhelmingly passed a resolution submitted by LBJ giving him "all necessary measures to repel any armed attacks against the forces of the United States and to prevent further aggression" in Vietnam. That measure, known as the Gulf of Tonkin Resolution, gave the government the legal authority to wage war in Vietnam against the Viet Cong and North Vietnamese.[8]

In a nationally broadcast address late in the evening of August 4—sometimes known as "the speech that launched the Vietnam War"—LBJ gravely told the American public about the "hostile actions against United States ships on the high seas in the Gulf of Tonkin." Johnson said he would not tolerate any "act of aggression" against U.S. military forces and that he had immediately ordered retaliatory action against North Vietnam.

"Yet," LBJ said, "our response, for the present, will be limited and fitting. We Americans know, although others appear to forget, the risks of spreading conflict. We still seek no wider war."[9]

Johnson may not have sought a wider war, but the American war effort in Vietnam widened considerably following passage of the Gulf of Tonkin Resolution. The first American combat troops, members of the Third Marine Division, landed in Vietnam early in March of 1965, followed by hundreds of thousands more army, marine, navy, air force, and even coast guard personnel. By 1968 the massive buildup peaked with some 530,000 American troops on the ground in South Vietnam.

That included a significant number of Special Forces personnel. The first SF troops, twelve members of the 14th Special Forces Detachment, came to Nha Trang in 1957 to train a group of South Vietnamese Army Rangers.[10] Soon the SF mission in Vietnam expanded and concentrated on organizing minority groups—primarily the dozens of indigenous tribal peoples known as Montagnards in the Central Highlands—into paramilitary units under the guidance of SF teams. Those units were known as the CIDG (Civilian Irregular Defense Group).[11]

In September of 1964, a month after passage of the Gulf of Tonkin Resolution, the 5th Special Forces Group took over all SF operations in South Vietnam. Fifth SF set up its headquarters in Nha Trang, a resort city on the coast of Central Vietnam. Not long after that, as Barry put it in his book, rumors swept Fort Bragg that "practically the entire Fifth Special Forces Group was to ship out by the end of the year."

The rumors turned out to be true. Barry—who had been promoted to spec 5 (the equivalent of buck sergeant) in July—received his orders for Vietnam on October 7, 1964. He would ship out on December 27. In the interim came more training at Fort Bragg. "We were issued gear and weapons—machine guns, mortars, recoilless rifles. We studied booby traps and practiced demolition," Barry wrote in his autobiography. "We were given briefings and books on Vietnam."[12] The training also included several weeks of Vietnamese language classes.

In early November, not long after his twenty-fourth birthday, Barry made out a will leaving everything to Lavona, who was pregnant with their first child. Then came a big farewell party at the 82nd Airborne's NCO Club at Fort Bragg, where Barry brought his guitar and played "The Ballad," among other songs. Then he and the other Green Berets had several weeks of leave before shipping out.

Barry and Lavona had hoped their baby would be born at Bragg. But that didn't happen. On December 2 they packed up their Ford Falcon and headed north so Lavona could deliver the child in Lehighton surrounded by her family. Lavona began having contractions in the car when the young couple reached the Pennsylvania line. She gave birth at Gnaden Heutten Memorial Hospital the next morning, December 3, 1964.

It was a boy. Barry named him Thor. "I had happened to read about the Scandinavian god of thunder and his hammer," Barry wrote. "I thought Thor a good, strong name for a boy and Lavona agreed."

Barry left the next day—but not for Fort Bragg. He took a bus to New York City, where he visited the Music Music Music offices on Broadway.

He wanted an advance against future royalties from sales of "The Ballad." Chet Gierlach said no, but he asked Barry to send tapes of anything new that he wrote in Vietnam.

Then it was back to Fort Bragg. Barry Sadler shipped out for the war zone, along with forty-seven other Green Berets, making up four twelve-man teams. They flew out in the rain on December 27, 1964, aboard a giant U.S. Air Force KC-135 Stratotanker.

The plane made stops at Travis Air Force Base outside San Francisco, in Hawaii, on Wake Island, and at Clark AFB in the Philippines, where the men spent the night.

The next day they flew into Tan Son Nhut Airport on the outskirts of Saigon. The plane touched down in the capital of the Republic of Vietnam at around 8:30 on the morning of Sunday, December 29, 1964.

CHAPTER 5

A LUCKY ONE

"When we went out on combat operations, it definitely wasn't 'hearts and minds.'"
—FORMER SPECIAL FORCES LIEUTENANT AL WILHELM

In their first few minutes in Vietnam, Barry and his fellow Green Berets struggled with their top-heavy rucksacks stenciled with their names, ranks, and service numbers and jammed with personal items. That included two types of fatigues, olive-drab greens and cammies, both with jump school silver wing patches on their chests and the Special Forces shoulder patch—a gold upturned dagger crossed with three lightning bolts—on their left sleeves with an "Airborne" tab directly above it.

The men had three types of headgear: the eponymous berets, camouflage baseball caps, and the helmets the men called steel pots. They wore their newly issued Tropical Combat Boots (aka, jungle boots) with heavily cleated black rubber soles and leather and cotton canvas upper soles with water drains. They also carried a raft of medical supplies and communication equipment.

The Green Berets landed at the bustling Tan Son Nhut Air Base on a hot and humid winter morning. The heavy air was redolent with the pungent odor of diesel fuel, mixed with wafts of rancid raw sewage and rotting garbage. More than one American who stepped out onto the tarmac at Tan Son Nhut remarked that the smell brought to mind burning excrement. Sometimes it was. The standard method of disposing the stuff at American bases in Vietnam was pouring gasoline into sawed-off fifty-five-gallon barrels hauled out of rudimentary latrines and setting the noxious mixture on fire.

Not long after deplaning, the men received their weapons. Each picked up a newly developed M-16 assault rifle, the superlight, gas-operated weapon that put out a deadly stream of semiautomatic or full automatic fire at the touch of the trigger. The SF teams' arsenals also included a variety of other weapons, most of which were inherited from earlier teams that had deployed back to the States. They included Winchester model 12 pump-action shotguns; .45-caliber pistols, compact .45-caliber M-3 submachine guns known as Grease Guns; .45-caliber Thompson submachine guns; .30-caliber M-903 Springfield bolt-action sniper rifles; and rifle-like, shoulder-fired M-79 grenade launchers.

Then came a hurry-up-and-wait, seven-hour stint sitting on the tarmac killing time at Tan Son Nhut. Finally, after dark, the men trudged up the rear loading ramp of a C-123 prop transport—the main form of fixed-wing transportation during the war—for a rocky 200-mile flight to Nha Trang on the South China Sea.

Sadler and company spent that night in moldy Korean War–era tents inside the heavily fortified 5th Special Forces compound in Nha Trang. "The main building was a beautiful old French mansion surrounded by a wall and barbed wire," said screenwriter and director Patrick S. Duncan, who paid a visit while serving with the 173rd Airborne Brigade during his Vietnam War tour. The compound also included a lounge where the Green Berets drank beer and played slot machines. They called it the Playboy Club.

"It looked like a frat house and smelled like old sweat socks," Duncan said.[1]

Barry, who was not unfamiliar with guns and rifles, heard his first shots fired in anger that night. "In the middle of the night, I was aroused by the crackle of small-arms fire," he wrote. The crackle came from Viet Cong guerrilla fighters outside the compound's perimeter.

Barry grabbed his weapon, ready to do battle, he said, "but we were ordered to stay in our quarters because we didn't know the place. Our people beat off the attackers without casualties."[2]

Two days later Barry and a group of other Green Berets boarded a twin-engine U.S. Air Force high-wing DH4-C Caribou transport plane for the short flight inland to Pleiku in South Vietnam's rugged Central

Highlands. A corps of the South Vietnamese army (known as ARVN, an acronym for the Army of the Republic of Vietnam) troops had its headquarters in that large city. Pleiku also was home to a Special Forces command and control team that worked with the local Montagnards and provided logistical support to other U.S. Army forces in the area.[3]

Viet Cong snipers sometimes took shots at the low-flying Caribous. "To foil them," Barry wrote, "the Caribou came down to the red earth in a steep dive, reversed its propellers, and blew red dirt all over the place."

An NCO herded the Green Berets into an armored personnel carrier lined with sandbags. The men wound up in different SF camps. Barry went to work as a replacement medic at Camp Plei Tanang Le, a tiny SF outpost forty-five miles east of Pleiku just inside the Cambodian border deep in the mountainous Highlands.

Soon thereafter, he received a letter from Lavona in which she enclosed a photo of herself holding their newborn son, Thor—"the first picture I ever saw of our baby," Barry wrote in his autobiography.

Barry treated his first patient at the dusty outpost surrounded by heavy scrub bush: a Montagnard who had taken shrapnel wounds in a leg and had also stepped on a punji stick—a sharpened bamboo booby trap often smeared with excrement that the Viet Cong deployed along jungle trails throughout South Vietnam.

Barry then moved to another nearby camp where—among other things—he treated his first rat bite. Then he was sent to a third Green Beret outpost, Camp Soui Doi. The Special Forces mission there—as it was in the other Central Highlands detachments—consisted primarily of leading Montagnard CIDG fighters on patrols to try to find and snuff out Viet Cong infiltration routes, as well as working on "hearts and minds" civic action programs and psychological warfare operations.

In late February Barry took an abbreviated training course in psychological operations (Psy Ops in military parlance) at Camp Goodman, the Special Forces compound—complete with a well-stocked bar—in downtown Saigon about three miles from Tan Son Nhut. He then flew back to the Highlands and checked into what would be his fourth and last unit in Vietnam, Special Forces Detachment A-216 at Plei Do Lim.

The area around Plei Do Lim, Barry wrote in his autobiography, "was beautiful country, a plateau of lush grass with little patches of jungle, banana groves, and Montagnard villages all around."[4] The detachment's compound, sitting at nearly 2,200 feet above sea level, was named Camp Hardy in memory of Capt. Herbert F. Hardy Jr., the commanding officer of another SF detachment who had been killed in action near the Cambodian border on March 4, 1964.

When Barry arrived Camp Hardy had about a dozen buildings inside a rectangular perimeter encircled by a wall of sandbags and barbed wire. Beyond that was a second heavily fortified perimeter. Outside the wire the men arrayed deadly Claymore anti-personnel mines, command-detonated remote control devices that spew out hundreds of steel balls in a sixty-degree, fan-shaped arc. As Barry put it: Hardy "was a model of security," a "strong camp, very well set up, with many defenses. We worked on them constantly, frequently changing things."

The outer perimeter, Barry wrote, "had only one entrance, with all kinds of weapons trained on it. There were underground bunkers, individual foxholes, and numerous fortifications and positions connected by a trench running around the edge of the camp. There were ditches joined with punji sticks and claymore mines."[5]

The camp also had a communications facility that was partly underground and a mess hall. Nearby was a Montagnard village where some 200 CIDG fighters lived with their families. The Camp Hardy complex also included an airfield with a 2,800-foot runway capable of handling Caribous, C-123s, and the larger C-130 Hercules, as well as a helicopter landing pad.

"The camp was located with the purpose of being a magnet village for others, which put us in the position of doing Civil Affairs types of things as part of our mission," Al Wilhelm, A-216's executive officer when Barry arrived, said.[6] Barry Sadler joined Billy D. Johnson and William LeGrand as the third medic on the team. That job entailed doing Civil Affairs (also known as "hearts and minds") work in the field and at Camp Hardy. Sadler, LeGrand, and Johnson treated Montagnard men, women, and children virtually on a daily basis, performing myriad medical tasks that included doing minor surgery, giving inoculations, treating injuries, and even performing rudimentary dental work.

"We're overgrown social workers," Barry told *Life* magazine in March of 1966. "We try to show [the Vietnamese people] we want nothing from them. We don't want their land or to sleep with their women or to take their food. It's a big job and a satisfying one and it works the hell out of you. The V.C. are doing the same things but we can offer these people in two years what it would take the V.C. 20 years to give. The best friend we have is medicine."[7]

Barry "saw lepers, treated cases of cholera and typhus, cut abscesses out of spines, pulled teeth, and delivered babies," he wrote in his autobiography. "Delivery of a baby was the simplest thing in the world. We just stood around to see that nothing went wrong."[8]

In the month of March alone, Sadler and Johnson—"a stocky, blond, blue-eyed man about my size, from Newtown, Missouri," in Barry's words—performed 1,097 outpatient procedures on Montagnard fighters, their dependents, and civilians. Sixteen patients required overnight stays at the camp dispensary; 295 people received treatment from Sadler and Johnson when they were outside the camp on medical patrols. Among other things the medics provided treatment for lacerations, punctures, fragment wounds, sprains, burns, and infected old wounds. The diseases they treated included dysentery, measles, chicken pox, mumps, tuberculosis, malaria, worms, and rheumatism.[9]

During their medical patrols outside the wire, the medics conducted sick calls, many for children. The villagers "often asked me to leave medicine [with them] so that they could continue treatment," Barry wrote. "We couldn't do that, since anything we left would be confiscated by the VC. But we told the patients and their families that if they came to Plei Do Lim, they would be treated. Many did so."[10]

The medical calls took place at random times and places. If the Green Beret medics "had given notice," Barry wrote, "or had attempted to maintain a regular schedule or route, we probably would have been murdered by the Viet Cong." In the villages, he wrote, "mothers would bring out their children. The ill would gather, and we had all the patients we could handle. We'd put patients who were crippled or seriously ill in the truck and bring them back to camp. We kept some for weeks, feeding and treating them."

The medics also treated their own team members who had been injured or wounded. And they accompanied Montagnards into the field on combat and reconnaissance patrols and ambushes.

Barry took himself out of action for three weeks because of a medical situation of his own—a bad case of hemorrhoids. He left Plei Do Lim on April 1 for Nha Trang, where he underwent an operation at the Army's 100-bed, 8th Field Hospital not far from the 5th Special Forces Compound.

Barry brought his guitar along. During his recovery he showed up at the compound's bar and played "The Ballad of the Green Berets." "I recall Sgt. Sadler sitting on the front porch of the old French villa on the beachfront in Nha Trang strumming his guitar and humming or singing and writing or rewriting the song," said former Green Beret Art Reed.[11]

The work of the young military nurses at the hospital inspired Barry, he later said, to write a song in their honor. That tune, "Salute to the Nurses," contains the lines: "And all of the men in this war-torn land/ Salute the nurses of Vietnam."

"He serenaded us several times, and even wrote a song to us," then twenty-four-year-old U.S. Army captain Osa H. Jensen, who treated Barry at Nha Trang, told a newspaper reporter a year later. "We were more than medical attendants to the men. We were their mothers, sisters, and confidants. They seemed very eager to talk to a girl and I guess we represented the girl from home away from home."[12]

Barry spent nearly three weeks at the Nha Trang hospital. He returned to Camp Hardy on April 21.

Just about every week a two-man SF team at Camp Hardy would take a group of Montagnard fighters outside the wire on patrols looking for the enemy. It worked on a rotation system, so each Green Beret went out once every six weeks or so. The two Americans took charge of platoon- and sometimes company-size Montagnard units. The Montagnards were equipped with, as Barry put it, a "lethal hodgepodge" of mismatched (and old) weapons: early twentieth-century Springfield .22-caliber rifles; similarly ancient bolt-action Mark I Lee-Enfield repeating rifles, the main weapon used by British forces during World Wars I and II; and a variety of shotguns and French light machine guns.

"When we went out on combat operations like that, it definitely wasn't 'hearts and minds,'" Barry's former XO Al Wilhelm said. "It was more often to destroy a village that had been harboring or supporting" the Viet Cong. In certain parts of the surrounding country, "the whole area was presumed to be hostile," Wilhelm said, "in the sense that there were no loyalties to the [South Vietnamese] government. I didn't find the people to be that troublesome, but we did more often than not find that that's where the communists—the VC—tended to operate."

On one such mission Barry and the Montagnards discovered a huge cache of rice, which they promptly burned. On another the men "tramped about a bit, burned some fields and returned," Barry wrote. "It was just a search, something to keep the VC aware that we were there," he explained. "By the end of the patrol, we had six suspects, and two of them turned out to be Viet Cong." The men questioned the VC and then sent them to the South Vietnamese Special Forces headquarters in Pleiku.

During downtime Barry and the rest of the team members did what soldiers do in those situations: They slept in, took naps, sunbathed, listened to the radio, read, and wrote letters home. They also drank a lot of beer and played a lot of cards, mostly poker. Since it was usually brutally hot in the daytime, everybody, Barry wrote, "observed siesta time, from about 11 a.m. to 1 p.m. or later." It was "so hot during the day and we slept so poorly at night, what with the rats and other small animals, we really needed our naps. My narrow underground bunk, in which the logs were still sprouting greenery, was musty and moldy but was about the coolest spot in camp."[13]

Barry was known as the guy in the unit with the guitar. "He'd pick and sing a little bit," Jimmy Walker, who succeeded Al Wilhelm as the unit's XO, said. "He even tried to teach me how to play it. He'd show me some chords and stuff." Barry "brought his guitar to camp," Wilhelm remembered, "which is a nice thing. That's a positive thing when you have somebody who can play and entertain and help people forget and relax for a little bit."

Barry Sadler wrote two songs while he was at Plei Do Lim. "Garet Trooper" mocks a rear-echelon soldier who "fought from Saigon to Nha Trang in every bar, that is, and only with the girls." "Letter from Vietnam" is a love song from a solider to his woman back home. That tune, Barry said, was inspired by his wife, Lavona, who was in Pennsylvania working two jobs, at a rug mill and waiting tables at the Big Chief drive-in restaurant.

"When I heard about this," Barry said, "I had a fit and made her give up the second job." Soon after, he wrote "Letter from Vietnam," which contains the words:

> Oh, Lord I'm tired and sad,
> And I want you, oh, so bad.
> I've been away so very long;
> Now I want to go home.
> So remember that I love you;
> That, my dear, is true.

On March 6, 1965, an army Public Information team from Saigon paid a visit to Camp Hardy. The crew shot some movie footage of the camp and the Montagnards and interviewed the SF guys. Someone told the Public Information Office people that Barry was singing and playing his own tunes, including a song about the Green Berets. Not long after that, on March 23, a pilot landed a small aircraft at Plei Do Lim, sought out Spec. 5 Sadler, and told him he had orders to take him out on a mission.

Barry "thought he did something wrong," Lavona said.[14]

"Where am I going?" he asked.

"Saigon," the pilot said.

"What for?"

"I don't know. I just have orders to deliver you to Saigon."[15]

Barry jumped on the plane, carrying his rifle—"cruddy, filthy, and needing a shave," he later said. He didn't find out exactly what the army had in mind for him until after the plane landed in Saigon. It turned out that a PIO major who had been at Plei Do Lim on March 6 wanted to film him singing "The Ballad" in Saigon. He also wanted Barry to write a song on the spot in honor of Maj. Gen. Delk Oden. A West Point graduate who had commanded a tank battalion in World War II, Oden was about to return home after having headed the Army Support Command in Vietnam since July of 1963.

"In a few minutes, I had something," Barry said, "a sort of ode to Oden, with lines about fighting and flying." That made the PIO folks happy. They procured a clean uniform for Barry, as well as a guitar, and put him up for the night. The next day he played his ode at Oden's farewell party. When he finished a Green Beret in the audience asked him to do "The Ballad." The next day the PIO filmed him singing the song in front of a bunker in Saigon. Film of that made its way on to American television.

Not long after that, back home at her mother's house in Pennsylvania, Lavona Sadler was getting ready to give her baby boy his afternoon bottle. "I had to pretty soon wake him up," Lavona said. "So I was just sitting there and thought I'd catch the national news first. It came on around six. And all of a sudden Barry was on TV singing 'The Ballad.' It was so weird. There he was, good looking and everything else and with that smile of his. And I was all alone in the house. There was no one there I could yell, 'Hey, look!'"[16]

It was a "bittersweet," moment, Lavona said, seeing her husband alive and well in the war zone, but at the same time knowing he still had nine months more of his one-year tour of duty to serve in harm's way in Vietnam.

Barry flew back to Plei Do Lim on March 30, 1965. While he was gone, on March 26, Sgt. Billy Bean, the unit's heavy weapons man, was bitten by a rat and evacuated to the hospital at Nha Trang for a rabies shot. The next day, March 27, catastrophe struck: At around five o'clock in the afternoon during a fierce thunderstorm, a lightning bolt hit the camp's perimeter. The lightning ignited thirty-six Claymore mines, spraying the inner perimeter and the Montagnard barracks with a deadly curtain of steel pellets.

The grisly toll: twenty-three Montagnards and suspected VC (who were being held as prisoners) killed and sixty-nine wounded. Only one American got hit. Staff Sgt. William LeGrand took pellets in the head and stomach and was evacuated to Nha Trang. He died on April 28 at the hospital at Clark Air Force Base in the Philippines. LeGrand, who joined the army when he was seventeen in 1950 to fight in the Korean War, was thirty-two years old. He left behind a wife and two daughters.

The only other American who lost his life at Plei Do Lim while Barry served there was one of the youngest guys on the team, twenty-three-year-old staff sergeant Raymond Joe Vrba Jr. On May 25 Vrba and 1st Lt. Daniel Hudson piled eighty-four CIDG fighters, two translators, and two ARVNs into two-and-a-half-ton trucks (known as deuce-and-a-halfs) and went into the bush. They were looking for the enemy after the VC had ambushed a wood-cutting detail. The men split into two flanks and began walking down both sides of a remote road. Vrba's element marched into the killing zone of a Viet Cong ambush. Hudson and his men tried to flank the ambush but had to fall back because of unrelenting enemy fire.

When the shooting stopped, six CIDG fighters were dead, four were wounded, and one was missing. Raymond Joe Vrba Jr. of Waco, Texas, perished in the crossfire.

Vrba had only recently arrived at the detachment. He and Sadler were bunkmates at Camp Hardy, and Barry had taken Vrba out on his first five-day patrol just a few days earlier. After the fatal ambush, Barry wrote, "I had the task of identifying Vrba's body and shipping it out, along with his personal belongings."

Barry Sadler paid tribute to Vrba—whose wife was about to give birth to their first child when he was killed—in his song "I'm a Lucky One."

> But at night when I sleep, I know my dreams will be
> About my friends I left across the sea
> I'll hear Vrba, Young, and Horn laugh again out loud
> We'll all be together in a happy crowd[17]

Sometime in mid-May, while out on patrol with the Montagnards, Barry Sadler walked into a punji stick that ripped into the side of his left knee. In his book Barry did not give the date the incident took place, saying only that it happened "a few days" before Memorial Day.[18] His official Purple Heart citation reports that the date was May 16.

Soon after it happened—but not until after Vrba died on May 25—Barry checked himself into the 8th Field Hospital in Nha Trang for treatment. Oddly, Detachment A-216's official Monthly Operational Summary for May does not mention the Sadler punji stick incident, nor does it say anything about Barry leaving Camp Hardy for treatment in Nha Trang any time that month, nor does it list any Americans in his unit as wounded in action that month.

One possible explanation: Because Barry at first didn't think the wound was serious, he did not report it, and his departure for Nha Trang simply fell through the organizational cracks and never made it into the summary.

"I have no memory of Barry walking into a punji stick," Jimmy Walker said in 2015. "But it's very possible this occurred and he said nothing to anybody because he was self-treating." As for the fact that the Operational Summary does not mention neither the incident nor Barry leaving for treatment, "people left almost all the time," Walker said. "It could be that Barry left to get medical supplies—or we could have been running low on beer."[19]

In his 1967 autobiography Barry wrote that he "bumped into a *punji* stick in the tall grass" while leading a Montagnard patrol. He said that he well knew that the feces-covered booby traps could cause serious problems. But, he said, "I had been taking an antibiotic because of a touch of dysentery, and the wound, in my left leg near the knee, seemed slight." So, Barry said, he simply pulled the stick out of his leg, cleaned the wound with a cotton swab, applied a bandage, and "finished the patrol."[20]

That "was a mistake," Barry admitted, as his leg subsequently swelled up and he developed a serious infection.

Barry gave the same basic story to interviewers when the "The Ballad of the Green Berets" hit big in 1966 and later whenever the topic came up. "We were on a regular routine patrol, a search and destroy operation," he told an Associated Press reporter late in February 1966. After the stick ripped into his leg, Barry said, "I cleaned the wound out. I was the medic in our team, so I know more about what I'm doing than the other guys. Apparently, I didn't know quite enough. A day or two later the contamination caused my leg to get a massive infection and abscess."[21]

He told *Life* magazine that after the stick gashed his leg, he "cleaned the wound, put on a strip of tape and stayed with the patrol."[22] A week later, the article said, Barry "was in the Nha Trang hospital," his "leg swollen double and throbbing with infection. To contain it, doctors carved out a strip of flesh three inches long and 10 inches wide. Out also came a mass of nerves, rendering a large portion of his leg permanently numb. Says Sadler, 'A little V.C. whittling a stick of bamboo put $100,000 worth of training out of commission.'"

Given the fact that Barry identified Vrba's body on May 25, he most likely flew off to the 8th Field Hospital in Nha Trang (where he had been treated for hemorrhoids in April) a day or two after that. Barry wrote that he already was in the hospital at Nha Trang on "the last day of May or the first of June"[23] when the VC hit the nearby airport with mortars. He said he pulled out his IV tubes, jumped out of his hospital bed, ran out the door, and "found me a hole, and waited for things to quiet down. When they did, I went back inside, attached the IV tubes and went to sleep."

Soon after that (either June 1 or 2), Barry joined a group of other wounded men as they piled into an Air Force C-119 "Flying Boxcar" cargo plane, which had been fitted out with medical litters to transport bed-bound and other patients. A few hours later the plane landed at Clark

AFB in the Philippines and Barry checked into the hospital there—"a big, beautiful, modern, air-conditioned place," he wrote in his autobiography. He would be there for the next seven weeks.

The infected leg did not respond to penicillin, Barry wrote, so the doctors at Clark "kept the wound open and draining for several days. They then closed it with wire sutures." Barry managed to take his guitar with him on the medical evacuation flight from Nha Trang to the Philippines. During his recovery at Clark, Barry sat in on a hospital concert given by a USO troupe of singers. He sang "The Ballad" and a song called "Bamiba," which he had written in Nha Trang. That tune plays tribute to 33 Biere, a local beer known as Ba Moui Ba in Vietnamese, which the troops called "Bam E Bam" or "Ba Me Bam."[24]

His songs, Barry wrote, "drew more applause than the USO troupe's songs from the men in the hospital."[25]

"You're a lucky one." Those are the words an officer at Clark used in mid-July when he told Barry he would be sent back to the States for more treatment. Those also are the words that inspired Barry to write the song with that title in honor of Vrba, Young, and Horn. It took him just "a few minutes" to write it, Barry said.

Barry Sadler left the hospital at Clark on July 20, 1965. He once again joined a group of wounded men on a military transport. This time they were heading home.

The plane stopped in Japan and at Travis Air Force Base in California, where Barry and the other patients spent the night at the base's hospital. Barry—who had not told Lavona he was wounded or had been in the hospital—called her that night with the news. The next day the medical plane began dropping the other patient/passengers off near their stateside posts. It took two days before Barry arrived at Fort Bragg's Womack Army Medical Center.

He wasn't in great shape. He had lost more than forty pounds, weighing in at around 140. His cheeks, Barry said, were "sunken." His eyes "looked different," his hair "was cropped short," and he wore "oversized pajamas." When Lavona Sadler arrived at the hospital, after driving to North Carolina from Pennsylvania, she did not recognize her husband.

"He was very skinny, very gaunt—terribly gaunt," Lavona said. "I was walking by him and then he called my name. He was in a hospital bed and I honest-to-gosh didn't recognize him at all. He had these wire stitches in his leg. He told me he had stumbled on a trap."[26]

Barry would walk with a slight limp for the rest of his life.

CHAPTER 6
THE RIGHT MAN WITH THE RIGHT SONG

"I wrote it for the git-tar"

—BARRY SADLER, AUGUST 1965

Barry recovered rapidly at the hospital at Fort Bragg. Soon, he was well enough to spend nights at an on-base guesthouse with Lavona and check back into the hospital during the day for treatment. The couple agreed that once Barry recovered, they would live off base.

"He told me to look for a house near the base," Lavona said. "So I found one and we bought it."[1] It was a small ranch house in a small subdivision. "We signed up for it," Barry wrote in his autobiography, "without my seeing it."[2]

Near the end of July, Barry had all but fully recovered. The hospital released him, and he went on convalescent leave. He and Lavona drove their blue Ford Falcon to her sister's house in Pennsylvania to retrieve seven-month-old Thor. After they drove back to Fort Bragg, Lavona stayed in North Carolina and took a job as a nurse's aide at Cape Fear Valley Medical Center in Fayetteville.

Barry used the rest of his leave to drive to New York City to see Chet Gierlach and Phyllis Fairbanks at Music Music Music. The reason: Barry thought he could capitalize on the widespread popularity of a newly published novel that lionized the work of the Army Special Forces detachments in Vietnam: *The Green Berets*, by Robin Moore.

Born Robert Lowell Moore Jr. in 1925 in Boston, Robin Moore was a descendant of the famed Lowell Boston Brahmin family. His childhood and adolescence couldn't have been more different from Barry's hardscrabble upbringing. Moore, whose father co-founded the Sheraton Hotel chain, went to Boston private schools and then joined the army during World War II. He served as a nose gunner on B-17 bombers in the U.S. Army Air Corps. After the war he graduated from Harvard, worked in the brand-new medium of television for a while, and then did advertising and marketing work for Sheraton for eight years.

Robin Moore became enamored of the Green Berets in the early 1960s. When he approached General Yarborough—reportedly with the help of a former Harvard classmate, U.S. Attorney General Robert F. Kennedy—about writing an in-depth book about the Green Berets, the marketing-savvy general readily agreed. He suggested that Moore go through SF training, which he did for nearly a year. Moore then went to Vietnam, where he lived and worked with Special Forces units for about five months beginning in January of 1964.

"I planned and researched" the book "originally to be an account presenting, through a series of actual incidents, an inside informed view of the almost unknown marvelous undercover work of our Special Forces in Vietnam and countries around the world," Moore wrote in the book's introduction, which he titled "Badge of Courage." But, Moore said, he encountered "major obstacles and disadvantages in this straight reportorial method." So he decided he "could present the truth better and more accurately in the form of fiction."[3]

Moore—and his publisher—made no secret of their unalloyed admiration for the men of the Green Berets. "Brilliant, inspiring tales of the little known but crucially important arm of U.S. defense, the crack teams of the Special Forces," the book's cover blurb proclaims, "true-life heroes who have made the Green Beret a badge of honor in the jungles of Vietnam and the world over."

Published just as the first American combat troops landed in Vietnam in March of 1965, the book struck a chord with the American public. It also "did as much as anything to elevate the Special Forces to national prominence," the Vietnam War historian Christian Appy noted.[4]

The Green Berets quickly became a big bestseller, the first book about the Vietnam War to do so. By the end of the year, it sold nearly 100,000 copies in hardcover. Then came the paperback, which also took off, selling more than 1.2 million copies in the first two months after it came out in

November. It stood as the nation's top-selling paperback well into the spring of 1966.[5]

Chet Gierlach and Robin Moore happened to be friends. Sometime during Barry's visit to New York City in August of 1965, Gierlach, Phyllis Fairbanks, and Moore had a discussion about Barry's song and Moore's book.

The song's "fate is inevitably bound up with the book," Fairbanks said. "Its author is a very close friend."[6]

According to Barry, Robin Moore suggested to Gierlach that he change the title of the song to "The Ballad of the Green Berets" (making the last word plural) to tie the song to the book in the public's mind. Gierlach did so, and then he had a little-known North Carolina singing group called The Hunters cut a demo, which he sold at cost to Avon Books. It was a promotional stunt, in which Avon handed out the record to booksellers to promote the upcoming paperback edition of Moore's book. That's also how Barry's picture made its way onto the cover of the soon-to-be huge-selling paperback.

Fairbanks, Barry wrote, called an Avon executive after she'd heard that the company hadn't decided on a cover image. "I have a real trooper here," she said. "Why don't you take a look at him?"[7]

Avon took a look. They liked what they saw, and they sent the recruiting-poster-handsome twenty-four-year-old to a well-known New York City commercial photographer, Lester Krauss. He posed Barry from the neck up with just a hint of his open-collared uniform showing, green beret, of course, perched on his head, staring resolutely just off camera. The words on the cover of the ninety-five-cent mass market paperback all but shouted: "The Green Berets: Robin Moore's flaming blockbuster novel about a new kind of solider in a new kind of war."

Barry said he received a fifty-dollar "model's fee" for the cover. But he would get much, much more out of that sitting. A few days later he met Robin Moore for lunch at the venerable (founded in 1868) New York City Athletic Club. The two met hit it off. Moore promptly arranged for Barry to move from the small hotel in Manhattan where he was staying into a suite at the Sheraton East, no doubt getting the free room through his Sheraton family connections. During lunch Barry mentioned that he could use a new guitar. That very afternoon, Barry said, Moore took him to a pawnshop on Eighth Avenue and bought him a guitar for $140.

Moore told a slightly different version of that story. "I was asked to help Barry with the lyrics," he told a newspaper reporter in March of 1966 when "The Ballad" was the best-selling song in the country, "and I was glad to do it. He's a fine boy. You know, when he returned to the states, he didn't have his guitar with him. It was wounded in Vietnam. So, I loaned him $140 for a new one."[8]

Whether it was a loan or not, getting that pawnshop guitar in Barry's hands was not all that Robin Moore did. In return for half an interest in the song, Moore "wrote a new third verse, added his name, and agreed to do all he could to sell it," Barry said.

Phyllis Fairbanks said that she and Chet Gierlach had marketing in mind when they arranged for Moore to contribute to the song. "We put the author of the book, Robin Moore, on the ballad," she said. "He did, in fact, contribute a couple of verses. Our feeling was that with this kind of limelight coming up, the publicity involved would benefit everyone."

Gierlach and Fairbanks also arranged for Barry to appear on *The Barry Gray Show*, a late-night New York City radio talk show on WMCA-AM. They also set up a two-hour sit-down for Barry with another of their pals, the popular syndicated columnist Bob Considine, who also happened to be a friend of Robin Moore's. Considine's "On the Line" commentary column appeared in scores of newspapers across the country.

Bob Considine wrote two fawning columns on Barry on consecutive days during the first week of August. In the first one the hawkish Considine gave Barry free rein to boost the American war effort in Vietnam and to denigrate those (relatively few) Americans opposed to the war. In his columnist's blunt style, Considine described Barry (incorrectly) as a native of San Francisco who "is against the Viet Cong and against anybody over on that side of the world or here at home who gives his enemy aid and comfort."

Calling Barry "an old 24," Considine said he was wounded in Vietnam and was "hobbling around New York these days with his friend Robin Moore, author of the best-selling book about the extraordinary Special Forces men whose valor in Viet Nam has moved the Viet Cong to put a bounty on their green-bereted heads."

Considine went on to quote Barry—who "seethes with war"—at length, extolling the Americans fighting in Vietnam, as well as the South Vietnamese military and the Montagnard fighters, and denigrating the Viet Cong. "We can win this war in three or four years," Barry told Considine, "if they let us. I mean we can win unless we get fouled up in one of those Korea-type situations.

"We're hurting the other side bad, chasing them, bombing them, burning their places and their food. We don't take many prisoners in Viet Nam, but most of those we do take say they are hungry. The VC isn't getting the recruits it once did."

Then Barry sounded off on one segment of the tiny American antiwar movement. "I got sick, while they were working on my leg at Fort Bragg, reading in the paper that some American college group was taking up a collection to buy medicine for the VC," Barry said. "First time in my life I was ashamed to be an American. Why, if those people knew one tenth of what the VC does to poor innocent people who only want to be left alone! The terrible tortures and terror. And here we are—some of us—trying to help them."

Considine ended the column with a big plug for Barry's song. The "sergeant," he wrote, "has put his convalescent time to good use. 'They say Viet Nam's a war without a song,' he said with a grin that wiped years off his seamed face. 'Now it's got one: "The Ballad of the Green Beret." I wrote it for the git-tar.'"[9]

The second column opened with what Considine called a "hairy" war story Barry told him. It involved a Montagnard suspected of stealing penicillin for the Viet Cong. To prove it, loyal Montagnards, Barry said, filled some empty penicillin containers with strychnine. The next day the suspect took off with the containers.

"He returned," Barry told Considine, "but three days later was mysteriously killed." The Montagnards "were delighted. They explained that the strychnine must have killed some Viet Cong VIPs because only high-ranking VC are given penicillin. The VC, in turn, had been obliged to kill our thief."

Considine then quoted Barry expounding on life at Plei Do Lim. "Our camp is 50 miles from nowhere," Barry said, "but we have ice, we bribe pilots to fly us beer and Coke—pilots are nutty enough to go for creepy VC weapons for souvenirs—and we always have plenty of meat in our deep freezer, wild pigs and buffalo we shoot."

The column ended with Barry explaining that the Montagnards were quite taken with the American movies the Green Berets showed once a month in the compound. They "love our movies, believe everything they see on the screen," Barry said. After showing a science fiction film, Barry said, his Montagnard counterpart came to him and said, "Docksie, you got ray-gun for me? I want one. I kill beaucoup VC with American ray-gun."

Meanwhile in New York City, Barry recorded four new songs, including "The Badge of Courage," an ode to the first Vietnam War Medal of Honor recipients. He also recorded another version of "The Ballad," using several lines that Moore suggested. Moore then paved the way for Barry to sign with the William Morris Agency, the top entertainment talent agency in the nation. "Robin and I thought this took care of everything," Barry wrote.[10]

Moore flew to Vietnam to write a series of articles for the Hearst newspaper chain. Barry drove to Pennsylvania, where he and Lavona hooked a U-Haul trailer filled with their modest collection of furniture, including some that Lavona's family had given them, to the back of the Falcon and drove back to Fayetteville. Barry went back on active duty, starting with a desk job at the hospital at Fort Bragg. He also did some hand-to-hand combat instructing. In November he took a trip to Leadville to see his mother and brother.

The first large battle of the American war in Vietnam took place just about the time Barry returned to Fort Bragg: a fierce four-day fight on November 14–17, 1965, near the Drang River in the Central Highlands not far from Plei Do Lim. In what became known as the Battle of the Ia Drang Valley, a heavily outnumbered 1st Cavalry Division battalion faced off against two regiments of North Vietnamese Army troops. While inflicting heavy losses on the NVA, the Cav lost 234 dead and nearly 300 wounded.

The Battle of the Ia Drang Valley proved to be an important turning point in the Vietnam War. Before November 14 a total of 1,100 Americans had died in the war, "most of them by twos and threes in a war where Americans were advisers to the South Vietnamese battalions fighting Viet Cong guerrillas," former war correspondent Joe Galloway, who witnessed the fighting at Ia Drang, wrote. "Now the North Vietnamese Army had arrived" and the fighting—and the number of American troops in Vietnam—escalated significantly.[11]

By the end of the year, the number of American military personnel on the ground in South Vietnam jumped to some 185,000.

The William Morris Agency never did get Barry Sadler a recording contract. But Robin Moore's entertainment connections finally paid off in November. At a get-together after he had given a speech on November 18 in Maplewood, New Jersey, not far from New York City, Moore told his friend Clancy Isaac, a colorful, savvy marketing man (and World War II veteran), about Barry and the song. Isaac put in a call to RCA Victor Records, setting up a meeting with Dick Broderick, the company's license manager. Broderick agreed to listen to Barry's demos. The rest is pop music history.

Broderick, Barry wrote in his autobiography, "had ears" and convinced the RCA higher-ups "that this was the right tune, right place, and right man with the right song."

"I took it to RCA Victor," Gierlach later said, "and everyone flipped over his voice. It was the fastest signing of talent you ever saw."[12]

The following day, November 24, 1965, Gierlach called Barry, telling him the good news: RCA wanted to sign him to a recording contract and cut an album as soon as possible.

"I had gotten in five days what I had been seeking for more than two years," Barry said. "They wanted me to come to New York as soon as I could get leave. I sent a telegram canceling my William Morris contract and got to New York on December 2."[13]

Barry signed with RCA that morning in Broderick's office. The twenty-five-year-old staff sergeant who could not read a note of music received a decent $500 advance. He went right to work with Andy Wiswell, a Grammy-winning A&R (Artist & Repertoire)[14] man and producer who had worked with Judy Garland, Perry Como, and Harry Belafonte, among others. Barry also signed a management contract that day with Victor Catala, a friend of Wiswell's. He then flew back to Fayetteville, where he wrote five more songs.

Barry flew back to New York City early on Saturday morning, December 18, ready to record sixteen songs. RCA wanted a dozen for the album.

At around 8:00 a.m., Barry walked into Studio A at the RCA Building on East 24th Street, wearing his Class A dress uniform. Veteran songwriter, arranger, and conductor Sid Bass—who had worked with Frankie Valli and the Four Seasons, Paul Anka, and Connie Francis, among many others—had a fifteen-piece orchestra and a male chorus ready to go. Barry doffed his uniform jacket, loosened his tie, and in the next two-and-a-half hours recorded four songs—"Lullaby," "Letter from Vietnam," "I'm Watching the Raindrops Fall," and "Badge of Courage." Then everyone broke for lunch.

After lunch Barry, Bass, and company recorded "The Ballad." There "was a stir among the musicians and also among the RCA executives outside the glass" as he launched into it, Barry said.

Then came "Bamiba," "Saigon," and "Salute to the Nurses," before everyone knocked off for dinner at six o'clock. After chowing down at a nearby Italian restaurant, the group reconvened in the studio and recorded the other songs that would go on the album: "I'm a Lucky One," "The Soldier Has Come Home," "Trooper's Lament," and "Garet Trooper." The session ended at eleven o'clock that night.

"During that nine-hour recording session," a friend of Gierlach wrote, "Gierlach himself lost five pounds. He estimates Sadler did about that. They put 12 songs on platters."[15]

RCA released the single of "The Ballad" on January 11, 1966. The album, titled "Ballads of the Green Berets," hit the record stores on January 20.

CHAPTER 7

A HOT NEW SINGLE WITH A READY-MADE MARKET

"I don't consider myself a performer. I'm not used to playing before audiences."

—BARRY SADLER, FEBRUARY 1, 1966

When "The Ballad of the Green Berets" burst on the scene early in 1966, the American public overwhelmingly supported the U.S. war in Vietnam.[1] Aside from Democratic senator J. William Fulbright of Arkansas, who chaired the Senate's Foreign Relations Committee, very few members of Congress spoke out against the widening war. What would become a widespread antiwar movement in 1968 had yet to move very far beyond small, sporadic demonstrations led by leftist student groups and pacifists.[2]

President Johnson reflected that strong support at the very beginning of his nationally televised January 12 State of the Union Address. Saying that the war "must be the center of our concerns," Johnson said that his administration would "not permit those who fire upon us in Vietnam to win a victory over the desires of all the American people."[3]

The American news media's coverage reflected the public's strong support of the war. News magazines, newspapers, and television news programs consistently provided upbeat war coverage, reflecting a World War II–style pro-administration, support-the-troops attitude—along with a significant dose of anti-communism.

"Today, South Viet Nam throbs with pride and power," *Time* magazine enthused a few months before "The Ballad" came out. "The remarkable turnabout in the war is the result of one of the swiftest, biggest military buildups in the history of warfare. Everywhere today South Viet Nam bustles with the U.S. presence."

Wave "upon wave of combat-booted Americans—lean, laconic and looking for a fight—pour ashore from armadas of troop ships," the article continued. "Day and night screaming jets and prowling helicopters seek out the enemy." The Viet Cong's "once-cocky hunters have become the cowering hunted as the cutting edge of U.S. fire power slashes into the thickets of Communist strength. . . . As one top-ranking U.S. officer put it: 'We've stemmed the tide.'"

The national folk music revival, which had begun in the 1940s, had hit its peak in the mid-1960s. Politically, the folk scene leaned heavily leftward. Only a handful of folk songs critical of the war in Vietnam (and war in general) gained some popularity. That included two Bob Dylan tunes, "Blowing in the Wind" (a big hit for the popular folk group Peter, Paul, and Mary) and the strident "Masters of War"; as well as two songs written and performed by Phil Ochs, "What Are You Fighting For?" and "I Ain't Marching Anymore"; along with Pete Seeger's "Bring Them Home."

Except for Peter, Paul and Mary's "Blowing in the Wind," the other antiwar tunes—although popular among folk music aficionados, including many college students—did not have much impact on the national cultural or political landscapes. One popular song did, though: P. F. Sloan's doom-and-gloom "Eve of Destruction." A version of the song by Barry McGuire hit number one on the pop charts in September of 1965. Although the Vietnam War is not mentioned in the song, "Eve" opens with words that castigate the war's policymakers and those doing the fighting:

> The eastern world it is exploding
> Violence flarin', bullets loadin'
> You're old enough to kill but not for votin'
> You don't believe in war but what's that gun you're totin'

The strong national support for the Vietnam War in early 1966—which soon would begin to ebb steadily as American casualties mounted—had a significant impact on the rapturous reception Barry's song received. "The Ballad" came out "three months before public opinion turned," Clancy Isaac said a decade later, slightly exaggerating the time frame. "When we were selling 'The Ballad of the Green Berets,' the protesters were the bad guys. Three months later they were the good guys. It was perfect timing. I must say that I handled the exploitation very well."[4]

Isaac had a willing partner in RCA Victor in the "exploitation." The big record company brought out the song and the album with a huge marketing and publicity blitz—"one [of] the most extensive record campaigns in RCA Victor history," *Billboard* magazine reported.[5] "Key Victor executives [were] in attendance" at the December 18 recording sessions, *Billboard* noted. "Top level conferences were held during the following week to map advertising, promotion and press strategy."

The first thing RCA did was place an ad in the music trade publications tying the single to the Robin Moore book. "The best-selling book inspires a timely new song—'The Ballad of the Green Berets,'" the ad read. "As timely as today's headlines! Backed by heavy consumer advertising, here is a hot new single with a ready-made market of millions who have read the best-selling book, 'The Green Berets.' Composed and sung by Staff Sergeant Barry Sadler, who served with the Green Berets in Vietnam, here is the glory and heroism of the men who make up The U.S. Army Special Forces. Sadler's set for an appearance on the Ed Sullivan Show, January 30. Watch for Staff Sergeant Barry Sadler—and watch for the album 'Ballads of the Green Berets'—coming soon!"

RCA also put together a lavish promotional kit that included a bio of Barry, photos of him in uniform, and a brochure explaining what the Special Forces was all about. The kit went out on January 17 to radio stations, newspapers, and record stores. Avon joined the marketing blitz by inserting a photo of the album cover in all new printings of *The Green Berets* paperback, which was among the best-selling books in the nation. In turn, RCA plugged the book on the liner's album notes.

Said liner notes, by the writer Arnold Falleder, went heavy on patriotism and adulation for Barry and for the Green Berets. "The album of plaintive Vietnam war songs," the notes say, "is the creation of Staff Sergeant Barry Sadler (who, incidentally is the young trooper pictured on the cover of the AVON paperback best seller, 'The Green Berets'), a combat veteran of the Vietnam war."

The "Green Berets," Falleder explained, "are a skilled and highly trained fighting force similar to the celebrated American Rangers and the British Commandos of the Second World War. The special group within the Army carries out exacting missions beyond the scope of regular troops."

The album consists of "songs of men in action, sung against impending death, loneliness, despair and hardship, performed by a survivor of those experiences." Sadler's "compositions are part of a great tradition that binds brave men together through history."

He "writes and sings in the tradition of country songs of the American West, reflecting his own personality and background; yet we're sure that many years from now these songs of Sergeant Barry Sadler will be recalled as a true expression of the Vietnam combat soldier's feelings during the time of that fierce encounter."

The day the single came out, January 11, 1966, Barry signed a contract with Sullivan Productions, Inc., to appear on *The Ed Sullivan Show*. He received $1,000 for the gig, the equivalent of about $7,300 in 2017 dollars, about three months' pay for an active-duty army staff sergeant. Barry flew to New York City for the broadcast on Sunday evening, January 30. He sang "The Ballad" live on the nation's most popular and longest-running variety show.

The Sullivan show had started in 1948 and had become a family Sunday-night institution. In the pre-Internet, pre-DVR year of 1966, with cable television in its relative infancy, tens of millions of Americans gathered in front of their TV sets every Sunday at 8:00 p.m. to watch Ed Sullivan. On tap every week: an eclectic vaudeville-like parade of singers, comedians, and novelty acts with cameos from politicians and sports figures, hosted by the notoriously wooden Sullivan, a former newspaper columnist.

Elvis Presley caused a national sensation when he appeared on the show, swiveling his hips, in 1956. So did the Beatles, who sang in front of an audience packed with screaming teenaged girls in 1964. There were no screamers in the audience when Barry walked on stage to polite applause wearing his dress greens on episode twenty of the nineteenth season of *The Ed Sullivan Show*. Barry wore spit-shined, bloused jump boots and—of course—a green beret. The only decorations on his chest were his jump wings and his Combat Infantryman Badge.

Two comedians, Dick Capri and Jackie Vernon, also were on the bill, along with a group of clog dancers called Les Faux Follets; the "precision archery team" of Markworth and Mayana; a favorite Sullivan puppet, the Italian mouse Topo Gigio; the Four Tops (who did a medley of their hits); the singer/guitarist Jose Feliciano; and television star Dinah Shore. The mayor of Montreal, Jean Drapeau, took a bow from the audience.

Barry looked slightly ill at ease, nervously fingering the hem of his jacket, as he walked out on stage and stood alone alongside a large image of the Special Forces emblem. But he performed the song flawlessly, looking steely-eyed and stern—and handsome—with a bare-bones musical accompaniment featuring a rat-a-tat military drumbeat and an off-camera backup chorus.

Flawlessly, that is, considering Barry was no Frank Sinatra. But his limited singing range on *Ed Sullivan*—and on the single and album—worked well enough with the simple, three-chord folk-like melody with no high (or low) notes to hit. His clipped, pleasant, if undistinguished, voice fit the song's steadfast declaration of fidelity told in simple rhyming couplets. In short, Barry's voice's shortcomings and his songs' often simplistic and corny words hardly mattered. Barry's message, his military bearing, and his status as a wounded veteran of the Vietnam War—aided by widespread support for the war and the men doing the fighting there—struck a powerful emotional chord with millions of Americans, including Vietnam veterans.

"I remember seeing him on *The Ed Sullivan Show* singing 'The Ballad' and I thought, 'Whoa, this is some kind of guy here. I'm impressed,'" said retired Marine Corps captain Dale Dye, a writer, actor, and movie technical adviser who did a tour of duty in Vietnam. "The song was catchy and it touched certain heartstrings among military people. It certainly worked for me."[6]

Walter Anderson, who also served as a U.S. Marine in Vietnam and who went on to become the editor of *Parade* magazine, was similarly impressed when the song hit. "I arrived back in the States in December 1965," he said. "Like many of my fellow vets, I was moved by the song, which—though it was specifically about the Green Berets—seemed to speak to and for us all. My buddies and I would play it on jukeboxes wherever we could—I guess as a sort of statement."[7]

When "The Ballad" was getting all that airplay, "we were in hog heaven; we had our own song," said former Special Forces staff sargeant Felix "Pete" Peterson, who had just returned from Vietnam when the song hit. "You have to remember that people didn't know who we were. When I would go home on leave to Wisconsin, people wanted to know if I was in the French Foreign Legion."[8]

The song "was released as a single just as I was starting Basic Training," said the novelist David Willson, who was drafted into the army in 1965. "We had radios that we kept on whenever we could get away with it, and it seemed the song was being played constantly. Leroy Bearmedicine, a member of the Blackfeet Indian Nation, a gifted singer and guitarist, had brought his guitar and he led evening singalongs featuring 'The Ballad of the Green Berets,' which he sang very tongue in cheek.

"My happiest memory of Basic Training is all of us booming the words 'jump and die.' We also sang various parodies. 'The Ballad' seemed designed to propagate them."[9]

"The Ballad" inspired more than one young American to join the army. "You had the newsreels" and "The Ballad," said Bill Branson, who enlisted on March 18, 1966, when the song was at its peak of popularity. "I was anticommunist. I thought they were evil and whatnot. I loved it when our politicians gave it to them. I believed in the Domino Theory. I believed we were going to free those people and we should. That was our role in the world. This was our generation's war—I didn't want to miss it."[10]

The song also inspired some men fighting in Vietnam. "It's more than just a song. It's a shared story, an anthem to valor and sacrifice, patriotism and victory," said Jim Kurtz, who served as a platoon leader with the Army's 101st Airborne Division in Vietnam in 1966. "'The Ballad,'" he said, "was the Vietnam [War] anthem.... I thought I wanted to be a hero and that Vietnam was the place to be heroic and that's what the song said.

"It was kinda like [the fight song] 'On Wisconsin.' We were going to march through the country and win the game, save the day."[11]

A few Special Forces men did not embrace the song. "I hate to be called a 'Green Beret,'" said John Opshinsky, who served as a radio operator briefly with Barry at Plie Do Lim. "A hat? I'll tell you what, the hat was lousy. I hated it. It served no purpose. It couldn't keep the sun out of your eyes. It was hot. It was uncomfortable."

As for Barry's song, "I just didn't care," Opshinsky said. "It was more or less the truth about our training and such, [but] I didn't jump to die; I jumped to live. I don't know about anybody else."[12]

The marketing and publicity blitz, the *Sullivan* appearance, and a February 11 spot on the popular ABC-TV *Jimmy Dean Show* variety show (other guests: The Andrews Sisters and the country music singer Billy Grammer) paid off. The record became hugely popular, and nearly all the media coverage contained little but positive things about Barry, the song, the Green Berets, and the war in Vietnam.

"Wounded Veteran Writes Song on Vietnam War," the headline of a typically upbeat article—this one in the *New York Times*—proclaimed. "A combat veteran of the war in Vietnam, who does not read music, is the composer of the fastest selling ballad that RCA Victor has had—with the exception of some of Elvis Presley's—in the last seven years," *Times* reporter Louis Calta wrote.

"Green Berets," Calta explained, "is a nickname for members of the Army Special Forces trained to carry out missions beyond the scope of regular troops." Barry—described as a "25-year-old red-haired soldier"—said that he had a few "leery moments" doing the *Sullivan* show. "'As long as the audience didn't have any rocks,' he recalled with a smile, 'I felt safe.'"

Barry also told Calta that he wanted to stay in the army, but the song's instant success changed his plans. You "can't pass up the economic advantages of being an entertainer," Barry said. "It has given me a home, a car and a steak every day, if I want it. I don't consider myself a performer. I'm not used to playing before audiences. Personally, I would prefer to play and sing before friends—it's more relaxing. But the Army has been very kind to me."

When asked how his wife felt about the hoopla, Barry said, "I don't think she believes it. She says I'm a dirty old sergeant."[13]

Newsweek magazine called the song "a warmly worded, coolly sung tribute to the tough, parachute-jumping commando-like Special Forces unit, nicknamed 'The Green Berets,' of which [Barry Sadler] is a member." Barry "sings in an untrained, pleasant voice," the article said, "and his songs are simple ballads about soldiering in South Vietnam—a war that tough, 25-year-old S/Sgt. Barry Sadler knows personally."[14]

In a four-page, photo-heavy spread, the widely popular *Life* magazine proclaimed: "The folk-rock of anti-Vietnam-war ballads has been drowned out by a best-selling patriotic blood-churner." It "is a march-beat salute to Americans who die in Vietnam 'for those oppressed,' and it was written by Barry Sadler, 25, who served as a combat medic with the U.S. Army Special Forces in Vietnam."

The song's lyrics, the article said, "while sometimes sentimental and uncomfortably banal . . . often express the foot soldier's feelings in a language he understands."[15]

A widely reprinted United Press International (UPI) wire service article on Barry led with: "The fastest-rising singing star in the country today is a young Army sergeant who composed his songs during breaks in the fighting in South Vietnam," which was not quite true. Barry, who "is unable to read music," the UPI reporter pointed out, "has a natural ability for composing country-western songs" and "is a good composer and excellent singer, and he probably could pick his spot on television."[16]

Another wire service article described Barry as "a stocky, square-jawed, 25-year-old all-American type." Simplicity "and the ingenuous quality of his lyrics is the combination that makes Barry's songs so touching," the article opined. "His voice is pleasant, natural and has the quality of a country singer."[17]

Barry's hometown newspaper, the Leadville *Herald Democrat*, joined in the enthusiasm. "The ballad, 'The Green Berets,' with record sales now past the 300,000 mark, is to the Viet Nam conflict what 'There's a Star Spangled Banner Waving Somewhere' was to World War II," the paper reported. "Leadville's interest in the song, the book of the same name, and the conflict itself has been heightened by the fact that the composer of the song, Sergeant Barry Sadler, is a Leadville native whose mother lives here."[18]

An Associated Press profile of Barry began with: "Last May, Staff Sgt. Barry Sadler counted 15 new stitches in his left leg that covered a fresh wound from a filth-laden pungi stick. Now he's happily counting the royalties from a song about his outfit—the Special Forces." The song, the article explained, "is a sentimental tribute to the Special Forces men who are trained at Fort Bragg to fight as and against guerrillas."

Barry "supports his wife and 13-month-old son largely on his Army pay," the article noted. "A Special Forces spokesman says a staff sergeant receives about $271 a month 'plus allowances.'"

Barry said: "I could drive a Cadillac, but I have a Ford. It's economical. It gets me where I want to go. I don't need one of those big chrome-plated things. I'm not a very good driver anyway. Speed scares me.

"I could have—oh, a three-story house, anything I want. But I can afford steak on a sergeant's pay. This is a flash thing. Two years from now, I'll be forgotten."[19]

A music critic for a small-town Massachusetts newspaper wrote that whenever Barry's song is played, "you can be sure it will start people talking. It's a sad song, but it isn't. I can't explain it really. All I can say is that if you have a chance, listen to the song."[20]

A newspaper columnist in a small Ohio town wrote early in March that the single and album "have sold 2 million copies. Sadler's first venture into the alien jungle of Tin Pan Alley could earn him $250,000."[21]

A brief article in the *Augusta* (Georgia) *Chronicle* used the occasion of the song's success to rebuke antiwar folk singers. "Other folk singers commercialize on war, anti-war, the military service and how to stay out of it, and draft burning," the article said. "Sadler is a medic trained to handle anything from bug bites to major surgery. Besides that, he's a pretty good singer."[22]

An editorial on "The Ballad" in a small Missouri newspaper lambasted rock-and-roll music and the nascent antiwar movement and pushed for victory in Vietnam. Barry's song "is a tune with a catchy lilt . . . , a song of direct action but not the hip swiveling, gyrating kind that has featured rock and roll music and its successor," the editorial said. Barry's song "may inspire some of the pickets and peace demonstrators to put on a uniform and try to win the coveted green beret."

Now "that the American people know what can be done with a good musical score and words that are not a jumble of jungle chatter, but make sense," the editorial concluded, "they may be willing to forsake rock and roll for all time. Next to the conquest of the Viet Cong, the war could produce no greater victory."[23]

Not all the reviews were raves. A Springfield, Massachusetts, music critic said that Barry's songs "are more maudlin than manly, and tinged with the commercialism that springs from the Nashville school of folk art."[24] An *Atlanta Journal-Constitution* critic called "The Ballad" a "sappy, manipulative, marching dirge."[25]

An article in *Time* magazine described Barry as "probably the closest-cropped, ruggedest (Black Belt in judo) and most musically illiterate performer on the pop charts." Give Barry a subject and a guitar, the article explained, "and he comes up with a song in ten minutes. RCA Victor arrangers transcribe the work for him, which he describes as 'kind of intermediate between ballad and calypso.'"

Then, "with cracking, lackluster tenor and a backing of RCA trumpets, or fiddle and humming voices, he croons away. For the most part the ballads are banal and ridden with sentimentality." If the Vietnam War, the article archly concluded, "has produced a true war poet, he is no doubt too busy fighting to write."[26]

Timothy S. Mayer, writing in the *Harvard Crimson* student newspaper, blasted the song and the album, characterizing them as "lifeless and ersatz." Arranger Sid Bass, Mayer said, was "forced to reach deep into his bag of tricks, coming up with virtually every phoney-baloney studio recording technique of goosing one non-existent voice and twelve non-existent melody lines into a passable record."

Barry's words, Mayer added, "are united by the common theme of self-congratulation," and "generally these songs are the dull and repetitious celebration of America's Best, who are apparently as devoid of personality as they are of cowardice."[27]

Linda Mathew, writing in the *Los Angeles Times*, echoed that criticism of Sid Bass's studio "bag of tricks." They failed to make "one nonexistent voice and 12 insipid melodies into a passable record," she wrote. The "whole album lacks the touches of black humor, the sense of conflict at hand, that made earlier war songs stick in the mind."

Although Barry's diction ranged from "the heavily eloquent ('What is the badge of courage?—It's sweat and blood and tears') to the quasi-lyrical ('Lay the green sod o're me'), his lyrics," Mathew opined, "are united by the common theme of self-congratulation. Sometimes they approach the sickness of 'Teen Angel' as in 'Trooper's Lament,' where 'As he fell through the night—His chute was all in flames—A smile on his lips—He cried out the girl's name,' but generally these songs are the dull and repetitious celebration of America's best."

Still, Mathew said, "however lifeless and ersatz the songs in this album may be, enough of them refer to the subject material of other ballads (prostitution in 'Saigon,' inter-service rivalry in '[Garet] Trooper,' and military discipline in 'Bamiba') to indicate that, in some radically different form, a few of them might indeed have been penned in the DMZ."

Her conclusion: Aside from "references to 'freedom' and 'those oppressed,' these songs are apolitical and blithely unconcerned with whom we are fighting or why. Sadler's interests, apparently, do not transcend 'fighting soldiers from the sky.'"[28]

Boston Herald reviewer George Forstythe called the album "a mournful record, unnerving more than entertaining." Perhaps, Forsythe said, "it is because we are too close to Vietnam and this is a conflict of great controversy and uncertainty. I have no idea where this album will go, but

I don't feel that it will be a too-popular item. And this is with all due respect to a great fighting outfit."[29]

Both the song and the album, it turned out, became extraordinarily popular. And it wasn't as though there was no competition. In 1966 the Beatles, the Rolling Stones, and Bob Dylan—as well as Simon and Garfunkel, the Mamas and Papas, the Righteous Brothers, the Lovin' Spoonful, and other rock bands—produced memorable music and sold millions of records. But none created a national sensation along the lines of what happened with Barry Sadler and "The Ballad of the Green Berets."

"When the song came out, we had three or four phone lines in the studio and they were lighting up with people asking me to play 'The Ballad' twice or three times," said the author Chip Bishop, who came home on weekends from Boston University to host a Sunday night Top 40 radio show in the winter of 1965–1966 on WWON in Woonsocket, Rhode Island.

"I had to put the brakes on. I could only play it once an hour," Bishop said. "But I would play it and dedicate it to PFC Jones from his sweetheart back home in Woonsocket. Every lonely girl out there wanted to dedicate that song to her boyfriend in Vietnam."[30]

The song "was only supposed to be local," Lavona Sadler said, "for the military, the Special Forces. We didn't think it would go nationwide. It just took off."[31]

Lavona was correct. Sales of both the single and album "took off like wildfire," as Barry put it.[32] By February "The Ballad"—with a retail price of less than a dollar—had sold more than two million copies, in addition to sales of over one million of the 33 rpm album, which retailed for around $4.50 in stereo and $3.50 in mono.

The song appeared on the *Billboard* Top 100 for the first time on February 5. It soon supplanted Nancy Sinatra's "These Boots Are Made for Walkin'" in the No. 1 spot. It stayed at the top of the charts for five weeks until slipping to No. 5 on April 9. The Righteous Brothers' "(You're My) Soul and Inspiration" moved to No. 1, followed by "Daydream" by the

Lovin Spoonful, "19th Nervous Breakdown" by the Rolling Stones, and "Bang Bang" by Cher. The Beatles' "Nowhere Man" was No. 6.

Early in March "The Ballad" also stood at No. 1 on *Billboard*'s Top 40 Easy Listening chart. No. 2 was "Crying Time" by Ray Charles. Barry's song also made *Billboard*'s Hot Country Singles list for the week ending March 5, reaching No. 13. As far as individual markets, early in March "The Ballad" was either No. 1 or No. 2 in Baltimore, Boston, New Orleans, New York City, Philadelphia, Pittsburgh, Detroit, Miami, San Francisco, and Seattle.[33]

If a song's worth is measured in how many times other performers record cover versions, "The Ballad" ranks fairly high. One discographer found forty-one cover versions of Barry's song, including twenty-four that came out in 1966.[34] That list includes Tony Martino, Ray Anthony, the Boston Pops Orchestra, Teresa Brewer, Duane Eddy, Ferrante & Teicher, Dick Hyman, the Lonesome Valley Singers, Dolly Parton, Johnny Paycheck, Kate Smith, and the U.S. Army Field Band & Chorus.

At first Barry "enjoyed the excesses that he was exposed to," Bill Parrish said. "He told me when he did *The Ed Sullivan Show*, he was walking down Fifth Avenue in New York and a carload of girls went by whistling and hollering at him. He told me, 'If this keeps up, I'm gonna enjoy stardom.' And, believe me, he took good advantage of that stardom."[35]

But things soon changed after General Yarborough realized the marketing potential of Barry and his song. He quickly reassigned Barry to the Fort Bragg Public Information Office—not to do PR work at Fort Bragg, but to make appearances all over the country, singing his song and singing the praises of the Green Berets. Or, as *Time* magazine put it, touring "the country as a flesh-and-blood singing recruiting poster, and performing before big audiences from Atlantic City to San Francisco."

Starting in the second week of February, Barry spent the next fifteen months mostly on the road doing radio and TV shows, appearing and singing at county and state fairs, festivals of all sorts, recruiting rallies, and veterans and patriotic group meetings.

He wasn't entirely happy about it.

"In a lot of ways he liked it and in other ways he did not," Lavona Sadler said. "It kept him forever from doing what he liked doing—soldiering. He told me he was just a glorified recruiter."[36]

CHAPTER 8

A DIRTY, OLD STAFF SERGEANT

"Nowadays, if you're not protesting something, you're a square."
—BARRY SADLER, FEBRUARY 19, 1966

With sales of the album skyrocketing, Barry, Gerry Gitell, Robin Moore, and RCA "naturally profited beyond our wildest dreams," as Barry put it in his autobiography.[1] He told writer Robert Powers in 1971 that after getting his first $250,000 royalty check, he deposited $200,000 in the bank and brought $50,000 in cash home to Lavona, dumping it on the floor in front of her in their living room.[2]

The Sadlers paid off the mortgage on their house in Fayetteville. They bought a color TV. Barry also splurged on "a few [mostly German] World War II weapons and other souvenirs, some cameras and a telescope that I had been wanting," he wrote in his autobiography. The Sadlers also bought his and her Jaguars. His was a black convertible; hers, a blue hardtop.

"He bought me a new one," Lavona said, "and himself a secondhand one."[3]

Almost immediately after the song hit, Barry announced that he would turn over a large chunk of his royalties to a nonprofit foundation to provide college scholarships for children of Green Berets and other service members killed or seriously wounded in the line of duty. He did so, Barry said, to help his fellow GIs.

"I just thought it was about time someone remembered them," Barry said. "Nobody remembers a soldier until he's dead. I'm making money on songs about my buddies. I feel some of it should go back to their families."[4]

The Barry Sadler Foundation incorporated in New York. The board of directors included James A. Skidmore. A sales executive for New

Jersey Bell Telephone Company, Republican Party activist, Marine Corps reserve officer, and strong supporter of the war in Vietnam, Skidmore was national president of the U.S. Jaycees. The foundation, which has long since disbanded, was in existence at least until the early 1970s.

How many scholarships did it fund? Barry never went into detail about the foundation in public—nor did he do so to his closest friends—after 1967. Bob Barkwill, Barry's manager from 1967 to 1973, said in 2015 that he had no memory of Barry discussing the foundation during those years. "He might have said something, but I don't remember," Barkwill said. "He didn't talk much about it if he did."[5]

Lavona Sadler said she had "no idea what happened" with the foundation. "I know that he gave ten thousand dollars" to set it up, she said. "But I don't know what happened to it."[6]

Barry Sadler's Pentagon-sponsored nationwide tour began with a February 12, 1966, appearance at a giant pro–Vietnam War rally in Atlanta. It ended in May of 1967 after Barry had performed at scores of events across the nation—almost all of which reflected American cultural and political values that were rapidly changing in 1966 and 1967 as what has become known as "the Sixties" was about to burst upon the national scene.

Barry was decidedly not a Sixties guy. Born in 1940 he did not fit in politically or culturally with the Baby Boom generation that was about to have a gigantic impact on American society in 1966. Barry was solidly a part of the World War II generation. In many ways the events and venues that embraced Barry from February 1966 to May 1967 represented a way of life that was about to be overshadowed by the earthquake of cultural changes that the rising Baby Boomers would embrace—from long hair, recreational drug use, and new forms of rock music to the Civil Rights, anti–Vietnam War, women's liberation, American Indian, and gay rights movements.

Certainly the home-town festivals, local and national Veterans of Foreign Wars and American Legion meetings, savings bond drives, state fairs, small-town TV and radio variety shows, patriotic group conferences

Barry Allen Sadler was born November 1, 1940, in Carlsbad, New Mexico. After his parents divorced in 1945, Barry and his older brother, Bob, fell into "a wandering life with our mother," he wrote, throughout the Southwest before settling in Leadville, Colorado.

UNIVERSITY OF TEXAS AT EL PASO LIBRARY, SPECIAL COLLECTIONS DEPARTMENT

During junior high and high school in Leadville, Colorado, Barry spent a good deal of time with his best friend, Delfino "Del" Gomez, and his parents and nine brothers and sisters. "They were extremely close; they were like brothers," Delfino's daughter Loretta Sparkman said of Barry and Del.

LAKE COUNTY PUBLIC LIBRARY, COLORADO MOUNTAIN HISTORY COLLECTION

When Barry joined the U.S. Air Force on June 2, 1958, he gave his home address as 118 W. 2nd Street in Leadville, the building that housed the Pioneer Club Bar and Café, one of the city's oldest and most famous drinking establishments. The Pioneer had a brothel on the second floor.

LAKE COUNTY PUBLIC LIBRARY, COLORADO MOUNTAIN HISTORY COLLECTION

Barry Sadler served as a radar technician in the air force for four years,
receiving his honorable discharge on
June 1, 1962. His time in the air
force included a one-year tour of duty
in Japan where, among other things,
he studied—and excelled at—martial
arts.

While stationed at Beale
Air Force Base in the
central California town
of Marysville, Barry and
his buddies Gary Zenger
and Paul Alford took a
short vacation to Hun-
tington Beach, California,
in 1961.

Barry joined the U.S. Army
on August 8, 1962, in Oakland, California, and volunteered for Special Forces
(Green Berets) medic training. During his nearly five
years in the army, he kept
a guitar with him almost
constantly.

Top: Barry (third from the right in the second row), arrived in Vietnam on December 29, 1964. After a short stint at the 5th Special Forces headquarters in Nha Trang, he spent the next six months as an A Team medic in the rugged Central Highlands.

UNIVERSITY OF TEXAS AT EL PASO LIBRARY, SPECIAL COLLECTIONS DEPARTMENT

Center: Special Forces Detachment A-216 at Plei Do Lim where Barry served from February 1965 until he was wounded by a punji stick in late May. The detachment's compound, at nearly 2,200 feet above sea level, was named in memory of Capt. Herbert F. Hardy, Jr., who had been killed in action on March 4, 1964.

JIMMY WALKER

Bottom: Camp Hardy had about a dozen buildings inside a rectangular perimeter encircled by a wall of sandbags and barbed wire. Beyond that was a heavily fortified second perimeter arrayed with deadly Claymore anti-personnel mines. Nearby was a Montagnard village where some two hundred indigenous troops who worked with the Green Berets lived with their families.

JIMMY WALKER

Special Forces lieutenant Jimmy Walker, who served with Barry at Plei Do Lim.

Barry in camouflage fatigues on patrol with the Montagnards.

Barry spent most of his time in Vietnam performing medic duties, but also went out on patrols with Montagnard fighters near Plei Do Lim.

Eating rice balls and fish while on patrol.
UNIVERSITY OF TEXAS AT EL PASO LIBRARY, SPECIAL COLLECTIONS DEPARTMENT

The Green Beret medics made it a point to reach out to Montagnard villagers around Plei Do Lim, treating men, women, and children.
UNIVERSITY OF TEXAS AT EL PASO LIBRARY, SPECIAL COLLECTIONS DEPARTMENT

On the back of this family photo of his wife, Lavona, and oldest son, Thor, Barry wrote, "This is the first picture I ever saw of our baby. Lavona sent it to me in Vietnam." Thor Sadler was born on December 3, 1964, in Lehighton, Pennsylvania, Lavona's hometown, when she and Barry were home on leave before he left for Vietnam.
UNIVERSITY OF TEXAS AT EL PASO LIBRARY, SPECIAL COLLECTIONS DEPARTMENT

Barry Sadler recorded "The Ballad of the Green Berets" and eleven other tracks on December 18, 1965, in New York City. RCA released the single on January 11, 1966, and the album, "Ballads of the Green Berets," on January 20. The single would go on sell some nine million copies and become the top *Billboard* Hot 100 hit of the year.

LSP-3547 STEREO

Ballads of the Green Berets
SSgt Barry Sadler
U.S. Army Special Forces

The Ballad of the Green Berets
Letter from Vietnam
I'm a Lucky One
Garet Trooper
The Soldier Has Come Home
Salute to the Nurses
I'm Watching the Raindrops Fall
Badge of Courage
Trooper's Lament
Bamba
Saigon
Lullaby

Arranged and Conducted by
Sid Bass

RCA VICTOR
DYNAGROOVE
RECORDING

Barry's photo on the back of the CD version of the record album, which retailed for around $4 in 1966 and sold more than two million copies.

The army sent Barry out on the road to promote the album—and to boost recruiting. He appeared at scores of events from early February 1966 until just before he left the army in May 1967. The last one took place on April 12, 1967, where Barry helped promote the sale of U.S. savings bonds in Washington, D.C.

After he got out of the army, Barry tried his hand at acting. He appeared in one film and had small parts in four TV westerns, including three episodes of *Death Valley Days*.
STUDIO STILL

Barry, his wife, Lavona, and their two young sons, Thor and Baron, moved into a four-bedroom, 4,000-square-foot ranch house on a five-acre plot on the eastern edge of Tucson in September of 1967.
DAVID LEE GUSS

The Sadlers' house, covered in burnt adobe brick, had a swimming pool and a swing set in the backyard, which looked out over a stark desert landscape. For privacy's sake Barry left the previous owner's name on the driveway's wrought iron fence.
DAVID LEE GUSS

From the time he was a boy, Barry was fond of weapons. He passed that on to his young sons, Thor and Baron, growing up in Tucson.
DAVID LEE GUSS

Right: Barry collected Nazi military memorabilia, including uniforms and weapons. He posed for a magazine shoot with what appears to be a German C96 Mauser semiautomatic pistol wearing a German army cap from World War II.
DAVID LEE GUSS

Below: Barry's extensive collection included a Schwimmwagen ("Swimming Car"), a rare amphibious vehicle designed during World War II for the German army by Ferdinand Porsche and his son Ferry.
DAVID LEE GUSS

Barry never came close to matching the success of "The Ballad," although he made two other albums in the late sixties and early seventies, along with several forgettable singles.
DAVID LEE GUSS

Barry kept the bulk of his collection of World War II German and other military memorabilia in a small room in his house in Tucson. It included swords, pistols, hand grenades, caps, an M-38 gas mask, and uniforms such as an Allgemeine SS officer's tunic with the Nazi armband and an SS field grey tunic. He also owned Hermann Göring's signet ring and a signed, special edition copy of Hitler's *Mein Kampf*.
DAVID LEE GUSS

Barry and Lavona moved to Nashville in March of 1973. He began spending a lot of time at the Hall of Fame Motor Inn's lounge with cronies from the music business. The men called it the "Hall of Shame" or "the Shame."

On November 1, 1977, Barry's thirty-seventh birthday, a small Nashville book publisher brought out Barry's first novel, *The Moi*—a book-length version of a screenplay he had commissioned. The pulp fiction Vietnam War novel centered on a Green Beret soldier who is captured and repeatedly tortured by the North Vietnamese.
BOOK JACKET, COURTESY OF ROB ROBISON

Sometime early in the fall of 1978, Barry started seeing Darlene Yvonne Sharpe, a 24-year-old aspiring country singer who worked as a barmaid at the Natchez Trace Lounge in Nashville.
METROPOLITAN POLICE DEPARTMENT, NASHVILLE, TENNESSEE

Barry shot and killed Darlene Sharpe's ex-boyfriend, the washed-up country music singer Lee Emerson Bellamy, in the parking lot outside Darlene's apartment in Nashville on December 1, 1978, telling the police he was acting in self-defense.
METROPOLITAN POLICE DEPARTMENT, NASHVILLE, TENNESSEE

Barry was arrested on June 1, 1979, and charged with second-degree murder. He later pleaded guilty to voluntary manslaughter and served less than thirty days in the minimum-security Nashville Metro Workhouse.

METROPOLITAN POLICE DEPARTMENT, NASHVILLE, TENNESSEE

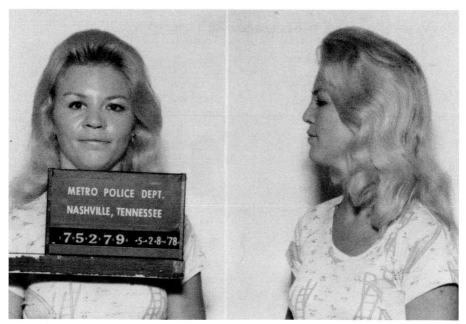

Darlene was charged with accessory after the fact in the Bellamy murder. She pleaded guilty and received a sentence of one year probation.

METROPOLITAN POLICE DEPARTMENT, NASHVILLE, TENNESSEE

Barry co-wrote a pulp fiction detective novel, *Nashville with a Bullet*, with his buddy Billy Arr. It came out in December 1981.

BOOK COVER, COURTESY OF ROB ROBISON

Barry used variants of this picture, taken in Tucson in 1971, on the covers of most of the twenty-two *Casca* books he wrote from 1979 to 1988.

DAVID LEE GUSS

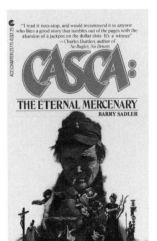

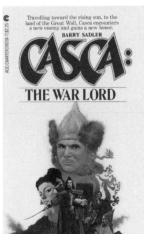

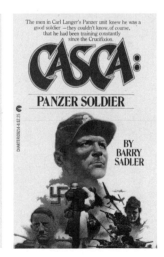

Above Left: The first *Casca*, published in July 1979.
Center: *Casca* No. 3, published in April 1980.
Right: *Casca* No. 4, published in September 1980.

BOOK COVERS, COURTESY OF ROB ROBISON

Barry left his wife and three children in Nashville and moved to Guatemala in 1984. He spent a lot of time at the Don Quixote bar at the Hotel Europa in Guatemala City.
SOLDIER OF FORTUNE MAGAZINE

Barry and his friend Ben Rosson went into the military equipment–selling business in Guatemala.
SOLDIER OF FORTUNE MAGAZINE

Barry would occasionally perform at the bar, which was adorned with a poster touting his *Casca* books.
SOLDIER OF FORTUNE MAGAZINE

Barry constantly surrounded himself with weapons during his four years in Guatemala, including what likely is a Romanian copy of the famed Russian assault weapon, the AK-47, with an up-front pistol grip.
BILL PARRISH

Barry told people he did mercenary work with the Contras, who fought against the communist-leaning Sandinista government in Nicaragua.
SOLDIER OF FORTUNE MAGAZINE

Barry dispensed free medical care to his neighbors in Guatemala, most of whom could not afford to pay a doctor.
ROB ROBISON

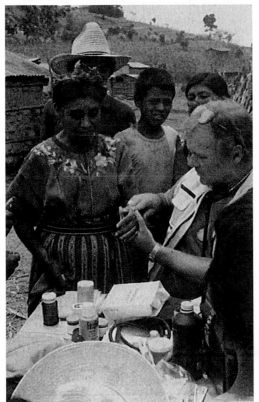

Barry paid medical visits to Mayan villages, where many Indians lived subsistence lives.
SOLDIER OF FORTUNE MAGAZINE

With his friend and literary agent Rob Robison, of Nashville, on a trip to visit Mayan ruins in Honduras.
ROB ROBISON

Barry's mother, Blanche "Bebe" Sadler, was at the center of a bitterly contentious lawsuit over who would direct his medical care after he was shot in the head in Guatemala City in September of 1988, brought back to the States, and confined to a VA hospital bed.
RICHARD T. CONWAY/*PLAIN DEALER*

and meetings, military balls, and other events that welcomed Barry were established parts of many Americans' lives. Many remain so today. But in February of 1966, as Bob Dylan wrote two years earlier, the times most definitely were a-changin' as what became known as the Generation Gap began to split the Baby Boomers and their parents' World War II–era generation. Barry, who was born in 1940, fit in solidly in outlook with the older side of the Generation Gap.

Take that first event on February 12. Some 10,000 people sat through the drizzling rain at what is now called Atlanta–Fulton County Stadium at a rally organized by an Emory University student organization called Affirmation Vietnam. Pro-war student groups would soon become a rarity on college campus. None would even come close to putting on a well-attended pro-war rally with appearances by top-tier government leaders and other dignitaries for the duration of the war.[7]

Barry kicked things off at the Atlanta rally by singing "The Ballad." He received a huge ovation. Then came chest-thumping speeches by an august lineup that included Secretary of State Dean Rusk, conservative activist Anita Bryant, Georgia governor Carl Sanders, Georgia's two U.S. senators, Richard Russell and Herman Talmadge, Atlanta mayor Ivan Allen, South Vietnam's ambassador to the United States, Nguyen Duy Lien, and Emory University president Sanford Atwood.

"Let us consult our courage—and not our fears," Secretary Rusk, an ardent Vietnam War hawk, told the crowd. "The integrity of the pledged word of the United States is the principal pillar of peace throughout the world."

A small group of antiwar protestors marched outside the stadium. One carried a sign calling for peace. "They bring that sign to the wrong address," Rusk said.[8]

The following week, on February 18, *The Army Hour*, a weekly radio program distributed on NBC to stations across the nation on Sunday afternoon, broadcast Barry singing "Badge of Courage" from the recording made the year before in Vietnam. The next day, February 19, 1966, the U.S. Army officially awarded Staff Sgt. Barry A. Sadler the Purple Heart for his punji stake wound. The order noted that the incident took place on May 16, 1965.

A few days later, on Tuesday, February 22, Barry made his first appearance at a local event, flying to Liberal, Kansas, where he and the U.S. Army Golden Knights skydiving team headlined the International Pancake Race. The race, an offbeat piece of boosterism, is a friendly competition between Liberal and Olney, England, in which women sprint down a city street flipping pancakes. It's held on Shrove Tuesday (Mardi Gras), the day before Lent.

Throughout his tour Barry used his platform—mainly newspaper, radio, and television interviews and brief speeches to his audiences—to promote the Green Berets, to give his views on the Vietnam War, and to sound off against those who protested the war, including musicians. Protest songs, he told a Washington (D.C.) *Star* reporter, "might have had a nice sound but not many people pay attention to the words. Nowadays, if you're not protesting something, you're a square."[9]

Barry also often spoke about his personal life, as people regularly asked him about growing up, how he got started in music, what happened to him in Vietnam, and his future plans. Barry told a *Dallas Morning News* reporter on a layover at Love Field, for example, that he wanted to go back and fight in Vietnam, but Lavona was not thrilled about it. "But I wear the pants in my family," Barry said. "Soldiering was the way I made my living."

When asked if he wanted his young son to be a Green Beret, Barry replied: "Thor was the god of thunder. When the time comes, he'll make his own decision. But he might as well serve with the best."[10]

A culture clash of sorts erupted when Barry went to Boston at the end of February for the ten-day Winterfest Folkfest at the recently built War Memorial Auditorium (now known as Hynes Veterans Memorial Convention Center). One local newspaper columnist predicted that Barry's pro-war message would win over the predominantly peacenik folk music crowd. With the huge success of "The Ballad," Barry has "spit in [the] faces" of antiwar folksingers, the columnist Jim Droney wrote, "and come up with something that's got the kids all over the country moving in another direction maybe."

Describing Barry as "no uncombed kid," the columnist said that the song's popularity "brings a different influence on the kids."[11]

The "kids" greeted Barry warmly when he walked on stage on Saturday night, February 26. However, according to one reviewer, the crowd clearly favored the folkies Phil Ochs, Richard and Mimi Farina, and Jean Redpath. Barry "clumped out onto the War Memorial Auditorium stage to the cheers of the Winterfest audience," Jim O'Reilly wrote. "Either stage fright or combat fatigue impelled him to leave after three songs. The anti-war sentiments of the later folkists somehow seemed more cleverly expressed and more warmly received."[12]

Barry sounded off against the antiwar crowd to another Boston reporter. The huge popularity of "The Ballad," he said, reflected the nation's overwhelming support for the war in Vietnam. "The vast majority of Americans are behind our efforts," Barry said. "Those who protest are irritating—like mosquitoes."[13]

When asked if his sudden success changed him, Barry replied with a "brief, tight smile," the reporter noted. He said: "It would be hard to recognize changes in yourself, but I think I've been a dirty old staff sergeant for too long—cleaned too many latrines and shined too many buttons—for anything to change me much."

At his next stop, in Tucson—to perform at a Southern Arizona Livestock Association dinner and then at the NCO club at nearby Fort Huachuca—Barry spoke at length to a reporter about the Vietnam War and about those who opposed it. "Combat in Vietnam is our secondary mission," Barry said. "Trying to get the people to be pro-Saigon is more important. We attempted a lot of social reform work. We wanted to show them we will help them if they give us a chance.

"Now you see the result of that work. The North Vietnamese are having to pour more and more troops into the south because the indigenous population is refusing increasingly to support them. . . . Though we [the Green Berets] have sometimes been referred to as the Peace Corps with guns, our kill ratio shows that when it comes to fighting, we are beating the enemy by the numbers."

When asked about draft card burners, Barry did not hold back. "They're a bunch of vomits," he said. "Demonstrating is their right, but burning draft cards? No, sir, I can't go along with that. This is a political war as well as a military one. I think we elected our leaders and we should follow them."[14]

Around that same time eighteen University of Minnesota students and two faculty members wrote a letter to pop music radio stations in Minneapolis and St. Paul. In it the stridently antiwar students called for the stations to stop playing "The Ballad," the No. 1 hit song in the country.

"The idealization of an elite corps of American fighting men contains elements which historically parallel the development of the infamous elite Nazi SS Corps," the letter said.[15] No newspapers quoted Barry's reaction, but there's little doubt what he would have said had he heard about the letter. It wouldn't have been delicately phrased.

Barry, on the other hand, would have heartily agreed with a Mrs. Ruth Grimm of Omaha, Nebraska, who expressed an infinitely more widespread view about the song and the Green Berets and the war in Vietnam. "The song is impressive," she wrote in a March 8, 1966, letter to the editor of the *Omaha World Herald*. "America needs more such men who are proud to fight for America and what it stands for. Some men would rather face prison than fight for their country."

During the first week of March—when John Lennon of the Beatles caused an international sensation by telling a reporter that the Beatles were "more popular than Jesus"[16]—*Life* magazine published a mostly fawning spread on Barry and the song. It included—in true *Life* magazine style—five large black-and-white photos: one of Barry in Vietnam wearing jungle fatigues going over a map with his Montagnard fighters, a cigarette dangling from his mouth and an assault rifle hanging from his shoulder; one of Barry strumming his guitar in his neatly pressed Green Beret fatigues in front of a reconstructed Vietnamese village at Fort Bragg; a photo of Barry simulating hand-to-hand combat at Bragg; one of him singing in the RCA studio with Chet Gierlach and Sid Bass; and one of Barry grinning broadly while holding up fourteen-month-old Thor, who's wearing a mini Green Beret outfit.

Back on the road Barry sang "The Ballad" at a dinner RCA put on at the annual National Association of Recording Merchandizers Convention in New York City on March 7. Also on the bill: stand-up comedian

Myron Cohen, an *Ed Sullivan Show* perennial. That same week RCA's Japanese subsidiary announced that it would be mounting a huge marketing and advertising campaign with the aim of selling a million copies of "The Ballad."

"There is every indication at present that the folk song boom is coming to Japan," Takeo Koto, the Victor Company of Japan's head of publicity, said. "Up to this date, however, we have had no hits in this vein, with the only exception of [the antiwar] 'Where Have All the Flowers Gone' three years ago. Now we are completely set for this drive, which involves publishers, radio and TV stations and of course, us."[17]

"The Ballad" did well in Japan, and in a few other countries, including Switzerland, the then West Germany, and what then was called the Union of South Africa, where it was translated into Afrikaans.

"The French liked it, too," Barry said in 1972. "But they changed the name to 'Passport to the Sun,' which I never could figure out. The French have always had a sore spot about Indochina."[18]

Barry's next gig took place at New York City's Lincoln Center's Philharmonic Hall, a March 13 appearance at a big American Parkinson's Disease Association fund-raiser. Barry headlined the program, which included the comic Pat Henry, best known for being Frank Sinatra's opening act, and the folk singer Nancy Ames. Later that summer Ames had a modest hit with "He Wore a Green Beret," a not subtle attempt to latch on to the popularity of Barry's song. Written by Frank Catana and Peg Barsella, "He Wore" is told by a woman whose "true love," a Green Beret, dies in Vietnam. "Though my love died," the song concludes, "I'm proud to say/His son will wear/The Green Beret."

With "The Ballad" still at No. 1, Barry appeared at the ninth annual Grammy Awards in New York City on March 15. In those days the Grammy Awards ceremonies were not televised live (a recorded TV special aired later in the year) and included only a handful of live performances. The main event took place at the Beverly Hills Hilton, but the 1966 Grammies included simultaneous programs in New York, Nashville, and Chicago. Roger Miller and the Statler Brothers performed live in Nashville. The comedian Godfrey Cambridge and Barry were the only live acts in New York City. Since "The Ballad" was released in 1966, it was not eligible for a Grammy that year. It did not win the following year.

In an interview about a week after the Grammies, Barry told a reporter that "The Ballad" and his other songs were neither pro- nor anti-war. "They are 'heart-of-the-soldier' songs," he explained. "They try to tell of a soldier's duty, of his pride, his unforgettable encounters with deprivation and suffering, his unending dangers, lucky triumphs, deep loneliness, and his love of country.

"No one hates war more than a soldier who's been in the heat of the battle. But if the objective is noble, one can't deny its glory, either."[19]

Meanwhile, the fighting in Vietnam had amped up considerably. The same week that Barry spoke of the dangers of war, the U.S. Military Command in Vietnam announced that 80 American troops had been killed that week, 816 wounded, and 17 missing in action or captured by the enemy. The previous week 100 men had been killed, 808 wounded, and 8 went missing.

NBC News aired a special one-hour report called "Vietnam: The Home Front" on Friday night, April 1. Produced by Chet Hagan and hosted by veteran newsman Frank McGee, the program looked at the emerging Vietnam War hawk-dove split through interviews with private citizens and members of Congress. The program opened with McGee sitting behind a news desk with "The Ballad" album cover displayed prominently behind him and Barry's song providing the background soundtrack.

"The song is indicative of the national preoccupation with a deadly jungle war in a far-off place," McGee said, while black-and-white footage of Barry recording "The Ballad" in the RCA studios rolled. "Sergeant Sadler's plaintive folk songs about Vietnam find their way into recruitment for the war, especially for the Nurse Corps." Then came footage of a recruiting event at Louisville General Hospital in which nursing students intently listened to Barry's "Salute to the Nurses."

The following night, Saturday, April 2, Barry showed up on the broadcast of *The Hollywood Palace*, an ABC TV variety show taped before a live audience in Los Angeles. Martha Raye hosted the show that week. An outspoken proponent of the Vietnam War and much beloved by the troops, Raye made many trips to the war zone, as she had done during World War II and the Korean War. In Vietnam she often wore a Green Beret uniform, complete with beret, and was made an honorary SF colonel.

That night's show included performances by the comedians Allen and Rossi and George Carlin, the singers Chad and Jeremy, and the dancer Ann Miller. A good number of men and women in uniform sat in the front rows of the audience.

"Anyone who's been to Vietnam can appreciate how beautifully Staff Sergeant Barry Sadler's songs have expressed the emotions and courage of our men over there," Raye said as she introduced Barry. "The sergeant himself, a wounded battle veteran, is here with us and we're very proud to have him on *The Hollywood Palace* tonight. Here he is, Staff Sergeant Barry Sadler of the Green Berets."

Barry walked confidently to center stage, wearing his green Class A uniform and jump boots, as he had on *Ed Sullivan*. This time five ribbons in two rows, including one for his newly issued Purple Heart, were on his chest.[20] Six actors in Green Beret uniforms stood at parade rest in the background as Barry resolutely sang "The 'A' Team"—an ode to the "strong and true" twelve-man "invincible" Green Beret units—a song that didn't make it onto his album.

The first verse is:

> Twelve men strong and true
> Twelve men fight for you
> On their heads a beret of green
> Twelve men, invincible, the A-Team

After it ended Barry and Martha Raye met at center stage and she addressed the audience. "Ladies and gentlemen," she said, "Barry has accomplished a rarity in the recording business. He just received two gold records, one for his album and another for his single record. And now he's going to sing the big one, 'The Ballad of the Green Berets.'"

Which Barry did. The six men in the background did a bit of marching to the opening of the song and then stood in silhouette behind Barry as he sang the song flawlessly. After the applause died down, Raye presented Barry with the two gold records.

"You deserve 'em," she said.

To which Barry replied: "Thank you, Martha, but as a fellow wearer of the green beret, I'd like to thank you on behalf of the men in Vietnam. You brought 'em live entertainment with laughs when they needed it the most."

Raye said she was "very grateful for the opportunity and I can't wait till I go back. And that'll be soon. Thank you once again for being here tonight, Barry. God bless you."

As he walked off the stage, Raye threw Barry a hand salute, and then said she would be right back as the show segued into a Windex commercial.

The following Monday, April 4, 1966, the southern Colorado correspondent for Denver's *Rocky Mountain News* paid a visit to the Pioneer Bar in Leadville. When they play "The Ballad," at the Pioneer, the correspondent, W. T. Little, reported, "which is quite often, the patrons and hired hands all but stand to attention." The reason: "the manager, Robert (Bob) Sadler, 30, is the brother of Staff Sgt. Barry Sadler," who wrote "The Green Berets," a "composition dedicated to the gallantry of U.S. fighting men in Viet Nam."

Bob Sadler told the reporter that his brother was in Fort Bragg "and he has no plans on leaving the Army as far as I know. The money he's made from 'The Green Berets' hasn't made too much change in his life."[21]

Bob Sadler was misinformed. Barry was not in Fort Bragg at that time. And Barry, in fact, had definite plans to leave the army. What's more, the song already had made monumental changes in Barry's life—and would do so until his dying day.

CHAPTER 9
A YOUNG, CREW-CUT TROUBADOUR

"I don't think the success has changed me much."
—BARRY SADLER, JULY 1966

As his nationwide tour moved into its third month, Barry kept up the frenetic pace. On March 27, 1966, he flew to Maryland and spent the better part of a week glad-handing at a giant job fair—the Jaycees Career Opportunities Exposition—at the Baltimore Civic Center. After returning to Fort Bragg, he flew to nearby Florence, South Carolina, late in the afternoon of April 4, to lip-sync "The Ballad" and "Letter from Viet Nam" for a local TV show.

When Barry got off the plane at the Florence Municipal Airport, the city's mayor presented him with a key to the city and a "handful of admiring teenagers" asked for autographs.[1] Barry hustled off to the TV studio, taped the songs, and flew back to Fort Bragg late that night.

Back at the base Barry took part in the official welcoming party at the Special Warfare Center for a special visitor, John Wayne, the famed movie actor. Wayne had just received word that the Johnson administration would cooperate with him on a pro–Special Forces, pro–Vietnam War movie he planned to star in and direct based on Robin's Moore's book. Wayne and his son Michael, who would produce the film, took the VIP tour at Bragg.

Two months later John Wayne spent three weeks in Vietnam visiting the troops. He also took time to narrate a Department of Defense documentary. Entitled "A Nation Builds Under Fire," the thirty-minute film put a totally positive spin on the American war effort—"the strangest war which America has ever been in," as John Wayne put it. Wearing army fatigues, Wayne narrated the movie with a Vietnamese village north of Saigon in the background. The main theme was how the United States was helping South Vietnam "build itself into a nation." The movie included heroic images of American and South Vietnamese fighting men, serving, Wayne said, "the cause of freedom."

Castigating the Viet Cong as "cutthroats and terrorists," Wayne called the South Vietnamese a "worthy and brave ally."

On Saturday morning, April 16, Barry served as grand marshal at the four-day Wilmington, North Carolina, Azalea Festival. Lavona came along—one of the few times she joined Barry at one of his events. At the Friday night ball before the next day's parade, Lavona was sitting at a table reading a book when Barry made his entrance into the room.

"I remember these two real pretty girls had their arms intertwined with Barry as they were walking him forward," Lavona said in 2015. "I just kept reading."[2]

The Azalea Queen that year was Ulla Stromstedt, a Swedish-born actress then appearing in the popular TV show *Flipper*. In addition to Barry the other festival celebs included TV bandleader Mitch Miller and comedian Larry Storch, the co-star of *F Troop*, another popular TV show of the day.

Around that time Barry told a *Time* magazine reporter that he was trying not to let "The Ballad"'s big sales and all the attention change his life. "I hope I have enough character not to let this blow my head out of proportion," he said. "I'm government property until March 1967 [actually May], and then I'll probably get out and into the entertainment world."[3]

Barry had said something similar to syndicated Hollywood correspondent Dick Kleiner a few weeks earlier in Los Angeles while taping *The Hollywood Palace* TV show. After getting out of the army, "I'll try and make a buck," Barry said. "But if it doesn't work, I've made enough on this one song so I don't have to worry for a while."[4]

Meanwhile, RCA and Barry's publisher, Music Music Music, continued to push their hot commodity. The marketing effort included Music Music Music sending radio deejays personally autographed copies of

"The Ballad" sheet music to use for promotions. All the jocks had to do was mail in a written request.

In mid-April, with sales of the "The Ballad" still strong, RCA released "The 'A' Team" as a single. The two-minute, seven-second tune, which Andy Wiswell produced, debuted at number 79 on *Billboard* magazine's Hot 100 chart for the week of April 23. It reached as high as number 28 in late May and stayed on the charts for a few more weeks. But "The 'A' Team" single never came close to matching the stratospheric success of "The Ballad." Nor would anything else Barry would put on vinyl.

Barry spent two days in Charlottesville, Virginia, as a special guest at that city's annual Dogwood Festival. He flew into town on April 19 and served as grand marshal for the festival parade the next day, waving to the adoring crowd from the back seat of a brand-new 1966 white Oldsmobile convertible.

Earlier that day Barry attended the dedication of Charlottesville's Dogwood Vietnam Memorial. The memorial honored U.S. Army spec 4 Champ Jackson Lawson Jr., a First Cavalry Division trooper from nearby Earlysville, Virginia, who had died in a helicopter crash in Vietnam in November 1965. The memorial, which now contains the names of all the other local men who died in the Vietnam War, is believed to be the first Vietnam veterans memorial in the nation.

After the dedication Philip Page, a twelve-year-old sixth grader, walked up to Barry to ask for his autograph. "The song was a hit at the time and when I saw the sheet music at Stacy's Music Shop downtown I bought it, and took it with me to the Dogwood Festival," Page said. Barry made a big impression on the boy. "He was in full uniform," Page said. "He seemed tall and broad shouldered. I had never seen a Green Beret before. He was handsome, looked like a football player. To a twelve-year-old kid it was like looking at a knight. I asked him to sign my sheet music and he did gladly."[5]

Ray Severn, who was sitting in the front row on Main Street for the parade, saluted Barry as he went by in the Olds. "He had a big ole smile," Severn said, "and he saluted me, seeing me saluting him."[6]

Barry showed signs in Charlottesville that he was not exactly happy with the all-but-constant travel and public appearances. "He came in with no clothes except for what he wore and a little [toiletry] kit and a guitar case," said Al Maracaibo, one of the festival's organizers. "When he came off the plane, he had his uniform on, open neck, with a white T-shirt. I guess he figured he'd wear the same clothes all the time he was here." One of the other organizers, an army reserve officer, Maracaibo said, told Barry "he had to shape up a little bit, clean himself up."[7]

Barry "was very well received" at the parade and other events he took part in. "He was a pleasant person to be around," another Dogwood Festival organizer, Jim Schisler, said. "But he wanted to be fighting; he voiced that. He also voiced that he didn't like what he was doing. He wanted to be doing his job, what he was trained for and what he was good at."[8]

Barry said just that in a 1971 interview. "I was a good soldier," Barry told Robert Powers, "a good medic. That's the kind of success I wanted." When the song hit big, he said, "I didn't know what was happening. The next thing I knew, senators and congressmen wanted me to speak with them and the Pentagon ordered me on tours to drum up more interest in the war."[9]

A few days after Barry returned to Fort Bragg from Virginia, a North Carolina state trooper stopped him for speeding in his new Jaguar. "He told the trooper," a North Carolina newspaper reported, "'I was just driving along listening to the radio and didn't notice my speed.'"[10] Barry paid a fine of $24.55.

A few days later, on April 28, Barry flew to Atlanta to play "The Ballad" and two other songs at the annual luncheon meeting of the Metropolitan Atlanta Chapter of the American Red Cross at the Marriott Motor Hotel. At a press conference before the event, Barry answered questions about his Vietnam War tour of duty.

"It is a tough, dirty life," Barry said, slightly embellishing his war experience. "The Green Berets are a guerrilla outfit. We live in the jungle for the most part. For weeks at a time all we see are ourselves, the jungle and the Vietnamese natives. There isn't much glamour attached to living on a diet of rice, in a stinking hot jungle, and forgetting what it's like to have a bath or not being shot at."

On this occasion Barry chose not to criticize antiwar demonstrators. "I like to think one of the reasons we are in Vietnam is so these people can continue to think what they want to think, even if I don't agree with them," he diplomatically said.

When asked repeatedly what he thought about the Johnson administration's Vietnam War policies, Barry "carefully skirted all questions," a reporter wrote. He snapped at another reporter who asked a question in that vein. "That was stupid," he said. "You should have known better than to ask me something like that."[11]

The following day Barry arrived in Winchester, Virginia, for the thirty-ninth annual Shenandoah Apple Blossom Festival. On Friday, April 29, Barry once again assumed parade grand marshal duties. That night he danced at the Queen's Ball with Queen Shenandoah XXXIX, Elizabeth Jane Henderson of Winchester, England.

Barry returned to the RCA recording studio in New York City sometime early in the spring and rapidly recorded a second album's worth of tunes with Sid Bass once again doing the arranging and conducting. Titled "Ssg Barry Sadler of The Green Berets Sings 'The "A" Team,'" the album hit the record stores near the end of May. As was the case with "The 'A' Team" single, the album did not come close to "The Ballad" in terms of sales or popularity, even though RCA hyped it as the next "Ballad."

Despite the hype, Barry didn't like the way RCA marketed the album. "I don't really feel they tried too much to promote it," he said in 1973.[12] RCA did pay for an ad in the June 18, 1966, issue of *Billboard*. It read: "'The "A" Team' Takes Over . . . where 'The Green Berets' left off! Watch history repeat as this new album follows Barry's hit single up the charts. Better stock it heavy!"

History, however, only repeated itself in that the new record followed the same musical formula RCA cooked up for the first one. "The uniformed folk singer," one reviewer wrote, has "a new album in much the same military-flavored tempo. 'The "A" Team,' an excellent kissin' cousin of the Green Berets ballad, [is] another military swinger with deep patriotic tones." It's "an interesting set, which, no doubt, will set off another round of TV guest appearances for Staff Sgt. Barry Sadler."[13]

There would, indeed, be many more TV and other appearances. But the new album didn't make the *Billboard* Top LPs chart until the first week of July, when it limped in at number 132. It dropped off the list entirely two weeks later. Sales were decent—the album sold around 100,000 copies, Barry said in 1972—but nothing close to what "The Ballad" and its album sold. Why didn't "The 'A' Team" hit the big time? Undoubtedly because the album's hastily written and recorded songs—with the exception of the catchy title track—were entirely forgettable.

"The Ballad" remained a hot commodity, though, and Barry hired marketing man Clancy Isaac to work some licensing deals. By late April an official Barry Sadler button had been produced and distributed to chain stores across the nation. *Newsweek* reported brisk sales as "the buttons are already a coveted item among the nearly 200,000 members of the fast-growing Barry Sadler fan club."[14]

"We've been very cautious in licensing products," Isaac told *Newsweek*. "We don't want to turn Sergeant Sadler into a carnival figure." Nevertheless, Isaac said he was looking into a line of Barry Sadler toy guys and field-ration kits, as well as—no surprise—actual green berets. *Newsweek* reported that an unofficial green beret "was selling briskly at a Times Square novelty shop." For "some reason," the shop's owner said, "they're very big with women."

For some reason Clancy Isaac never made a deal for those toy guns, field-ration kits, or berets.

Back on the road again, Barry flew from Fort Bragg to Louisville on May 3 to be the honorary grand marshal of the Pegasus parade, the downtown event held on the Thursday before the running of the Kentucky Derby. Lavona accompanied him. She proved to be adept at crowd control, coming to Barry's rescue after they arrived at their hotel and a crowd of what a local reporter called "eager teenagers" surrounded Barry. Lavona immediately whipped out an attaché case and gave each teen an auto-graphed Barry Sadler note card. Barry flashed his wide smile at the young people clutching their autographs, and then he and Lavona hustled into an elevator, taking them far from the adoring throng.[15]

Barry arrived in Danville in southern Virginia on May 7 to be the guest of honor at a local VFW post banquet. Calling him "an authentic hero of the war in Viet Nam," a local newspaper reported that the "rug-gedly handsome little soldier delivered one of the briefest after-dinner speeches on record." Barry opened with "a little joke," the paper said in a front-page article. To wit: Special Forces men "used to get up and run five miles before breakfast, then go out and bite snakes or something. But now, we all go down to the theatre and have singing lessons."[16]

That was the extent of Barry's speech. He then took question from the audience of about 100 VFW members and guests. What do SF men think about antiwar demonstrators, someone asked. "We don't think any-thing about it," Barry answered. "You can get together 40,000 people to protest anything. It's the 190 million who stay home that count."

Did the United States belong in Vietnam? Barry avoided answering, as he had the last time someone asked that question in public in Atlanta. "I don't know," he said. "I'm not a politician. We elect people to determine our policy. It's our job to carry out their policy."

He ended the Q&A by humbly thanking the VFW members for their service. When his audiences cheer, Barry said, "they're not applaud-ing me, they're applauding you for what you've done in past wars and for all the soldiers and what they're doing today. As long as you're behind us, we'll do the job and do it right."

At the dance following the banquet, Barry, billed as the "guest vocal-ist," sang "The Ballad."

A few days after Barry returned to Bragg, he gave a special tour of the Special Warfare Museum. This time the VIP was Randy Boone, a songwriter and actor who was born in Fayetteville and starred as a singing cowboy in the TV show *The Virginian*. A reporter from the Greensboro, North Carolina, *Daily News* tagged along.

"Barry likes to affect a tough attitude," the reporter wrote, but "it is a thin camouflage for the warm, sensitive person underneath."[17]

After the tour Barry introduced Boone and the reporter to Lavona and Thor. He went on to speak with mixed feelings about his success. "They tell me I've made more than half a million dollars" from the song and album, he said, "but I can't believe it." He sounded off again about draft card burners, calling them (again) "a bunch of vomits." Barry gave Randy Boone a gift as he was leaving, a dagger from his German weapons collection.

Barry flew to Chicago on May 16 to be an honored guest at the annual Chicago Police Department Recognition ceremonies. The department presented him with an engraved police nightstick to mark the occasion. Lavona joined Barry in Chicago, having flown in from Pennsylvania after visiting her family. "Barry was already there," when she arrived, Lavona said. "So I went to his hotel. But they wouldn't give me the room number in case I was a nut. Then, when they found out I was Barry's wife, they gave us one of those fancy suites."[18]

A few days later Barry spent four days at Fort Gulick in the then U.S.-owned Panama Canal Zone, the home of the 8th Special Forces Group and other U.S. military units. According to Bill Coombs, who was stationed at Gulick at the time, the sergeant running the SF NCO and officers clubs asked for Barry to perform to help boost business. But when the general in charge of the Canal Zone found out, he ordered Barry to sing at all the military clubs in the zone and not to play in any civilian bars.

Barry "did not follow orders," Coombs wrote. "I know he appeared and sang a song or two at several places in Colon. He may have done the same thing on the Panama City side as well."

Barry also told Coombs that RCA Victor gave him $1,500 "to spend as he wished" during his time in Panama. "That was quite a bit of change," Coombs said, "when you could get a rum and Squirt downtown for fifteen cents."[19]

John Gissell, Barry's buddy from SF medic training, was with the 8th SF Group at Gulick at the time. Gissell remembered that Barry "had an Army escort officer taking him around," and saw him sing in the local VFW hall.[20]

Going through U.S. Customs at the Miami airport on the way back to Fort Bragg, Barry ran into a newspaper reporter from Omaha, Nebraska. The inquiring reporter asked how Barry's tour was going. "I don't plan to keep this up much longer," Barry replied. "I'm making a lot of money now but I don't enjoy all this moving around."[21]

But Barry—who was nothing if not a good soldier who obeyed orders—did keep moving. The second week of June he flew out to California, where he taped a week's worth of introductions to a series of war movies, including the 1958 film *No Time for Sergeants*, on KCAL-TV, an independent station in Los Angeles.

That week a new single made the country and pop music charts: the unabashedly patriotic "Day for Decision," a spoken-word effort by country music singer/songwriter Johnny Sea (born John Allan Seay Jr.). That five-minute, thirty-three-second endeavor—something of a rejoinder to "Eve of Destruction"—eventually made it to No. 14 on the *Billboard* country chart and No. 35 on the pop chart. It also spawned an album of the same name with tunes such as "God Bless America," "When Johnny Comes Marching Home," and "The Star-Spangled Banner."

The spoken song laments the state of America at home and abroad when "young men are dying for ideals that don't seem to mean too much to Americans anymore." America's "real trouble," Sea says, "doesn't lie in the rice paddies of Vietnam, in the masses of Red China, or in the diabolical intrigues to the south of us. The real trouble lies" at home in the form of a "disease which is slowly eating away at the heart of American lives." Said disease would be cynicism and nonbelief in god and country.

"We've killed all the sacred cows and destroyed all the images. And there's nothing left to respect. Old fashioned love of God, country, and family is passé. . . .

"Patriotism, the old hand-over-the-heart, flag-waving singing patriotism, has been condemned. . . . This 'better red than dead' cancer is more feared by the American soldier than all the communist mortar shells. It kills the vitality and spirit of America."

"Day for Decision" joined Barry's "Ballad" as the two most popular pop pro-military songs that resonated with many Americans during the cold war when anti-communist feeling was still high and the war in Vietnam hadn't yet turned into the divisive quagmire it would soon become.

Right around that time Barry-friendly columnist Bob Considine reported that the communist government of East Germany had banned the German version of "The Ballad," titled *Hundert Mann und ein Befehl*" (literally, "A Hundred Men and a Command"), which was "a smash hit" there. The East German communist leaders, Considine wrote, see "no good coming of clean living, right thinking, whitewashed East German youth going about [their] people's paradise whispering a tune whose words carry messages about the derring-do of crack American Army troops who are giving a very hard time to East Germany's splendid ideological comrades, the Viet Cong and North Vietnamese regulars."[22]

The army flew Barry to San Francisco in June to give a boost to its Nurse Corps Recruiting Program at the Presidio. "Full utilization was made of Staff Sergeant Sadler's visit to San Francisco, and the news media coverage gained by his presence was of great benefit to the recruiting program," the colonel in charge of the program wrote in the official letter of appreciation to Barry's commanding officer at Fort Bragg. "His ability to meet the press, radio and television was most noteworthy and his appearances were well received by all."[23]

After San Francisco came a trip to Washington, D.C., on June 25 to attend the OSS (Office of Strategic Services) Detachment 101 Association banquet at the Mayflower Hotel. The legendary World War II OSS leader general William J. ("Wild Bill") Donovan created Detachment 101 in April of 1942 in Japanese-occupied Burma. It became the first U.S. military unit to work undercover with a large guerrilla army—in this case, Kachin ethnic group fighters—deep in enemy territory. The men of OSS Detachment 101, also known as the American-Kachin Rangers, used unconventional warfare tactics that later became a model for the work done by the Green Berets in the Vietnam War.

"Barry was the banquet's special guest," said Allen Richter, a retired army colonel and the president of OSS Detachment 101 Association in 1966. "He was young, unassuming and soft spoken. He played 'The Ballad of the Greet Berets,' which brought a tremendous response. The 600-plus attendees gave him a standing ovation. He then presented Detachment 101 with a green beret and sword."[24]

Richter went on to say that when his term as president of the association expired, he handed the green beret that Barry presented to the group to his successor. He, in turn gave it to the next president "for safe keeping, and it went on to each succeeding president. It currently resides in Georgia with the last elected president."

After the OSS gig in Washington, Barry flew to Detroit, where he did a little recruiting, then, on June 28 and 29, he took part in the forty-sixth annual convention of the U.S. Jaycees, the "junior" U.S. Chamber of Commerce civic organization then open to men aged eighteen to forty. The Vietnam War—and the Jaycees' strong support for it—was very much in evidence at the convention, held at Detroit's giant Cobo Hall Arena.

The Jaycees staunchly supported the war. In a referendum its members backed LBJ's war policies by a twelve-to-one margin. Working with the Young Republicans and Young Democrats organizations, the Jaycees ran a national program that sent food and clothing to the people of South Vietnam.

The convention's first session opened in dramatic fashion. The arena darkened and a spotlight followed each of the fifty state Jaycee presidents as they solemnly marched into the hall carrying their state flags and then posted them on a huge four-tiered stage. Then Barry walked in—in his Green Beret uniform, naturally—carrying the American flag. The delegates rose and sang the National Anthem as Barry stood front and center holding the American flag. Then the Jaycees recited the Pledge of Allegiance.

After the flag-draped opening, former vice president Richard Nixon, who would become president in January of 1969, gave the keynote speech. Michigan's Republican governor George Romney—who would run unsuccessfully against Nixon for the 1968 Republican presidential nomination—also spoke. Vice President Hubert Humphrey spoke the next day. Barry sang "The Ballad." Miss America 1996, Deborah Bryant of Overland Park, Kansas, also made an appearance.

While Barry was in Detroit, the Defense Department announced that fifty-five American servicemen had been killed in Vietnam that week.

Barry had a busy Fourth of July weekend in 1966. He attended a joint meeting of local members of the American Legion, VFW, and the Disabled American Veterans in LaGrange, Georgia, south of Atlanta on July 3. Then he flew to LaCrosse, Wisconsin, to take part in an American Legion Fourth of July party. The next day he flew to Langley Air Force Base outside Norfolk, Virginia, for a ceremony in nearby Newport News at that city's World War I Victory Arch. The ceremony honored a group of seventy-five young men from the area—many of them friends from childhood—who joined the army under a program called the Tiger Platoon. The national commander of the American Legion spoke at that event, as did Virginia governor Fred Pollard and U.S. senator Harry F. Byrd.

In Chicago, on his way to Langley, Barry had given an interview to a newspaper reporter in which he talked about growing up, his musical abilities, and his post-military plans. How did he get started writing songs, the reporter asked.

"The reason," Barry answered, tongue firmly in cheek, "is because I'm such a lousy guitar player I never had the nerve to play someone else's stuff. And I'm still a lousy guitar player."

Barry—described by the reporter as a "young, crew-cut troubadour"—said that five record companies had turned down "The Ballad" before RCA said yes. "I don't think the success has changed me much," Barry said. "It's made some changes in me. The hardest thing to get used to, I think, has been the crowds. I'm not much of a partier. I don't like large crowds or loud noises or loud music, and it gets on my nerves a little bit. Being on the banquet circuit . . . can be rougher, I suppose than guerrilla warfare. I got a good elbow from hanging out at these bars lately, at cocktail hours. I sure don't have much time now for exercise."

When asked if the Robin Moore book helped make his song popular, Barry replied that it did. "And, I think," he added, "the song has probably helped sell a few copies for him, too. One thing is for sure, though, the public is now aware of the Green Berets. It used to be pretty aggravating when you'd go to a gas station and tell 'em to 'fill 'er up,' and the attendant would look at you and your beret, and say, 'My, you speak English well.'"[25]

On July 8 Barry took off again, this time to lend his star power to army recruiting events in three New Jersey cities: Newark, Atlantic City, and Paramus. SF master sargeant Forest Sutton served as Barry's official army escort on that jaunt.

Barry appeared on the cover of the July 9, 1966, issue of *KRLA Beat* magazine, published by KRLA-AM, a popular Los Angeles Top Forty radio station. In the cover photo Barry, in his SF uniform, half grins at the camera with an American flag next to him. The article, titled "Barry Sadler: 'You Don't Have to Shake Dandruff,'" includes a photo of Barry, again with a tight grin, looking at the camera with a lit cigarette in his right hand.

Calling him "the brash and outspoken American soldier who vaulted to fame" after "The Ballad" hit it big, the article mentioned that Barry had very little use for draft card burners, "dissenters," and "long-haired groups." Barry told the magazine that he wrote "The Ballad," in part, as an answer to the antiwar crowd. As for the new generation of long-haired rock and rollers, Barry said: "I don't think you have to have shoulder-length hair and shake dandruff over the first three rows to be able to sing."

What did he think of people who called his songs "trash"? It's "a free country," Barry replied. "People have the right not to like my songs, just as I have the right not to like them."

The reporter then asked Barry about a positive comment he had made on a TV show about killing a man running across an open field. Could he explain that? "I don't necessarily get pleasure out of killing a man," Barry replied. "Maybe I do from making a good shot. Just as a deer hunter likes to make a good shot, but I don't particularly like to kill a man."

What were his plans for the future? If he stayed in the army, Barry said, he "would be limited to a desk job. I just wouldn't feel right doing that. Somehow, I would never feel like one of the 'big boys.'" Barry said he hoped to leave the army, and to continue singing and recording "as long as there is a market for the type of songs that I do. I like making a buck just as much as the next fellow."[26]

After a break back at Fort Bragg, Barry drove to nearby Charlotte, North Carolina, to do a live TV appearance on Wednesday, July 20, on the regionally syndicated *Arthur Smith Show* on WBTV. Host Arthur "Guitar Boogie" Smith, who died at age ninety-three in 2014, was a nationally known guitar and banjo player. His old-fashioned variety show featured live country music, which he performed with his band, the Crackerjacks. He also interviewed guests from the worlds of country music, Broadway, Hollywood, and sports. Smith welcomed the little-known and the famous, the latter group including the evangelist Billy Graham and country music superstar Johnny Cash.

Barry traveled with a Green Beret demonstration unit from Fort Bragg to the Illinois State Fair, which ran from August 12 through August 21 at the fairgrounds in Springfield. The twelve-man Special Forces team put on special programs each of the fair's ten days. Also on the bill at the huge event: performances by the Beach Boys, Sam the Sham and the Pharaohs, Red Skelton, Carol Lawrence, Robert Goulet, Jack Jones, and George Kirby.

Barry played a small role at the giant forty-eighth annual National American Legion Convention, which took place in Washington, D.C., August 30 to September 1. He performed "The Ballad" at a luncheon at the National Press Club for some 300 former American Legion department commanders on August 30. That morning, President Johnson had addressed the convention's opening session at the D.C. National Guard Armory.

The American military in Vietnam, LBJ told some 3,000 American Legion Convention delegates, is "the best trained, best equipped, the best supported army that America has ever put on any field of battle. Their morale is as high as their firepower is great. They have encountered an enemy whose tactics are unlike those a modern American Army has ever faced before. And they are beating him in engagement after engagement, day after day."

Johnson spoke of the widely accepted American view that stopping the Viet Cong and North Vietnamese in Vietnam would prevent the spread of communism—aided and abetted by the Soviet Union and China—throughout the world. This was Johnson's version of the so-called Domino Theory first enunciated by President Dwight D. Eisenhower in 1954.

"Make no mistake about the character of the war," Johnson warned. "Our adversaries have done us at least one great service. They have described this war for what it is—in unmistakable terms. It is meant to be the opening in a series of bombardments—or, as they are called in Peking [Beijing], 'wars of liberation.' And if it succeeds in South Vietnam, as [Chinese military leader] Marshal Lin Pio [Biao] says, 'The people in other parts of the world will see that what the Vietnamese people can do, they can do, too.'"[27]

The convention also heard from, among others, Secretary of State Dean Rusk, Joint Chiefs Chairman general Earle G. Wheeler, and Richard M. Nixon. The future president spoke to delegates extemporaneously in the ballroom of the Washington Hilton Hotel the day after President Johnson's formal speech opening the convention. Nixon offered his own version of the Domino Theory, saying, "If Vietnam falls, the Pacific will be transformed into a red ocean and the road will be open to a third world war." Those "who predict the Vietnam War will end in a year or two," Nixon said, "are smoking opium or taking LSD."[28]

Barry's next stop: a TV guest appearance on *The Mike Douglas Show*, a popular, syndicated, daytime TV talk show taped in Philadelphia. The episode Barry appeared on aired on local TV stations during the first two weeks of September. The other guests included the opera star Patrice Munsel and the erudite TV host Bergan Evans. The singer Jerry Vale was Douglas's co-host.

Then came appearances at the weeklong Eastern States Exposition in West Springfield, Massachusetts, which was held September 17 through September 25. Barry performed five times, sharing the stage with—among others—Mike Douglas, George Kirby, the Andrews Sisters, a 4-H equestrian drill team, square dancers, and sheep-shearing and pony-pulling contestants.

Barry made a short jaunt to North Adams, Massachusetts, to perform at the town's nineteenth annual Fall Foliage festival's Teenage Dance on Main Street on Tuesday night, September 20. After being guest of honor at a welcoming dinner party at a local restaurant, Barry was driven with a police escort to a makeshift stage—the back of a flatbed truck in front of a park. Chaos ensued.

Barry's "arrival at 8:30 nearly precipitated a Beatles-style mob scene," a local reporter said, "as hundreds of screaming, gasping teenagers surrounded his car." When a group of teens started chasing the car, the local cops hustled Barry behind a row of stores and the overexcited fans went back into the street in front of the stage. A crowd that the reporter estimated at about 5,000 "cheered, shrieked and applauded his brief appearance on the bandstand." The teenagers screamed so loudly, that few could hear him sing "The Ballad" and the two other tunes he sang sitting on a stool and accompanying himself on guitar.[29]

Lavona and Thor flew to Denver with Barry for his next appearance, a two-day gig to help kick off the Mile-High United Way Drive. Barry's mother, Bebe, who still lived in Leadville, showed up in Denver to see Barry and Lavona and meet her grandson for the first time. The army assigned tough-as-nails Green Beret sergeant major William "Wild Bill" DeSoto to be Barry's Denver escort. Desoto, age forty-six, had seen combat in World War II and Korea and had done two Vietnam War tours.

Late that afternoon Barry and Wild Bill took part in a United Way rally at the Denver Civic Center. Barry also performed "The Ballad" at the local USO for a small group of staffers and active-duty service personnel and at the kick-off United Way dinner that night. Before that, at Fitzsimmons General Hospital—later known as Fitzsimmons Army Medical Center—Barry sat down in the hospital cafeteria, strummed a Silvertone acoustic guitar, and started chatting up the patients, most of whom were recovering from Vietnam War wounds.

Barry sang "The Ballad" and signed autographs and then went to a ward for the seriously wounded. He signed more autographs there and joked with the patients.

"How did you get that, doing squat jumps?" Barry jocularly asked a man with a bandaged knee.

"No," the guy answered, "I did it on the basketball court."

"Don't you wish you'd been over in Vietnam and got shot instead?" Barry said.

"I'm going to Vietnam as soon as I get out of here," the G.I. replied.

"In that case, you better get out on a basketball court before you go," Barry said with his sly grin.

In Denver Barry showed more signs that he was not happy with the all-but-constant traveling. "I'm not an entertainer," he told a newspaper reporter. "I do wish they'd let me sing something else for a change."[30]

Next on the Sadler tour: the annual Mountain State Forest Festival in Elkins, West Virginia. Once again Barry served as a grand marshal of a parade—the "grand feature parade," on Saturday, October 8. Steve Bruno, one of Barry's SF training buddies, happened to be in town for the festival as the woman he was dating (and later married) lived nearby. At the parade Bruno ran into another former fellow SF trainee, Dutch Meershaw.

"The streets are lined with people in this little town. Everybody turns out. We're like six, seven deep along Main Street," Bruno said. "The parade starts. Sadler's the grand marshal. He's sitting in this Cadillac convertible on the back on the trunk like Miss America, waving to everybody and smiling. Dutch starts yelling out his name. 'Saddie' we called him. And with all the cheering and people throwing panties at him and everything else that's going on he happened to catch a glimpse of Meershaw and he points to him and he says, 'Dutch.' There's a huge smile on his face.

"Sadler says, 'Get over here. Get over here.' And he tells the guy to stop the car. So we jump in the car and we're all the friggin' grand marshals of the parade. I'm waving at everybody and [Barry's] waving at everybody, Dutch is waving at everybody. We finally get to the end of this thing and he's surrounded by all these young girls."[31]

After Barry signed autographs for his adoring fans, the three men had lunch together.

"So you really made something out of yourself," Steve Bruno said.

"Guys, I can eat steak every night and drink twelve-year-old Scotch," Barry replied.

"I can't believe that silly song we were all playing with back in the day is on every radio everywhere," Bruno said.

"Neither can I, believe me," Barry replied. "I got this great duty. I came back from Nam and here I am going around the country as an ambassador."

Bruno asked Barry if he planned to stay in the army.

"I'm going to do this tour and get out," Barry replied.

Bruno did not see that as a good sign. "That was not what I wanted to hear," he said. "Barry had no idea what hit him. I knew that he still had no idea what he was into and what he could do if he really applied himself."

CHAPTER 10

THE BEST THING THAT EVER HAPPENED TO HIM

*"The Army stuff went real well, but you can't go on forever with it.
It'll probably be forgotten tomorrow."*
—BARRY SADLER, JANUARY 1967

RCA released two more Sadler singles in October and November of 1966:
the sappy "One Day Nearer Home" (clocking in at two minutes and nine
seconds) and the even sappier "I Won't Be Home This Christmas." The
latter amounted to two minutes and fourteen seconds of banality, ending with the lines: "Your picture I put next to my heart and/With it I'll
never part, so across the sea I stretch my hand/Merry Christmas, Merry
Christmas, from Vietnam."

Billboard predicted that Barry's Christmas song "could hit fast and
big."[1] It never hit at all—nor did "One Day Nearer Home."

It's likely that Barry recorded the four tunes—the B sides were the
forgettable "Not Just Lonely" and the lamentable "A Woman Is a Weepin'
Willow Tree"—around the time he did "The 'A' Team" album, although
none of the tunes made it onto the album. Sid Bass is listed as the arranger
and conductor on all four songs and Andy Wiswell the producer. Barry
co-wrote "I Won't Be Home This Christmas" with veteran songwriter
Leonard Whitcup.[2]

Barry's road trip continued in October. After the Elkins, West Virginia, shindig, he flew to Washington, D.C., to appear at the AUSA
(Association of the U.S. Army, a large nonprofit that supports the military) Annual Meeting. Once again Wild Bill DeSoto served as Barry's

official military escort. Barry turned twenty-six on November 1, and the army gave him a present: no gigs for three weeks.

That ended on Thursday, November 17, with a trip to Columbus, Ohio. Two days later Barry sang "The Ballad" at halftime of the annual Ohio State–Michigan football game. Barry performed with the Ohio State University Marching Band at what was dubbed the "Freedom Parade" halftime show.

The show's other featured guest, Green Beret 1st lieutenant Charles Q. Williams, had received a Medal of Honor for his courage under fire in June of 1965. During a fourteen-hour attack by a regiment of Viet Cong, Williams constantly braved enemy fire to save his men and fend off the enemy. In doing so, Williams took shrapnel, grenade fragments, and bullets in his right and left legs, left thigh, stomach, and right arm.

Barry flew back to the nation's capital early in December for a series of events. He showed up on Betty Groebli's *Capital By-lines*, an early afternoon, forty-five-minute local radio talk show on WRC-AM, on December 5. The British actor Michael Caine shared the microphone.

The next night Barry was signing albums at the city's best-known and most-popular Irish bar, Matt Kane's Bit 'O Ireland on Thirteenth Street downtown. Marine sargeant Robert Emmett O'Malley showed up, having just received the Medal of Honor from President Johnson. O'Malley had led a squad of 3rd Marine Regiment men through a bloody engagement against Viet Cong fighters during which he was wounded three times but refused medical care until his badly wounded men were evacuated. The night at the bar ended with Barry playing piano and O'Malley belting out Irish songs.

The next night Barry was guest of honor at a banquet sponsored by the D.C. Jaycees. Proceeds from the event went to Barry's foundation. That night a documentary produced by WGN Chicago, *The Heroes of Viet Nam*, aired on stations throughout the country. The half-hour show used words from Barry Sadler's songs to accompany footage of American service personnel in the Vietnam War.

Nineteen-sixty-six was a very good year for Barry Sadler. At year's end *Billboard* magazine anointed "The Ballad of the Green Berets" No. 1 on the "Hot Singles of 1966" chart—the industry standard, which ranks records based on radio play and sales. "The Ballad" came in at No. 10 on *Billboard*'s "Top Singles of 1966," a list based solely on chart positions. The "Ballad" LP also sat at No. 10 on *Billboard*'s "Top LPs of 1966" (based on chart positions).[3]

Nineteen-sixty-six was not a very good year for the American war effort in Vietnam. The number of U.S. troops more than doubled—from around 184,000 at the end of 1965, to more than 385,000 on December 31, 1966. More than 6,300 Americans died in Vietnam in 1966—nearly three times the total number of troops killed in action since the war had begun.[4]

How long would the war go on? Few Americans thought it would end in the near future. "I wish I could tell you what you have fought for—peace in the world—is just around the corner," President Johnson told a group of Vietnam veterans in Washington on December 15, "but there will be some long and difficult days ahead, days that will require patience, judgments, and understanding."[5]

Early in 1967 RCA Victor decided that the time was right for a third Barry Sadler album, one that de-emphasized the Green Berets. The result: "Barry Sadler Back Home," a collection of a dozen forgettable songs released in mid-January. Barry is smiling broadly in the photo on the album cover. He's wearing civilian clothes, a short-sleeved sports shirt, and is resting his left arm atop a guitar on his knee. Barry "sings love themes in a country mood," the back cover says.

"Nobody says it's the best voice in the Army, but with good orchestral backing supplied by Sid Bass [and] a cooperative girl chorus 'ooh-aahing,' [Barry] gets by," one critic said in a mixed, if generally positive, review of the album.[6]

"One Day Nearer Home," the single released in October, was on the album, along with its B side, "Not Just Lonely." Barry wrote three of the songs, "I Walk Alone," "Wind Take a Message," and "Come With Me." Sid Bass, who produced the record, co-wrote "Anymore" with Bob Crewe, who had co-written a string of No. 1 hits for the Four Seasons, including "Big Girls Don't Cry" and "Walk Like a Man."

The critics all but ignored "One Day Nearer Home." The radio stations didn't play it. Hardly anyone bought it.

That did not deter the U.S. Army from sending Barry out on the road again. Around the time the album came out, Barry spent two days back in Washington, D.C. He arrived in town to put in an appearance at the fifteenth annual Women's Forum on National Security at the Washington Hilton Hotel on January 24. The Vietnam War was very much on the minds of those who spoke and the delegates who attended, all of them representing women's auxiliaries of national veterans' service organizations.

John E. Davis, the national commander of the American Legion, gave a hawkish keynote speech. He called on the Johnson administration to expand the war by allowing U.S. troops to cross into Cambodia to raid Viet Cong sanctuaries and by lifting restrictions on bombing targets in North Vietnam.

"Let us re-examine all of the limitations now placed on our military to make sure these do not stand in the way of our vital objectives," Davis said. "Let us pile on the pressure until we have broken either the enemy's will or his ability to carry on the fight. When we hurt him hard enough long enough, we will have our victory. There is no other way."[7]

Martha Raye—who had just returned from entertaining the troops in Vietnam and did not attend the forum—received an award for distinguished service "in the cause of national security" at the event's closing session. Barry sang "The Ballad." Vice President Hubert Humphrey pressed the flesh at the end of the closing session.

The Vietnam War peace movement steadily picked up steam in 1967, especially on college campuses, even in places where pro-war sentiment remained strong. Dozens of students at the University of North Carolina

(UNC) in Chapel Hill, for example, began staging weekly one-hour silent vigils to protest the war in front of the city's main post office.

During the February 1, 1967, vigil, a group of pro-war UNC students put a stereo in the window of a dorm room and blasted out patriotic tunes, including "The Ballad," to taunt the silent protesters. The police shut down the music for violating an antinoise ordinance, so the pro-war group unfurled a sign saying, "the Viet Cong may be nice guys, but would you want your sister to marry one?"[8]

No antiwar demonstrators showed up in Washington, D.C., for the annual Valentine Ball put on by the Military District of Washington in the International Ballroom of the downtown Washington Hilton Hotel on February 3. The Army Band performed during the program. So did Barry Sadler, "singing some of his favorite songs as well as his 'Song of the Green Beret,'" a local newspaper reporter misreported.[9]

Nor were any peace people on hand the next day in Halifax, North Carolina, for the Boy Scout Patriotic Pilgrimage. Some 4,000 scouts attended the event in the small town near the Virginia border where a group of colonial legislators had signed the "Halifax Resolves" on April 12, 1776, the first official action by a colony calling for independence from England. On February 4, 1967, the scouts wrote letters to men serving in Vietnam and heard speeches from World War II aviator rear admiral Edward Outlaw and Medal of Honor recipient Charles Q. Williams and the song "The Ballad of the Green Berets" performed by Staff Sgt. Barry Sadler.

Barry gave an interview to an Associated Press reporter after he traveled back to Fort Bragg to talk about his post-army plans. "I'll be moving away from the military stuff into popular music—country and western and ballad," Barry said. "The Army stuff went real well, but you can't go on forever with it. It'll probably be forgotten tomorrow. That's why you have to keep working with new things."

Described by the reporter as a "chunky, 26-year-old Special Forces medic," Barry went on to say that the single and his albums had sold more than six million copies and that his songs had been translated into six languages. He said that he had saved or invested most of the royalties and that he was supporting himself, Lavona, and Thor "on his Army pay of $271 monthly and allowances and living in a modest, three-bedroom house."

Barry's plans, he said, also included producing a TV show on self-defense for women. And he saw himself making it in Hollywood.

"I still have a good chance for the movies," Barry said. "Since I've been a sergeant I figure I could play one."[10]

Barry had managed to sneak away from his promotional duties in 1966 to work with the veteran journalist and public relations man Tom Mahoney on his autobiography, *I'm A Lucky One*, which hit the bookstores the first week of February. One of the nation's best publishers, Macmillan, bought the book and brought out a quality hardcover with Barry on the cover, a duffle bag slung over his shoulder, in full Class A uniform, smiling knowingly into the camera.

"The soldier who wrote 'The Ballad of the Green Berets' tells what it's like to train in today's Armed Forces, to fight as a Green Beret in Vietnam, and to strike it rich as a balladeer," a blurb on the cover notes, managing to get the words "Green Beret" in twice in that one sentence.

The back cover contains three paragraphs by Robin Moore. "I would say," Moore says, "'*I'm* a lucky one.' Together we made the entire world aware of the brave men of the U.S. Army Special Forces, he with his ballad and I with my book." Adversity for Barry, Moore wrote, "turned to triumph, that's the fabric of truly moving, inspirational writing. *I'm A Lucky One* is a human and American document rich in this quality."

Barry, in essence, dictated his life story to Mahoney, a former reporter and editor at the *El Paso Times, Buffalo Times,* and *Look* and *Fortune* magazines. Mahoney had served in the Office of War Information in World War II and later did PR work for General Electric and a big ad agency, Young & Rubicam. Mahoney, who died in 1981, co-wrote several other books. That included *The Longest Auto Race,* about a 1908 around-the-world car race Mahoney wrote with race-car driver George Shuster.

I'm A Lucky One is not very moving or inspirational. It's a decently written, short account of Barry's life that often is vague about dates and places and is cluttered with filler and other non-autobiographical chronology detours. When Barry mentions getting a tattoo in Japan, for example, Mahoney adds three paragraphs about "why soldiers and sailors get tattooed." When Barry gets to November 23, 1963, Mahoney comes up with four paragraphs on the Green Berets and JFK's funeral, although Barry had nothing to do with that. When Barry first mentions the Montagnards, four pages of background follow, including a description of "the bravery and ingenuity" in Vietnam of SF captain Vernon W. Gillespie, whom Barry never met.

Most of the reviews were kind to this tepid book, offering mainly book reports summarizing Barry's life, with a sentence or two of praise for the book. *I'm A Lucky One* is "a complete and very human, first-person story," a reviewer for a Minnesota newspaper wrote, for example. It's "a uniquely American story, one that focuses on the life of an uncommon young man, but one that also gives an eye-opening picture of training and combat life in today's armed forces."[11]

A reviewer for a Florida newspaper had almost the same opinion. He called the book "a uniquely American story," one that provides "a vivid account" of "an uncommon young man" and "a stunning account of training and combat life in today's armed forces, and the Green Beret way of fighting in Vietnam."[12]

"The story of Barry Sadler could be the story of millions of men who enlist in the service and are proud of the service they give their country—except for the ending," a reviewer in Wisconsin opined. *I'm A Lucky One* "is written for all readers but teens will probably have more interest in it than adults."[13]

In one of the few reviews in a big-city newspaper, Bonnie Aikman of the Washington, D.C., *Evening Star* also offered a book report, spending much of the review summarizing Barry's life story. The story of his military training "is buoyantly, boyishly enthusiastic," Aikman wrote. "The style of his narrative," she said, with its "unabashed pride in his achievements," is "probably easily forgiven as the youthful bombast" found in "countless letters from young servicemen abroad." Barry "does sound like an abundantly good-natured fellow," she concluded, whose "appetite for new skills . . . appears to be as boundless as his facility for writing ballads."[14]

The book received only a few negative reviews. Clarence Doucet, writing in the New Orleans *Times-Picayune*, offered a mixed opinion. Calling the book "an easy-reading short review" of Barry's life, Doucet wrote: "This is not a deep book. It is a genuine review, though, of a life that has been to some interesting places and done some interesting things. No messages of sage advice fill its pages. It is essentially plain talk."[15]

College student Linda J. Greenhouse attacked the book in her review in the *Harvard Crimson* newspaper. Characterizing *I'm A Lucky One* as a "ghost-written hack autobiography," Greenhouse wrote that Sadler and Mahoney "ramble on for page after page; 185 in all, managing to turn what could have been a mildly enlightening tale of either a hillbilly in the New York publishing world or a soldier in Vietnam into an absolutely wretched book."[16]

Barry "doesn't take a step without offering a 2,000-word discourse on where he is going or where he has come from," Greenhouse wrote. Worse, she said, the book left "an uneasy aftertaste" because—despite the fact that Barry dedicated the book to those who didn't come home from Vietnam—he papered over anything negative about the military and the war in Vietnam.

"If Sadler brought back any genuine emotion at all from Vietnam," Greenhouse concluded, "it is simply that the Army and everything he did in it was the best thing that ever happened to him."

Barry did a few TV and radio shows to hype the book, but large newspaper and magazine reviewers ignored it and sales were so-so. That didn't stop the army from sending Barry back out on the road for the last four-plus months of his military career. On February 18 he spoke at the twentieth annual Patriotic Conference in Chicago sponsored by the VWF Auxiliary of Illinois. Barry made a brief speech at the conference's luncheon and took a few questions afterward. Barry, with Wild Bill DeSoto in tow, appeared at an event sponsored by the Downtown Optimist Club of Flint, Michigan, on March 11.

Two days later groundbreaking ceremonies took place at the recently renamed John F. Kennedy Center for Special Warfare at Fort Bragg for a memorial to SF soldiers who were killed in combat. The Special Warfare Memorial Statue—a twelve-foot-tall bronze of a Green Beret in Vietnam War jungle fatigues carrying an M-16 rifle—would be dedicated in 1969. All the funds for the $100,000 memorial statue came from private donations. Barry Sadler and John Wayne each donated $5,000 and former secretary of defense Robert S. McNamara wrote a check for $1,000 to build the statue.[17]

The last two events Barry undertook for the army were promoting U.S. savings bonds in Washington, D.C. The first took place on April 12, a rally aimed at federal workers held in the departmental auditorium of the U.S. Postal Service headquarters. The comedian Phyllis Diller and Barry were the star attractions. Diller told jokes. Barry sang a few songs, including "The Ballad." Afterward, a reporter wrote, "he posed for pictures with a lot of excited secretaries who happened to come to work with loaded cameras and new hairdos."[18]

Three days later, on April 15, 1967, the largest Vietnam War protest demonstrations staged since the war began took place in New York City and San Francisco. In New York a crowd estimated by police at between 100,000 and 125,000 marched from Central Park to the United Nations Plaza. Civil Rights leader Martin Luther King Jr. and activist pediatrician Dr. Benjamin Spock led the march. In San Francisco some 100,000 marched from downtown to Golden Gate Park, where the folksinger Judy Collins and rock bands Big Brother & the Holding Company with Janis Joplin and Quicksilver Messenger Service performed.

Barry's final army-sponsored event before he received his honorable discharge on May 4 had taken place three days earlier—a public "Share in Freedom" lunchtime savings bond rally held in front of the Treasury Department building at Fifteenth and F Streets in downtown Washington, D.C. The event included the release of fifty balloons, one of which contained a card entitling the finder to a $25 U.S. savings bond—and an appearance by the Green Beret balladeer, Barry Sadler.

Jane Rager, who did occasional part-time promotional work for the Treasury Department and who worked nearby, showed up in her homemade Uncle Sam suit to release the balloons. "When I arrived to do the photo op, someone said, 'By the way, Barry Sadler is here,'" Rager said. "I spent a couple of hours talking with him just making light conversation. He was a kind, humble soldier. He kept it professional. He seemed really quiet and shy—and the perfect gentlemen."

"I'm just a soldier," Barry told Rager before they parted. "I'm out of my element here."[19]

"The Ballad," Barry said in 1972, "really affected my career in the Army. I wanted to re-enlist. I did. I like medicine; it was my whole life." But the army made things extremely difficult for him. After "the song had died out and the fame was gone," he said, "they wouldn't have let me do my job as a soldier. I know it was partly because I had been wounded—but that wasn't all of it.

"The Army liked it when the song was current. It meant I could do enlistment programs. But when it was all done with, they wouldn't have had time for a sergeant who had made that kind of money. And I think the Army really likes for a man to be—well—un-public. I was a public figure, and that didn't make me fit for a soldier" in the army's eyes.

"If I had to do it all over again," he said, "I'd probably throw the song in a trash can. In the Army, I had a job I liked, people I liked, and something that suited me. I don't think I realized what a different world I got into after 'The Ballad' became so popular."[20]

On May 7, 1967, Barry Sadler walked into a nondescript administration building at Fort Bragg and signed the paperwork to receive his discharge. Barry did not want a ceremony. The army obliged. Nor did Barry pose for pictures after leaving the base processing office even though newspaper reporters and photographers waited outside the building.

A week earlier he had been awarded the Army Commendation Medal for meritorious service performed from October 13, 1965, when he came back on full duty following his injury, to May 3, 1967. That made six medals upon Barry's chest. The others: the Purple Heart, the Armed Forces Expeditionary Medal (for his service in Vietnam), the National Defense Service Medal (for honorable active-duty service), the Air Force Longevity Service Award (for four years of service), and the Good Conduct Medal.

"I wasn't the best soldier in the world," Barry said in 1979. "I received medals for staying alive but not for doing anything heroic."[21]

He may not have been a hero, but Barry Sadler conducted himself well while serving in the U.S. Air Force and Army. Except for normal GI hijinks, he stayed out of trouble. No official reprimands, no Article 15s (the nonjudicial military punishment for minor misconduct), no courts-martial. The undisciplined teenager grew into a responsible husband and father, a revered wounded war veteran—and a nationally known and respected singer/songwriter. And he made a pile of money.

Barry's future as a civilian looked promising. He had financial security. He was about to move to a big new home in a new city with his wife and young son. He'd be writing more songs and planned to make more records. He would give a shot at making it in the movies.

What could possibly go wrong?

CHAPTER 11
BEING A FAMILY

"We just wanted to live a normal life."

—Lavona Sadler

The Sadlers stayed in Fayetteville until October, three months after their second son, Baron, came along on July 12, 1967. Former staff sargeant Sadler, no longer working for Uncle Sam, happily took a long break from making appearances, doing just a few events on his own during the first six months after his honorable discharge.

"We just wanted to live a normal life," Lavona Sadler said.[1]

During the last week of May, Barry taped a segment on *The Al Capp Show*, a syndicated, hour-long TV talk show. Capp, best known as the creator of the *L'il Abner* comic strip, was an ardent Vietnam War hawk and outspoken critic of antiwar protesters. Although out of the army, Barry was billed as "Sgt. Barry Sadler" on the show, which also included an appearance by the flamboyant actress Tallulah Bankhead.

Barry didn't do another event for nearly four months. Then he flew to San Antonio on September 7 to perform at the fiftieth-anniversary salute to Kelly Air Force Base. Also on the bill: the Airmen of Note, the official USAF jazz ensemble.

Barry made good on his vow to try acting. He had met the long-time TV and film producer Robert Stabler in Los Angeles in the summer of 1966. Barry subsequently worked with Stabler as his military technical adviser on a Vietnam War movie script for a film called *Search and Destroy* that Stabler wanted to produce and shoot in the Philippines. That film never happened. But Stabler, who had been producing episodes of the long-running TV western series *Death Valley Days* since 1952, liked

Barry's looks—and his fame—and offered him a small part in an episode.[2] Barry accepted.

"I've been restless with nothing to do," Barry told a newspaper reporter in North Carolina. "So the acting profession seems to be an interesting challenge for me. I'll give it an honest try."[3]

Barry, Stabler said, "did a darn good job, and he'll do some more when we film in Tucson in a few months." Stabler kept his word and gave Barry small parts in two more *Death Valley Days* episodes shot in January of 1968 in Tucson. As far as Barry's acting, no one except Robert Stabler ever used the word "good" to describe it.

In September 1967, not long after Barry did that first acting gig on the *Death Valley Days* set outside Apache Junction, Arizona, the Sadlers moved to Tucson. They bought a large, four-bedroom, 4,000-square-foot ranch house on a five-acre plot on the eastern edge of the city. The house, covered in burnt adobe brick, had a swimming pool and a swing set in the backyard, which looked out over the stark desert landscape. For privacy's sake Barry left the previous owner's name on the driveway's wrought-iron fence.

Tucson today is a busy metropolis an hour's drive from the Mexican border, and about twice that distance from Arizona's much larger capital of Phoenix. Sitting at 2,600 feet above sea level and surrounded by dramatic mountain ranges rising from 6,000 to nearly 9,400 feet, the city lies in the northern reaches of the Sonoran Desert. Temperatures average eighty-two degrees year-round. In 1967 it had something of a split personality: A railhead and center of the cattle-ranching industry, Tucson also is the home of Davis-Monthan Air Force Base, one of the largest military installations in the country, and the University of Arizona, a preeminent land-grant university in the Mountain West.

"On any given day in Tucson in that tumultuous year of 1967, you could attend a cattle auction, an air show, a public lecture or poetry reading, and a rock concert," said the author Gregory McNamee, who has lived in Tucson and written about the city and its environs for many years.

"And not just by local-favorite acts like Linda Ronstadt's band The Stone Poneys, but also big national acts like the Doors and Jimi Hendrix."[4]

The east side of town, where the Sadlers settled, was at some distance from the action, a few miles beyond the sprawling Davis-Monthan Air Force Base in a dense forest of saguaro cacti. Most of the inhabitants of the east side in 1967 were Mexican and Anglo ranchers, as well as employees of mines in the mountains to the south and retirees.

Why the move to Tucson? Barry "just decided," Lavona Sadler said. "He had two lovely aunts, Hope and Joyce, who lived there. They were wonderful, wonderful people—completely different from his mother."[5]

Hope and Joyce "were very good to him," Barry's air force buddy H. D. Graham said. "He talked about them all the time. He didn't talk about his mother very much. He talked about his dad quite a bit, but I don't think he knew a lot about him. I think that was stuff he picked up from his aunts and uncles."[6]

Barry bought a house in Tucson for his brother, Bob, who was married and had three children. He paid for his mother Bebe's move to Tucson, as well. "I guess he wanted Bob to help him take care of business and get him out of the mines," Lavona said. "All Barry wanted to do, I think, was to be a family."

Bebe Sadler split her time in Tucson between Barry's and Bob's houses. "She was funny; she was smart; she was witty. There were a lot of good qualities about that woman," Lavona said. "But she wasn't like her sisters at all. She had a downright mean streak. She seemed to laugh at other people's hardships or try to make hardships for other people."

On November 11, 1967, ten days after Barry's twenty-seventh birthday, the episode of *Death Valley Days* he shot in September aired on TV stations across the country. In "The Informer Who Cried," Barry played Jackson, one of four bank robbers. The small part had very few lines, which was just as well as Barry delivered them in a wooden monotone. On the other hand, the teleplay was not exactly Shakespearean and his acting skills just about equaled those of the rest of the cast. Plus, he looked the part of a nondescript cowboy and seemed to handle his horse capably.

Next in what would be a short-lived acting career: a small role in his first—and last—Hollywood movie, *Dayton's Devils*. Written by journeyman screenwriter Fred De Gorter, produced by Barry's Hollywood buddy Robert Stabler, and directed by TV producer and director Jack Shea,[7] that forgettable film starred Rory Calhoun, a veteran of countless movie and TV westerns. The movie featured a young, voluptuous Lanie Kazan, making her Hollywood debut; Leslie Nielsen, who went on to fame as a comic actor in *Airplane* and the *Naked Gun* movies; and Georg Stanford Brown, the actor best known for his work in the 1970s TV cop show *The Rookies*.

Barry played Barney Barry, one of the antiheroes in a crime caper with a plot that borrowed heavily from the popular 1960 movie *Ocean's 11*. In *Dayton's Devils* a gaggle of sketchy ex-military men and one woman, led by the unbalanced, revenge-seeking ex-USAF Colonel Dayton (Nielsen), conspires to make off with the payroll at an air force base.

"I play the killer in the group of six specialists, you know, forgers and such like, who gets to kill a nice kindly old fisherman," Barry jokingly told a Tucson newspaper reporter just before the filming started. "We serve this ex–Air Force officer, who thinks the military mind will react in a predicable way—too slow to catch us."

Barry also told the reporter that he was planning to go back to Vietnam, and would be shooting a movie called *The Widow Makers* in the Philippines. He said he would be acting in the film—and writing the theme music.[8] None of that transpired.

An "avid collector of Nazi daggers, cutlasses, pistols, medals, uniforms—even an army of rare Nazi toy soldiers," the Tucson reporter wrote, "Sadler sits among his memorabilia and contemplates opening a bar in Tucson."

The Tucson bar did come to pass. Just before the end of the year, Barry opened the Beachcomber Bar at the end of a nondescript East Side

Tucson strip center about a half-hour's drive from his house. For a while the small bar offered Sunday-evening jam sessions, inviting all musicians to join in. But that never worked. Barry told some people that he would be performing at the Beachcomber, "but not on a regular schedule."[9]

Barry may have picked up his guitar once or twice and played at the bar, but he didn't spent much time there. "Barry didn't go out to it much," said Bob Barkwill, Barry's close friend and showbiz manager from late 1968 to the early 1970s. "We went out there a couple of times and had a few drinks. Barry would just sit and talk to people and then we'd leave."[10]

"He had a tiny stage in there. He had girls in there dancing," Robert Powers said. "The only time I was ever in it, there were some girls grinding away on the stage. They weren't topless; they were bikini grinding. It was a wannabe stripper bar, I guess."[11]

"I happened by and attempted to sell [Barry] a legal liability policy," former Tucson insurance man Ron Edwards said in 2016. "It was 9:30 a.m. and he seemed a little fuzzy. He was quite talkative, and said he had been a Green Beret and had written a song and he had received a substantial sum and was having a good time. My impression of him was he should not be a bar owner as he was his own best customer."[12]

Barry let his brother, Bob, "take care of the whole thing," Bob Barkwill said. "He was running it and handling the money."[13]

In the twelve months that ended when Barry opened the bar on December 31, 1967, more than 11,000 Americans lost their lives in the Vietnam War—an increase of more than 5,000 compared to the previous year. The figure for 1968 would be even higher.

Nineteen-sixty-eight, in fact, proved to be the height of the American war in Vietnam—and one of the most turbulent, traumatic years in American history. Much—but not all—of the turbulence and trauma had to do with the war in Vietnam, where the number of American troops hit its peak at more than 530,000.

The surprise Tet Offensive during the January 30 through January 31 Lunar New Year celebrations proved to be a turning point in the war.

Viet Cong and North Vietnamese army units attacked South Vietnamese and U.S. military and government installations throughout the country. South Vietnamese, American, and South Korean troops quickly repelled the enemy. But the fighting went on in Saigon for more than a week and in the ancient capital of Hue until early March.

Although a decisive military defeat for the enemy, Tet '68 proved to be a game-changing psychological victory for them. The massive, surprise offensive—covered in detail on U.S. television news shows and newspapers—shocked the American public, which had been assured that a U.S. victory was imminent. Tet convinced many in this country that the war could not be won and support for the Vietnam War waned considerably.

On February 18, 1968, the U.S. military reported a record number of American casualties for the previous week: 543 dead and 2,547 wounded.[14] On March 12 Senator Eugene McCarthy of Minnesota, running on an all-out antiwar platform, came close to defeating President Johnson in the New Hampshire Democratic Party presidential primary. On March 31, in a nationally televised speech, Lyndon Johnson shocked the nation when he announced he would not run for reelection and would try to start peace talks to end the war.

On April 4 the Rev. Martin Luther King Jr., the Civil Rights leader and Vietnam War opponent, was assassinated in Memphis. Large-scale riots followed in more than half a dozen large cities, including Baltimore, Boston, Chicago, Detroit, Washington, D.C., and Newark. On June 5 Democratic presidential candidate Robert F. Kennedy, the brother of President John F. Kennedy and an opponent of the Vietnam War, was assassinated at the Ambassador Hotel in Los Angeles. On August 28 and 29, a large-scale riot erupted in Chicago when the police and National Guard troops attacked some 10,000 antiwar protestors outside the Democratic National Convention.

As more than one observer has noted, 1968 was a year in which the United States suffered a nervous breakdown.

Barry Sadler, an ardent supporter of the war in Vietnam, went through no traumas or tragedies in 1968. He spent most of that year in Tucson and Los Angeles doing his TV acting and making occasional TV and radio appearances. In mid-January Barry filmed two more *Death Valley Days* episodes on a sound stage in Old Tucson, a replica of the city from its 1860s Wild West days that Columbia Pictures built in 1939. Barry commuted to the gig.[15]

In the first three months of the year, Barry made three appearances on *The Woody Woodbury Show*, a nationally syndicated daily TV talk and variety show taped in Hollywood. In late February he showed up on *The Sam Yorty Show*, a local Los Angeles TV talk show hosted by that city's outspokenly conservative former mayor.

Death Valley Days ran the episode "The Pieces of the Puzzle" on May 11, 1968. Robert Taylor, the series host, starred. Barry again had a bit part, playing a cowboy named Bill Truman. The plot had to do with who held claim on a large portion of land in Arizona from an old Spanish land grant.

In July Barry taped *The Les Crane Show*, a syndicated TV talk show, in Los Angeles. The topic was the No. 1 issue of the day: the Vietnam War. In a show Crane titled "Will the Real Patriot Please Stand Up?," Barry faced off against a fellow former Green Beret medic, Al Adams, and Los Angeles Valley College history and political science professor Farrell Broslawsky, both of whom opposed the war.

"Sadler was somewhat hostile, and we had a nasty exchange at one point, but when the show was over we were cordial with each other," Broslawsky remembered many years later.

The nasty exchange went something like this:

"We will never win if we are willing to continue a war of attrition. That would only create another generation that would continue to fight," Broslawsky said.

"That's how we *will* win the war," Barry replied, "by killing off the enemy."

"Does that mean killing the old and the young, women and children?" the professor asked.

"Yes," Barry replied.

"How would that distinguish us from the Nazis?" Broslawsky countered.

"We are *not* going to lose that war," Barry came back.

"At that point, Les Crane went to break," Broslawky said. "My impression of Sadler was that he was imbued with a set of military values that required obedience to orders regardless of the effect."[16]

The low-budget *Dayton's Devils* had nothing to do with the Vietnam War. The film arrived in movie theaters on September 19, 1968. It didn't stay long. Few critics paid attention to it; those who did noted that the movie's plot had giant holes, the screenplay was filled with inane dialogue, and the acting was on a par with Barry's work on *Death Valley Days*.

A. H. Weiler called the movie an "amateurish caper" in his short, dismissive review in the *New York Times*. Barry and the other actors, he wrote, have all "the dramatic impact of a Boy Scout troop on a hike" in a film that was "simply dull."[17]

Barry's third and last *Death Valley Days* episode, the Robert Stabler–produced "A Short Cut through Tombstone," aired on November 22, 1968. Less than a week later, the Thanksgiving-week episode of the long-running TV western *The High Chaparral*, titled "For What We Are About to Receive," hit the airwaves. Filmed earlier in the year in Old Tucson, the show would be Barry's only appearance on *The High Chaparral*. He played—no surprise—a young cowboy, the taciturn son of a cranky rancher. It was another small role in which Barry looked the part and delivered his few lines earnestly if awkwardly. It proved to be his last acting gig.

"I feel like acting for me is pretty much washed up," Barry said in 1971. "I think the world will survive without my face on the screen."[18]

"Barry wasn't an actor," Lavona Sadler said. "You have to get lessons unless you're a natural. There is no way without a god-given talent for acting that you can pull it off." Barry's few lines in the TV westerns, she said, "seemed stifled to me."

While he was on the set shooting *The High Chaparral* episode, Barry ran into Bob Barkwill, a thirty-eight-year-old cowboy singer, musician, actor, and agent working as an extra. The two men hit it off and very soon became close friends and business associates.

"He invited a bunch of the cast over to his place," Barkwill, who lived in Tucson, said. "We went over and had drinks that night at his ranch and got to be good friends. We had great times together. We all became close friends: Barry, Lavona, and the two children, Thor and Baron, who were just little kids."[19]

Bob Barkwill and the Sadlers remained close friends for more than two decades. Barkwill "was an instrumental part of our lives," Lavona Sadler said.[20]

Not long after Barry and Bob Barkwill met, they agreed to work together to try to get into the movie business. "We only had a handshake agreement," Barkwill said. "He told me, 'If you cheat me, you'll know what I'll do.' We joked about it."

Meanwhile, Barry used a big chunk of his royalty money to accumulate tens of thousands of dollars' worth of World War II German military memorabilia. He displayed the collection of ammunition, uniforms, medals, headgear, pistols, submachine guns, and other weapons in a small room of its own in his house.

"He had quite a collection," Barkwill said. "He had a bunch of the daggers given to fighter pilots and pictures of the pilots. He had a big copy of *Mein Kampf*, a rare edition autographed by Adolf Hitler. He collected Russian guns and German guns. He had Herman Goering's signet ring. He would let me wear it. He had a pistol with gold engraving on it. I think he got it from the actor Rory Calhoun he was good friends with. It was out of Hitler's collection."

"Growing up and seeing those items, I actually thought the Nazis won the war and I thought we were the Nazis," Thor Sadler said in 1989. "It was very romantic and appealing for a kid my age, four or five years old, and I got caught up in the regalia and the music." But Barry set his son straight on the legacy of the Nazis. "He told me," Thor said, "there is no music on the battlefield, only blood and gore and friends dying all around you, and nothing glorious or honorable in killing another man."[21]

Barry's Nazi collection included a Schwimmwagen ("Swimming Car"), a rare amphibious vehicle designed during World War II for the German army by Ferdinand Porsche and his son Ferry.[22] Barry bought the air-sealed, jeeplike vehicle from Hollywood Military Hobbies, a small shop on Hollywood Boulevard in Los Angeles.

"We used to take it out for long rides," Bob Barkwill said. "It had all the German markings on it. It was open and you could drive into the water and clutch in the propeller and drive across the lake. It once broke down on us out in the desert south of Tucson. Then we fixed the wiring. It leaked a little when we went into the lake."

On more than one occasion, Barry took the journalist Robert Powers out on joyrides at night—armed with assault rifles. "I remember bouncing over the countryside way out in the desert in the [Schwimmwagen] with a couple of M-16s and shooting in the night, acquiring verisimilitude for the things he was writing. That was Barry's idea, anyway," Powers said. "I'd sit on the right side shooting the M-16 with my left hand and he was sitting in the driver's seat, popping 'em out with just one hand."[23]

On occasion, Barkwill said, Barry would take the Schwimmwagen out for a spin in Tucson wearing a World War II German uniform. "Barry would like to dress up once in a while," he said. "He wore some German outfits at his ranch. Then we'd drive around. People saw us going around in Tucson and thought, I guess, we were nuts. But it was fun."

Barry and Bob Barkwill—who had moved to Los Angeles—started a film production company they called Eagle International Limited in rented office space at a Hollywood movie studio. "I was president and Barry, I think, was vice president," Barkwill said. "We had a little office at this studio where they shot *Beverly Hillbillies* and *Green Acres* and *Petticoat Junction*. My office was right next to George Burns and Eddie Albert."

People started coming to them with scripts, but Barry and Bob concentrated on working on a screenplay of their own, for a Vietnam War movie they called *Sergeant Sand*. The plot: A Special Forces sergeant is captured by the enemy and subjected to extremely brutal torture, including long stretches of being held in the jungle in a small cage.

"Barry thought of the whole thing," Barkwill said. "Barry was good at stories; he came up with a lot of them. We had a fella we met in a bar write us a movie script; his name was Rocky Graham. Barry dictated it to him. We sat down and wrote that thing out with him in a week, a week and a half."

Barry eventually put up about $150,000, and he and Bob Barkwill set out trying to raise the rest of the money to put the movie together. "In Hollywood you start talking to people," Barkwill said. "We hit a lot of bars. We went to a bunch up on Sunset Strip, [including] the Cock and Bull, a bar that most of the bigwigs would come around and drink at [at] night. We got to know a lot of people."

Barry and Bob did more than schmooze bigwigs at the bars. They did their share of just plain drinking and hanging out at the Whiskey A Go Go nightclub on Sunset Strip; they partied at a strip club called the Phone Booth on Santa Monica Boulevard; and they ate and drank at Dino's Lodge on Sunset.

"We used to sit at the bar with [the singer] Frankie Avalon," Barkwill said. "We met Michael Wayne and a lot of character actors . . . Yaphet Kotto, Max Baer Jr., Sunny Tufts. We'd sit there and drink all night with Sunny Tufts. Barry's drink was rum and Coke."

Sometimes at Dino's, Barkwill said, "they'd call Barry up on stage and he'd sing."

They visited Martha Raye at her house and Raymond Burr at his place. Burr, the star of the popular *Perry Mason* TV series, had visited Plei Do Lim to meet and greet the troops when Barry was there in 1966. Raymond Burr "invited us to come to his house when he was doing [the TV show] *Ironsides*," Barkwill said. "We watched a couple of episodes. He was a nice man and a funny guy."

Barry "and Martha Raye were great friends," Barkwill said. "We went out to her place a couple of times. She also invited us to visit her one time on the set of *The Carol Burnett Show*. [Raye] would talk about the times she went over to Vietnam and how she enjoyed helping the troops."

On more than one occasion, Barry turned off potential investors— and others. "Barry would sometimes hit people the wrong way," Barkwill said. "He'd just talk too much." One night Bob Barkwill introduced Barry to the actor Forrest Tucker, one of the stars of the TV series *F Troop*. "Forrest thought he could get Barry a guest spot," Barkwill said, but after having a drink or two with Barry, he said, "You can forget it." Why? Because "Barry would start with all these stories and get into the German stuff," Barkwill said. "I told him, 'You've got to be careful with what you say.'"

Barry and Bob eventually convinced several actors to be in the Vietnam War film, including Jeffrey Hunter, who agreed to play the lead. They lined up Robert Mitchum and Rory Calhoun for cameos. Hunter got excited about the film, and he went with Barry and Bob to Paramount Studios, where they pitched the idea to Michael Wayne, who ran his father's company. They also took it to Universal Studios. Wayne and Universal passed.

On May 25, 1969, Barry and Bob met with Hunter and his wife at their home in Van Nuys. "There was a guy in Florida who was going to give us the [rest of the] money to make the movie but he wanted to meet Jeffrey Hunter. He was a big fan of his," Barkwill said. So Hunter agreed to fly to Florida to meet the man. The following day, "I get a phone call that Jeff fell and they were taking him to the hospital. The next morning, the 27th, I get a call from my friend who said that he had died."

Jeffrey Hunter died at 9:30 that morning at Valley Presbyterian Hospital after undergoing brain surgery. He was forty-three years old. Barry and Bob went to his funeral, which turned out to be the end of their abortive movie careers.

"From that point everything seemed to fall apart," Barkwill said. "We disbanded the movie business."

Barry blamed the Hollywood culture. "The first thing I found out about Hollywood was that it's phonier than camouflage," he said in 1971. "I found out that Hollywood is based on the premise that everything is 100 percent go, five minutes before it bombs." Plus, he said, "there's an element in Hollywood, a pinkie, faggie element, and I turn 'em off right from the beginning."[24]

Bob Barkwill had another explanation for their lack of success. After eighteen months of trying to sell the movie, he said, "nothing happened. Nobody wanted to touch anything about Vietnam at that time. It was a sore subject."

Barkwill was correct. Until the late 1970s Hollywood did not exactly have an affinity for the Vietnam War. The American motion picture industry strongly supported World Wars I and II and came up with a handful of patriotic war movies during the Korean War. During the increasingly controversial Vietnam War, however, the studios avoiding tackling the conflict head on.

"Nobody wants to see a guy getting killed in the Vietnam War [in a movie] when guys are getting killed in the Vietnam War," a Universal Studios executive explained in September of 1967.[25]

There was one notable exception, however, John Wayne's *The Green Berets*. Filmed in the summer and fall of 1967 primarily at Fort Benning in Georgia—six months after Wayne had visited Fort Bragg and the Pentagon agreed to cooperate in making the film—the movie came out during the height of the Vietnam War in June of 1968.

Wayne directed. His son Michael produced. James Lee Barrett based his screenplay on Robin Moore's novel. The critics loathed it.

The Green Berets "is a film so unspeakable, so stupid, so rotten and false in every detail that it passes through being fun, through being funny, through being camp, through everything and becomes an invitation to grieve, not for our soldiers or for Vietnam (the film could not be more false or do a greater disservice to either of them), but for what has happened to the fantasy-making apparatus in this country," Renata Adler wrote in her scathing *New York Times* review. "It is vile and insane. On top of that, it is dull."[26]

Adler and other critics concentrated on the film's defiantly pro-war message and its giant lapses of Vietnam War verisimilitude. That included the fact that sixty-year-old John Wayne (who never served in the military) was two decades older than most Green Beret colonels—and about thirty pounds heavier than the chunkiest Special Forces officer serving in Vietnam.

"Authenticity," former Vietnam War correspondent Charles Mohr wrote, "is one of the earliest of several hundred casualties in the movie."[27] Not once, the British critic Gilbert Adair wrote, "does one get a sense of the lived experience of soldiers at war."[28] At times the movie seems to be "a Western, with the Viet Cong filling in for the Indians attacking an isolated outpost," the film critic (and Vietnam veteran) Brock Garland wrote. "Moreover at times, the VC attackers seem to be Japanese soldiers high on sake while making a last *banzai* charge in the name of the emperor."[29]

As for the movie's political message, Roger Ebert of the *Chicago Sun-Times* expressed the widespread critical view that the movie was little more than "propaganda . . . a heavy-handed, remarkably old-fashioned film." The movie imparted the message that in Vietnam, Ebert wrote, "we seem to be fighting a war for no particular purpose against a semi-autonomous enemy. . . . It appears that the war has been caused entirely by the enemy and that the enemy commits atrocities because he enjoys them. There seems to be no other issue. This is not only dishonest, but unfair."[30]

While the critics slammed *The Green Berets*, the film-going public made it one of the most popular movies of 1968. Made at a cost of some seven million dollars, the movie eventually grossed more than twenty-one million.

John Wayne unapologetically touted the film's pro-war message. "Because the critics don't like my politics, they were condemning the war, not the picture," he said in a *Playboy* magazine interview in 1971. "I don't mean the critics as a group. I mean the irrationally liberal ones. Renata Adler of the *New York Times* almost foamed at the mouth because I showed a few massacres on the screen. She went into convulsions. She and other critics wouldn't believe that the Viet Cong are treacherous—that the dirty sons of bitches are raping, torturing gorillas."[31]

Aside from meeting John Wayne at Fort Bragg in 1967, Barry Sadler had nothing to do with the movie based on the book with his picture on the paperback cover. As far as his song is concerned, the movie opens with "The Ballad," but not Barry's version. Instead, Wayne used a lavish choral arrangement produced by the composer and conductor Ken Darby.

"You'll notice that someone else is singing the song in the movie," Bill Parrish said. "That's because Barry's agent [Clancy Isaac] wanted too much money. Barry was pissed at him because he thought singing it would revive his career."[32]

Barry Sadler's career certainly did need reviving.

CHAPTER 12

A NICE GUY

"He was not your typical Ward Cleaver."

—THOR SADLER, 1989

In 1969 Barry and Lavona were living comfortably in their house with their two young boys and three dogs—including his German shepherd Odin—along with Lavona's two pet raccoons.

Lavona said that Barry doted on his two young sons, reading poetry and kids' books to them and spinning yarns that he made up. But Barry also practiced old-school strict discipline. When the boys misbehaved, he'd make them stand at attention. And he did not spare the rod.

"His favorite line was 'I'll whip you till your butts bleed,'" Thor Sadler said in 1989. "We always cried louder than it hurt. It was a con we learned." His father, Thor said, "was not your typical Ward Cleaver. . . . That didn't mean that he didn't love us."[1]

That summer Barry had all but given up on showbiz. He had spent the royalty money from "The Ballad" single and the album. His bar was not exactly thriving. It would, in fact, soon go bankrupt. "I was always a better consumer than an owner," he later said.[2]

His attempt to make it in Hollywood had failed. RCA had dropped him. He spent a good deal of time and energy searching for some type of money-making opportunity.

There was an occasional low-rent personal appearance. On Sunday night, February 9, for example, Barry helped judge an amateur dance contest at the Classic Cat nightclub in Hollywood. He got the job through the other "celebrity" judge that evening, the actor Rudy Acosta, who had a recurring role in *The High Chaparral*.

Early in March Barry showed up to sign autographs at a two-day sales event at Edwards Trailer Sales, a mobile home dealer in Marion, Illinois. Then came a five-night singing gig at Pete's Supper Club in Evansville, Indiana, followed by another personal appearance, this time at the grand opening of Big J's Shopping Center in Vincennes, Indiana, on March 15.

It was a far, far cry from *The Ed Sullivan Show*.

Barry's last TV appearance—another small part in a *Death Valley Days* episode called "The Oldest Law," which he had filmed a year earlier—came when that showed aired on March 29.

Barry Sadler turned twenty-nine on November 1, 1969. Two weeks later, on November 15, what is believed to be the largest antiwar protest in U.S. history took place in Washington, D.C. A crowd estimated to be at least 250,000—mostly Baby Boomers—gathered at the Washington Monument grounds that bitterly cold November day in a peaceful rally sponsored by the Vietnam Moratorium Committee. They heard anti–Vietnam War speeches from Senators Eugene McCarthy and George McGovern and listened to folksingers Peter, Paul and Mary, Arlo Guthrie, and Pete Seeger.

On November 19, 1969, the Special Warfare Memorial Statue—which Barry had supported with a $5,000 donation—was dedicated at the U.S. Army Special Operations Command Memorial Plaza at Fort Bragg. That same day Apollo 12 astronauts Pete Conrad and Alan Bean landed on the moon, becoming the second group of Americans to do so, following Neil Armstrong and Buzz Aldrin's historic Apollo 11 moonlanding in July.

As 1969 came to a close, the American war in Vietnam raged on, although casualties had begun to decline. For the week ending on October 11, for example, 82 American troops were killed and 1,315 wounded—the lowest weekly total since August of 1967. At the end of 1969, the number of troops in Vietnam was down to around 475,200. That year 11,780 Americans perished in Vietnam, about 5,000 fewer than the year before.[3]

In 1970 "The Ballad of the Green Berets" had long since ceased being a national sensation. But the song remained popular at Fort Bragg—and virtually everywhere else U.S. Army Special Forces men trained and plied their trade. That included the Special Forces Training Center at Camp Mackall adjacent to Fort Bragg, where instructors had their trainees stand up, come to attention, and belt out the first verse of "The Ballad" before the start of classes every morning.

The song also was part of a ceremony at Mackall after the men completed the training. "We had an informal, small formation," said Phil Milio, who volunteered for Special Forces after returning from a tour of duty in Vietnam early in the spring of 1970. "Each guy was called up individually and given our green beret. We shook hands and afterward we all sang the song. I thought it was a little bit over the top, but we were all really proud that we could wear the beret."[4]

In one of the handful of appearances Barry made in 1970, he flew to Fayetteville in November to do a few radio and TV interviews and visit the Fayetteville VA Medical Center hospital and a local detention center for teenagers. Bruce Love, then an active-duty army warrant officer, happened to be at Bragg visiting a friend who worked in the Public Information Office. Love wound up hanging out with Barry for most of the day he was in town.

"He was a nice guy," Love said in 2015. "He struck me as very down to earth, and he wasn't into himself. Even though I was in civilian clothes, once I was introduced, it was always 'Yes, sir' and 'No, sir.'"

Barry "looked like he didn't like the spotlight," Love said. He "got some good-gestured ribbing" from some Green Berets at Bragg. 'Oh, here comes one of 'America's best.'" But Barry "didn't mind the ribbing," Love said. "He wouldn't even answer back. He just ignored them."

Barry dutifully did the radio and TV interviews, answering questions mainly about Green Beret training, and putting in good words for the Fort Bragg–based 82nd Airborne and the Special Forces. He avoided questions about the war. When asked where he served in Vietnam, Barry said, "It's sufficient to say I served. I'm not a hero. The guys who didn't come back were. I lost too many friends over there so I would prefer not to have the light shine on my time."

At the VA hospital someone came up with a guitar and Barry played and sang "The Ballad" for a group of patients in the dining room. Then he went room to room, chatting with men—nearly all of them recuperating from Vietnam War wounds—at their bedsides.

"He would say, 'I'm proud of you, Welcome Home,'" Love said, "'I'm glad you made it. Don't ever let anybody put you down for a Purple Heart. You did your job.'"

At the youth detention center, Love said, Barry "spoke very frankly and very directly, and said, 'I was just like you. I was leaning toward the wrong path and the military got a hold of me and it really straightened me out and I got focused and you need to do that.'"

He then answered questions and told the teenagers: "The future is yours to choose what you would like it to be. You can continue down this road. They're building new prisons every day, but the army is taking people every day. It's your choice where you want to spend your life.

"If the military's not for you, then still make a good career out of something. Don't wait for it to be given to you. You have to work for everything. There are rewards to those who do that."[5]

Sometime during the year of 1970, Barry stood in front of a movie camera in his wood-paneled den in his house in Tucson. Wearing what looked like a blue jumpsuit, a clunky microphone draped around his neck and his portrait and two gold records hanging on the wall behind him, Barry recited the words of his small part in *No Substitute for Victory*, a film billed as a "Vietnam War Docu-Drama." Directed by Robert F. Slatzer—a screenwriter, B movie director and producer who claimed he secretly married Marilyn Monroe—the movie starred John Wayne.

The Duke, sitting in what looked like his office, offered his thoughts on the Vietnam War—what he called "facts of history," and introduced a group of Vietnam War hawks, including the journalist Lowell Thomas, retired army generals Mark Clark and Paul Harkins, retired navy admiral

U. S. Grant Sharp, Martha Raye, former Green Beret sergeant Peter Stark (who lost both legs in Vietnam), and Barry Sadler. Wayne and company sounded off about a worldwide "communist conspiracy" and the need to stop "communist aggression" in Vietnam and elsewhere. They castigated weak-willed American politicians, the American antiwar movement, and the American news media for aiding and abetting the enemy by working against the American war effort in Vietnam.

John Wayne and the other commentators discuss "our no win policy and restrictions on our fighting men, and our never ending wars for communism's conquest of the U.S.A.," one newspaper ad for the movie said.[6]

"It's time we spoke out about Vietnam," Wayne said in his opening remarks, "and the most obvious, yet the most ignored, threat ever faced by free people in the history of the world." He went on to condemn American "street demonstrators," American politicians, and "civilians" who called for an American withdrawal, saying, "We can't stop the war by giving up and we sure can't settle anything by trying to bargain with a winning enemy at the peace table."

Barry provided the viewpoint of a Green Beret medic. "We have a big job in Vietnam," Barry said, staring into the camera with a look of steely determination on his face—and with "The Ballad" playing in the background. He said that villagers all over South Vietnam "are constantly threatened by the Viet Cong and their North Vietnamese allies." South Vietnamese men are "often recruited into [the enemy's] armed forces, sometimes through propaganda, promises, [and] lies. When that fails, they don't hesitate to use force, terrorism, even butchering entire villages as an example to those who won't listen to their 'friendly' persuasion."

When the Viet Cong use force, Barry said, "they use these." He then held up what looked like a 1950s vintage M-1 rifle—"modern weapons, made in communist China and the Soviet Union, their communist allies."

Barry went on to explain what he did in Vietnam as the film showed grainy clips of Green Beret medics ministering to Vietnamese people. He then described conditions in Saigon, "a big city with a half million people in it and with worse traffic than you'll find in New York." He talked about life in the Mekong Delta region of South Vietnam, "twenty-eight-thousand square miles of the richest rice land in the world." That led into a description of the Strategic Hamlet Program in which the Americans and South Vietnamese uprooted entire villages and moved them into heavily fortified hamlets—a program that was all but universally regarded as a failure.

That program "so infuriated the communists," Barry said in clipped, measured tones, "that they stepped up their attacks on these unarmed, innocent people. Whole villages were burned to the ground. Farmers were mortared and machine-gunned in their rice paddies while trying to gather their crops. The attacks became more and more vicious and fanatical."

Barry seemed incredulous that what he called Viet Cong "terror tactics" didn't "inflame the Free World against the communists." And he was even more indignant that, "unbelievably," as he put it, "criticisms of our operations began to mount." That criticism—which was extremely rare when Barry was in Vietnam—was "frustrating for a soldier," Barry said, "halfway around the world fighting a war. It seemed like the enemy was the good guy in the white hats."

It was "as if the American public was only getting the information the reds wanted them to. In fact, I'd say the press has been more helpful to the enemy than a fresh division."

It's doubtful that Barry wrote the words he spoke in the film. However, there's also little doubt that Barry fully believed what he said.

No Substitute for Victory played for eight months, primarily in the South, Midwest, and West, beginning in early February of 1971. But it rarely was shown in movie theaters. The screenings took place in high school, junior high, and elementary school auditoriums; in social halls and hotel ballrooms; and at conservative college auditoriums in small cities and towns. Places such as Fort Walton Beach, Florida; Lubbock, Texas; Tipton, Indiana; Ukiah, California; Fond Du Lac, Wisconsin; Ogden, Utah; Caldwell, Idaho; Rockford, Illinois; and Prescott, Arizona.

Barry introduced the film at a meeting of the local Jewish War Veterans post in Tucson on April 4. He showed up at screenings at the Phoenix College auditorium on May 21 and 22.

Nearly all the screenings were sponsored by local TRAIN (To Restore American Independence Now) committees—ad hoc groups set up by the John Birch Society, a far-right-wing group. TRAIN, one newspaper reported, was a John Birch Society "nationwide network of local committees formed by citizens who believe traditional American principles should be reasserted in the U.S."[7]

In January of 1971, just before *No Substitute for Victory* began playing around the country, Tucson photographer David Lee Guss drove out to Barry's house for a photo shoot for an article that Robert Powers was writing. Guss made several return visits during the next three months. The two men did not exactly hit it off.

"Barry was edgy (on the verge of imploding), rude and abrasive to me," Guss said in 2015. "But, chameleonlike, he was far different with his family or with Bob Powers."

I "wore a beard then," Guss said, "which really set [Barry] off. When I was photographing him alone he muttered repeated, sarcastic references to bearded hippies." When the subject of Andy Warhol—who was making a gay western in Tucson at the time—came up, it "ignited a profanity-laden diatribe against what he called 'Hollywood fags.'"

Barry, Guss said, "seemed happiest when [he was] with his family, expounding on his weapons collection and firing his machine guns in the desert. He especially favored a Chinese-made one and one built in Prague. He said little, but did imply more than once that he ran guns in and out of Mexico, some sixty miles south of Tucson."

As Barry showed David Guss his Nazi memorabilia one day, the photographer asked him if a uniform with a swastika armband he had in a closet fit him. "He said it did," Guss said. "Just when he was on the verge of posing in it for me, Lavona entered the room, overheard the conversation, and quickly scotched any such foolish nonsense."[8]

By the end of 1971, Barry had run through every cent of "The Ballad" royalties. "I didn't know what to do with all that money," Barry told Robert

Powers. "There were a lot of people trying to help me out; the Internal Revenue [Service], for one."[9]

What do you do, Barry asked rhetorically, "with a quarter of a million dollars and more coming in each month? I didn't know what to do. I hired two lawyers, one just to keep track of what the other was doing. Then I hired an accountant and a few other business types. I lost the first million income from not knowing who I could trust and what to do. By the time I learned, it was too late."[10]

Barry said he didn't know the record business or how to manage money. "I never made more than $6,000 a year in my life," he said. "Between one thing or another, by the time the popularity of the song had died down, I didn't have much left. I went into the bar business and that went broke. I bought a condominium in the Bahamas and that's not too good. I spent a lot of money on my weapons collection—at least that's still worth something."

Barry said he was "trying to get together a collection of songs. And I'm looking for an album. I'm not interested in touring, but I like writing songs. I've painted a little, mostly war subjects, and I've done some welding and metal sculpturing. I like it. I get bored. I don't hunt and couldn't care less about golf." Barry also said he was working on a novel and selling insurance part-time.

He told a Tucson newspaper reporter in the summer of 1972 that he had started a battery-selling business called Arizona Basic Corporation of America. "We're going to do with batteries what Midas did with mufflers," Barry said. The company would be selling car, boat, and other batteries, Barry said. "For $2,500, you can make between $25,000 and $30,000 a year. It's nothing exciting, just common merchandising."[11]

The battery business never materialized. And nothing came of Barry painting, welding, metal sculpting, or insurance selling. The novel writing did pan out—but not until 1979.

Barry played a few gigs around Tucson before he and Lavona moved to Nashville in March of 1973. He sang at a steak fry put on by the Arizona Airborne Division at the Camelback Inn in Scottsdale on May 29, 1971. He appeared at the first annual Dance for Muscular Dystrophy sponsored by the Pima Jaycees at a hotel in Tucson on September 2, 1972.

Also on the bill that evening: Los Chanquitos Feos, a local young people's Mariachi group, and the Loren Nichel Orchestra.

Bob Barkwill had picked up two new clients in the early 1970s. One was Montie Montana, a cowboy actor, stuntman, trick rider, and roper, best known for roping President Eisenhower on the reviewing stand during the 1953 presidential inaugural parade in Washington. The other was Archie Campbell, the comedian, writer, and country music singer, one of the stars of the long-running, country-flavored TV variety show *Hee Haw*.[12]

That show was taped in a studio at WLAC-TV in downtown Nashville, the main reason Bob Barkwill moved there in 1972. He and Barry remained close friends, and Barry visited him in Nashville "to see what it was like," Barkwill said.[13] Early in 1973 Lavona and Barry left Tucson to join Barkwill in Music City USA.

"I decided on the move," Lavona said. "That was my choice, to go to Nashville. I got tired of the desert weather."[14]

Barkwill found a real estate woman in Nashville, and she found the Sadlers a small house in Hendersonville in the suburbs northeast of town. They made the move in February of 1973. Part of the reason had to do with the fact that Lavona had an inkling that Barry could re-kindle his musical career in the nation's home of country music.

"I didn't mention this [to Barry], but I thought he could get in with the music people" in Nashville, Lavona said, "and maybe he could do something—not play, but sing."

The singing thing did not work out. But a few years after the Sadlers moved to Nashville, Barry began an unlikely second act—as a very successful pulp fiction author.

CHAPTER 13
WHERE THE MONEY IS

"I'd like to play a medley of my hit."

—BARRY SADLER, 1970

Barry had been toying with the idea of writing fiction since he'd helped put together the screenplay for his Vietnam War movie that never went anywhere in Hollywood. Before he left Tucson, Barry sought out the writer Robert Powers for guidance.

His first idea was a novel based on Longinus, the legendary Roman soldier who ran his lance into Jesus on the cross. "I helped him out with some of that stuff," Powers said. "He knew I was writing and he came over to my place with the idea for a novel about a mercenary, but it wasn't fully developed. I might have been the one who told him to make it a series because that's where the money is."

About a week after Powers planted that seed, he said, "Barry said, 'Boy, that was a great idea,' and he stuffed a fifty-dollar bill in my shirt. I said, 'C'mon, man,' but back in 1972 fifty bucks was pretty good money." Later on, Powers said, "I helped him with the manuscript, but it never got anywhere."[1]

Barry and Bob Powers also worked together to try to turn the unsold Vietnam War screenplay *Sergeant Sands* into a novel in the spring of 1972. "As far as I know, he had played around with the idea for some time—the basics of it anyway, but it was hardly fleshed out in any way," Powers said. "So, that spring I began dictating a novel about a sergeant and his Vietnamese captor.

"The novel was finished in the summer and I hired a transcriber who took the [tapes] and did the transcription. Sadler and I executed a contract in case he ever did anything with it. Then he went to Nashville and I lost track of him in 1973."

The "basic idea" for the book, Powers said, was Barry's, "as was anything specific about general military life in Vietnam circa 1964–1969. The character development and the tensions and the yin-yang between the main character and the captor were pretty much all mine, as was the day-to-day writing. Barry never sat down at the typewriter or helped dictate. It was somewhat of a joint venture, but not a collaboration."[2]

After moving to Nashville, Barry continued tinkering with the Vietnam War novel, as well as with a series of action adventure stories in which the Roman soldier based on Longinus reappears in different wars, plus several other book ideas. He also tried to jump-start his musical career.

"When Barry came to Nashville, I got him some jobs," Bob Barkwill said. "He did some one-night stands up in Ohio, places like that. They all wanted him to sing that song. Then he sang other songs and kind of told some jokes."

One of Barry's standbys: "Hello. I'd like to play a medley of my hit."

For his first gigs Barry didn't have a band or use backup musicians. He'd come on stage alone with just his guitar. "He knew a lot of songs," Barkwill said, "and he was a good guitar player."[3]

On January 27, 1973, about a month before Barry and Lavona moved to Nashville, American and South and North Vietnamese negotiators signed the Paris Peace Accords after nearly five years of talks. The main provisions included the United States agreeing to withdraw its combat troops from South Vietnam and the North Vietnamese agreeing to release the 591 American prisoners of war they held. On February 12 the first American POWs—some of whom had been held captive since 1964—flew home to heroes' welcomes.

The impending prisoner release inspired Barry to write and record a song called "This Is the Last Song of War." He and Bob Barkwill produced it on a label they called Vietnam Veteran Records. They recorded the song at the Knoxville studios of Luke Brandon, an old friend of Bob's client Archie Campbell. "It was a lot cheaper to do it there," Barkwill said. "We cut it in a couple of hours."

He and Barry "wanted to have it pressed and out there when these guys were coming home," Barkwill said. But the pressing took longer than expected and the song didn't hit the streets until three days after the POWs came home. Barry and Bob nevertheless called a bunch of radio stations to hype it.

"We got quite a bit of airplay around the country," Barkwill said. But the unmemorable record—with "O, God, I Can Make It" as its B side—sold very few copies.

On May 27, 1973, a few months after he arrived in Nashville, Barry made his first appearance on a local TV show, *Mornings With Siegel*, the irreverent talk show host Stanley Siegel's one-hour gabfest, which aired at 7:00 a.m. The country music singers/comedians the Hager Twins were Siegel's other guests that morning.

That gig didn't pay, but Barry's "obsession," after he moved to Nashville, said Bill Parrish—who met him in a bar within a year after Barry moved there—"was to make money again. He had come to Nashville to try to make it in the music business. He couldn't get out of the starting blocks with that so that's when he decided to write books."[4]

Vietnam Veteran Records went nowhere. Bob Barkwill moved to California in 1974 and his business relationship with Barry all but dissolved, although they remained friends. Barry kept at the writing, but took low-rent singing gigs to pay the bills. Lavona went to work selling cars at E. B. Smith Chevrolet in downtown Nashville, the only woman on the sales force.

Barry sang "The Ballad" at a concert held in conjunction with a pro-celebrity golf tournament in Huntsville, Alabama, in September of 1973. That same month he was part of a "Sounds of Nashville" troupe that included Archie Campbell that did two shows at the Muncie Field House in Indiana. Barry showed up with a band early in November of

1974 at Country and Western night at the CPO Club at the Newport, Rhode Island, Naval Station. Barry and company performed, along with what was billed as a group of "Nashville's top performers." Admission for the show: $1.50.[5]

Barry appeared with country musicians Johnny Dollar and Jay Lee Webb at a country music festival put on by the Danville, Virginia, American Legion Post 325 on November 23, 1974, at the Old City Armory. Admission: five dollars in advance; six dollars at the door. Getting a jump on the nation's 1976 bicentennial, Barry formed Barry Sadler and His Spirit of '76 Country Music Show early in 1975. Among their few gigs: a benefit concert held March 3, 1975, at tiny Prophetstown High School in northwestern Illinois.

On May 17, a little more than two weeks after the Vietnamese communists took over South Vietnam, Barry did a one-night stand at the Flying V Ballroom ("The Midwest's ONLY Floating Dance Floor!") just outside the village of Utica, Nebraska.[6] Then came a benefit country music concert for the Madison, Ohio, Township Fire Fighters and Rescue Squad at Madison High School on June 14. Also on the bill: Grand Ole Opry performers Lonzo and Oscar (the duo best known for their comic song "I'm My Own Grandpa"), Leona Williams, and Elmer Fudpucker. Barry was billed as "Former Staff Sgt. and American War Hero."[7]

Back in Nashville Barry wrote a song called "Bless Them All" with longtime pop music producer, arranger, and conductor Chuck Sagle, who had worked with Carole King, Neil Sedaka, Tony Orlando, and Bobby Darin, among others. Sagle co-produced the single, backed with "For the Truth and the Right," which he also co-wrote with Barry. The former was a half-spoken eulogy for the Vietnam War and an ultraconservative rebuke to the "politicians" who ran the war to satisfy "their greed."

In the song Barry describes walking through Arlington National Cemetery, where he hears the voices of the 58,000 Americans who died in Vietnam, "calling through their tears and their pain, 'God forgive you, America, you let us die in vain.'" Barry then speaks the words: "as long as I stand as a man, no enemy foot shall tread upon this place, the campground of the dead." In between he sings the chorus: "Bless them all, bless them all, dear God, bless them all."

The song ends with another voice saying: "Left behind in Vietnam on April 28th, 1975, were our last two Marines killed while defending the Tan Son Nhut Airport near Saigon: Cpl. Charles McMahon Jr., Lance Cpl. Darwin Judge. Whether or not you can ever be brought back to Arlington, we want you to know you will not be forgotten."[8]

The song ends with Barry singing with great emotion: "Bless them all, bless them all, Oh, my God, bless them all. Bless them all."

"For the Truth and the Right" barely registered with the American music-loving public. Undaunted, Barry wrote and produced a patriotic album called "Of Thee I Sing" to try to take advantage of the nation's celebration of its 200th anniversary in 1976. The record—which featured country music singers/songwriters Merle Kilgore and Ed Bruce—got little attention and sold anemically. On a positive note, President Gerald Ford presented a copy of the album—along with several other gifts—to Queen Elizabeth and Prince Charles on the last day of their royal visit to Washington, D.C., on July 10 of the Bicentennial Year of American independence from England.

On August 21, 1976—eight days after the birth of his daughter, Brooke—Barry was grand marshal of a bicentennial parade in the small town of Martinsburg, West Virginia. That night he played from 10:00 p.m. to 2:00 a.m. at the Top Brass Club on Route 11 in Bunker Hill, West Virginia. Also on the bill: The String Dusters.[9] He also appeared at a July 1, 1977, "Pre-4th of July Party" with Webb Pierce and his band at downtown Nashville's short-lived Rhinestone Cowboy Club.

As those small-time and small-town gigs indicated, Barry's second try at a musical career went nowhere. With money short Lavona left E. B. Smith Chevrolet to take a job managing a convenience store to help pay the bills. She wanted Barry to give up music and start writing books.

"I said, 'Well, you know, Barry, you read a lot.' And that's when he started writing books," Lavona said.[10]

Barry made that decision while spending a good deal of his time hanging out in Nashville bars favored by country music singers, studio musicians,

Artist and Repertoire (AR) and PR men, and other industry types. The hangouts included the Commodore Lounge at the Vanderbilt Holiday Inn, the Country Corner Bar downtown, and the Natchez Trace on Old Hickory Boulevard in suburban Bellevue. Barry's favorite, though, was the Sound Track Lounge at the Best Western Hall of Fame Motor Inn near Music Row in downtown Nashville. Barry and his drinking buddies called it the "Hall of Shame" or "the Shame."

"A lot of people in the music business hung out there," Parrish said. "It was headquarters for Barry. He had breakfast of coffee in the morning. Then the bar opened at eleven. So he would hang out there until he headed home at five, six o'clock in the afternoon."[11]

As Parrish indicated, Barry was putting away more than his share of booze. "He drank. We all drank," said John Buchan, a writer who met Barry at the Hall of Fame in the late 1970s. "It was common in the afternoons and in the evenings to go to some of those places. We'd sit around and talk about the business."[12] Buchan said he "never saw Barry out of control because of his drinking. He was a big, barrel-chested guy and he could drink a lot, but I never saw him out of control, ever."

"Barry was a friend and I used to hang out with him at the Hall of Fame saloon," said Jay Diamond, a former country music disc jockey, road manager, and agent. "He usually hung out in the bar. I didn't drink; Barry did, oftentimes too much."[13]

Among the other country music folks Barry met and befriended at the Hall of Fame was Earl Owens, who ran a large public relations firm and managed some big-name country musicians, including Jerry Lee Lewis. Owens was a pal of Lafayette "Fate" Thomas, the sheriff of Davidson County, which includes the city of Nashville. Thomas, who served in that politically powerful position from 1970 to 1990, particularly enjoyed cozying up to the country music crowd.[14] So much so that he regularly deputized people in the business. The list of Sheriff Fate Thomas's card-carrying honorary deputies included Earl Owens, Johnny Cash, Porter Wagoner, Roger Miller, Hank Williams Jr., Roy Acuff—and Barry Sadler.

"I was with the Davidson County Sheriff's Department," Owens said, "and I got [Barry] a job down there, too." On December 7, 1976, Barry was officially made a deputy sheriff in Davidson County with the honorary rank of lieutenant "to execute any and all processes that may come into his hands and to maintain the peace and dignity of the State, and arrest any and all persons violating the Criminal laws of the State of Tennessee," as his ID card noted.[15] The ID card listed his height as 5'9", his weight as 190 pounds, his eyes as blue, his hair as brown, and his "build" as "medium." He received $700 a year in compensation.

Even though it was an "honorary" job, Barry would sometimes put on a deputy sheriff's uniform and go out in patrol cars. And he was armed, as the job included a permit to carry weapons. "He took care of prisoners, taking them places, arresting folks—if there were warrants, he went out and took care of those," Owens said.

"He also was working with canines," Bill Parrish said. "And I know he worked with a pretty skilled boxer there on footwork and so forth. Barry was pretty good at whatever he did."

"Barry said he taught sheriff's deputies self-defense and other stuff," Jim Sledge, a former Nashville Police homicide detective, said in 2015. "I don't recall if he really did or not. It would have been kind of unique that they would need that because in Davidson County the Sheriff's Department does not have arrest powers. They're not the police. They're not law enforcement. All the Sherriff's Department in Davidson County has is custodial power and serving civil process. You can't be pulled over by a sheriff's deputy."[16]

On November 1, 1977, Barry's thirty-seventh birthday, a small Nashville book publisher, Aurora Publishers, brought out Barry's first novel, *The Moi*—a $4.95 hardcover, book-length version of his *Sergeant Sands* screenplay. Barry dedicated the book to his sons, Thor and Baron, and his daughter, Brooke.

The Moi sunk into obscurity soon after it came out. As the journalist John Ed Bradley put it in a long profile of Barry in *GQ* magazine, the book "didn't sell enough copies to fill a shoebox."[17]

The book is "no *Apocalypse Now*, but it's a good story," a spokesman for Aurora told a newspaper report.[18] *The Moi* certainly is no *Apocalypse*

Now, Francis Coppola's phantasmagoric Vietnam War film that wouldn't hit the theaters until 1979.[19] But does *The Moi* tell "a good story"? Only if your idea of a good story is an intimately described account of unrelenting physical and emotional torture gleefully perpetrated upon a stalwart Vietnam War Green Beret sergeant by a sadistic, American-hating North Vietnamese army captain.

The book is filled with over-the-top action, much of it extremely violent. An enemy soldier's throat crumples "in a lump of ruptured cartilage and pulp" as an American strangles him. Two GIs are "stabbed repeatedly by the enraged" enemy after they try to surrender. The hero, Sgt. Mike Reider, is beaten with fists and sticks, has his Achilles heel severed, is stripped naked, harnessed in a yoke, led on a leash with a choke collar around his neck, muzzled, and made to drink and eat on his hands and knees out of bowls.

All this, plus comic book–worthy dialogue. "I am going to teach you to respect your superiors—you and all your fat, soft American brethren," North Vietnamese army captain Lim "hisses" to Reider. You "will crawl, and then bark, sit up, do tricks and eat like a dog and follow me around on a rope, and I will show this entire village that the Americans are nothing but dogs for a North Vietnamese officer."

You "imperialists are through, Reider," Lim goes on to say. "Your empire is crumbling. The day soon comes when America will sink into its own slime and strangle. Asia's day is dawning. And we will rise in our hundreds of millions and repay all you round-eyed dogs for your centuries of exploitation. . . . I hate you Anglo-Saxons! I despise the white skin of your bodies that will soon disappear from our land."

After that harangue, Sandler writes, Lim's "lips curled into a virulent sneer." Later Lim "giggled and writhed in devilish ecstasy and reveled" as he watched GIs being mowed down by his men.

The only book review of *The Moi* appeared in Nashville's morning newspaper, *The Tennessean*, ten months after it came out. Reviewer Walter Carter liked the book, calling the writing "clean and straightforward." Barry, Carter said somewhat enigmatically, "doesn't attempt any literary feats that he can't accomplish." If Sadler hadn't included the characters' backstories "he would no doubt be criticized for shallow character development and amateurish writing [see above]—terms which do not apply in either case." Carter said he found "a fascinating quality" to the story, even though when he finished, he had "the feeling of being bled dry."[20]

The Tennessean review notwithstanding, it's fair to say that Barry's first foray into fiction was an artistic and financial flop. But that did not deter him. Within eighteen months he would start churning out a chain of more than two dozen action- and violence-filled mass market paperback thrillers that would sell hundreds of thousands of copies.

Before that, however, Barry produced another clunker, a slender how-to book with an unwieldy title: *Everything You Want to Know About the Record Industry in Nashville, Tennessee, Country Music Capital of the World.* Barry had help with that one from Bill Rigsby, a Nashville piano player, singer, and songwriter known professionally as Billy Arr.

The two men met at one of the Nashville watering holes Barry frequented, and they soon became close friends. As he tended to do with other writers he befriended, Barry asked Billy Arr to collaborate on a book. Billy said yes. The two men brainstormed. They came up with the idea of a country music biz instruction manual using Barry's name and Billy's knowledge of the industry. They sold it to Aurora Publishers.

The 128-page, large-format book came out in the summer of 1978, retailing for $4.95. It has twenty-seven "chapters," some as few as one page, giving pointers on such nuts-and-bolts information as finding an agent, copyrighting songs, and putting a band together. It's filled with photos and lots of white space.

Billy Arr told John Ed Bradley that he and Barry "locked themselves into a room one weekend" and wrote the book in "all of eighteen hours," with, Bradley said, the "warm, brown odor of Jack Daniels on every page." Barry and Billy received a $4,800 advance, Bradley wrote, "enough for two solid months of partying."[21]

In the book's introduction Barry writes that he had "several reasons" for writing it. "The most important of these reasons is that I did it for the money"—a joke, but not far from the truth. Another reason: "I think I can fill a gap that exists in books about and concerning music."[22]

Everything You Want received a sort-of favorable review in the Nashville *Banner*. "Sadler's writing style is generally laid back and occasionally tongue-in-cheek, as he advises good ole boys (to the exclusion of good ole gals) to keep their day jobs and to lay off the booze," reviewer Stacy Harris wrote. She went on to call the book's pictorial layout "sloppy" and pointed out that Barry and Bill Arr copied a listing of industry contacts from a 1977 book without crediting the source.

Still, she called the book "excellent" and commended Barry for including his address and phone number for readers to call for more information.[23]

Walter Carter (who found *The Moi* "fascinating") wrote a mixed review in *The Tennessean*. He compared the book to "The Ballad," saying both were "simple and straightforward almost to the point of embarrassment." He called the book's pictures "useless," but Barry's advice "useful." Barry, he said, "does not beat around the bush."[24]

CHAPTER 14
THE ONLY HERO OF THE VIETNAM WAR

"I'm no Hemingway, but I think I can write an entertaining book."
—BARRY SADLER, 1978

Early in February of 1978, Barry gave an interview on the occasion of the publication of *The Moi*. He seemed to be in a feisty mood. Or he may have been playing with *Washington Post* Style Section reporter Stephanie Mansfield, telling her what he thought she wanted to hear—something Barry was wont to do. Nevertheless, he came out swinging.

There was egotistical bombast: "I'm the only hero of the Vietnam War," he said. "Name me two Medal of Honor winners. You can't. But everybody remembers me."

There was bluntness: "I'm a hustler. I do whatever I can to make a buck."

There was truth stretching: He was "producing music and writing songs" and had completed an album, Barry said. And planning a nationwide book tour. And contemplating going to South Africa to train mercenaries. And thinking about going back to Vietnam to fight the communists, something he "wouldn't mind" doing.

Mansfield asked about the Vietnam War and a recent wave of films dealing with it, including *Coming Home*, *The Deer Hunter*, *The Boys in Company C*, and *Go Tell the Spartans*. Barry blurted out: "I think it's a little bit belated, and personally, I feel it's nauseating. I lost of lot of friends over there. I'm still bitter."

He then went off on draft dodgers, gay people, African Americans, the women's movement, and illegal drugs. Antiwar protesting "was something for those kids to do," he said. "Everyone wants to be part of something. I have respect for the people who stayed in the country, but those that left showed a real lack of guts. A real cop-out."

Mansfield would not print what Barry had to say about gays and blacks, writing only that his comments "would make [the bigoted TV character] Archie Bunker blush." As for the proposed Equal Rights Amendment, Barry offered what in 2017 would widely be regarded as a sexist rant: "I don't know why you women want equality when you've been above us for so long. I happen to like opening doors for ladies. Let's talk about equality when you get into a foxhole with me, baby, carrying a fixed bayonet."

The interview ended with a lament about American heroes. "My kid watches that bionic man on television," Barry said. "Where are the Audie Murphys, the Cisco Kids, the Lash Larues?"[1]

Barry told an Associated Press reporter in March that he was through with recording and would be concentrating on writing. "I've turned down a couple of music contracts because they wanted to jump right back in the same old bag," Barry said. "I'll always dabble in music, but what I really want to do is write novels. I'm no Hemingway, but I think I can write an entertaining book."[2]

As for his previous recordings, Barry self-deprecatingly (if accurately) said that "they got worse. I listen to them now and want to cringe. I didn't know it at the time, but they were garbage." Barry didn't rule out the occasional singing gig, though, saying that he still enjoyed "doing it because it was so good to me. But it's difficult to go through life as a funny-looking hat."

When it came to talking about the Vietnam War, Barry went into ultraconservative mode, railing against weak-willed politicians, the news media, and the antiwar movement. "Most people," he said, "realize what we did was sell out. Peace with honor was garbage. It was no surprise when North Vietnam took over. I still stay a little bit hot about it. After all, out of 80 in my Special Forces class less than a dozen are still alive. And how do you tell families of 50,000 men [killed in Vietnam] that it's not important?

"I believe there were valid reasons for American involvement. We'd have done a service if allowed to do the job. We were not outfought, but were defeated morale-wise and press-wise much like the French were."

Later that year, in late November, Barry told a Nashville reporter about his latest project, writing a war memoir. If he did write a memoir—and it's very doubtful he did—the book never saw the light of day.

Barry also said he was working on an album of "country-pop songs of love, whiskey and women." If he was, it never was released.

The Moi, the article reported, was being "considered for a major motion picture." It may have been, but no picture—major or minor—came close to happening.[3]

Barry had begun working—with a handshake agreement—with Rob Robison, a Nashville country music talent agent, in 1977. The two men met—where else?—at the Hall of Fame lounge. "A lot of us would have breakfast or coffee in there in the mornings, a bunch of songwriters and others in the music business," Robison said, "and Barry was there and we got acquainted having coffee with everybody else. For some reason Barry and I jelled."[4]

One day in 1977 Barry asked Robison to read what he described as a draft of a novel. It dealt with the adventures of Casca Rufio Longinus, a Roman soldier condemned to live as an "eternal mercenary" because of his role in Jesus's crucifixion.

"Barry said, 'I've written something and I'd like you to give me an honest opinion,'" Robison said. "It was *Casca, The Mercenary*, a rough draft. I read it and I called him the next day."

Robison, a former World War II navy submariner, was leaving Nashville for a three-week tour in Europe with his client Carl Mann, the rockabilly singer best known for his 1959 hit version of "Mona Lisa." Robison told Barry, "Carl and I will be gone for three weeks, and if you haven't sold that book, I'll start a literary agency and sell it." Robison later recalled that at that time he "didn't even know how to spell 'agency.'"

When Robison returned to Nashville, Barry hadn't sold the book. "So we sat down and talked and decided I'd sell it," Robison said. "And I did."

Sadler and Robison—known to family and friends as Robbie—proved to be a very good team. In the next decade, working closely together, Barry produced and Robbie sold twenty-nine mass market paperback pulp fiction thrillers, twenty-two in the *Casca* series. Nearly all sold well, to the tune of hundreds of thousands of copies.

"I don't think Barry and I were ever off the same page because we both had the same thing in mind, and that was making some money," Robbie said. "I wanted hit books, period, because I knew with hit books I'd make money—and learn how to be an agent maybe."

Robison sold the first *Casca* books by cold-calling book editors in New York City. "I contacted some people, [including] a guy called Mike Seidman, the editor [at Grosset & Dunlap], and also Tom Doherty, who [today] owns Tor Books," Robbie said. "And I sold it."

Barry wanted a one-book deal. Robbie saw it as a series, and negotiated a four-book contract with Doherty. "And that," he said, "was the start of *Casca*."

That 1978 contract with Grosset & Dunlap's mass market paperback imprint, Ace/Charter, paid Barry $16,000—$4,000 for each book. He received $8,000 upon signing the contract and would get $2,000 when he finished each of the books.

Seidman initially was not impressed by Barry's work, although they would later become friends and collaborators. When he read the first draft of the first *Casca*, Seidman told Doherty: "This is a good idea. Too bad the guy can't write."[5] But Seidman and Doherty saw promise in Barry's wide knowledge of history and his idea of taking the eternal mercenary into wars and conflagrations across time.

When Barry received the $8,000 advance, John Ed Bradley wrote, he "temporarily retired from writing to do what he did best: kill time" at the Hall of Fame lounge and the other bars he frequented in Nashville. It was no secret that Barry drank heavily. Jack Daniel's was one of his favorites. He also had many sexual encounters with women—and he wasn't exactly subtle about it.

"Barry could have been a good writer—not a great writer—but he never put the meat to the bones," Lavona Sadler said. "He was too lazy. He would rather chase the skirts and drink."[6]

"He had a motor home, a Winnebago, I think, that he'd park outside the Hall of Fame," Bill Parrish said. "He would take a lot of [women] there. At various times I'd see Barry go through three different ones in a day. He had a tremendous appetite. That Winnebago was rockin' frequently outside there."[7]

Sometime early in the fall of 1978, Barry started seeing Darlene Yvonne Sharpe, a five-foot-three, blonde, twenty-four-year-old aspiring country singer who worked as a barmaid at the Natchez Trace Lounge. Darlene was born and raised in Fairview, Tennessee, a rural bedroom community in the far western Nashville suburbs. She started high school there, but because of a tumultuous home life ("conflicts with her mother," as she put it), she went to live with relatives in Royal Oak, Michigan, in the far northern Detroit suburbs, when she was seventeen.[8] Darlene graduated from Clarence Kimball High School in Royal Oak in June of 1972.

Two years later Darlene had a near-fatal car accident in Michigan that—among other serious injuries—left her blind in one eye. "She laid in the hospital for quite a while," Lavona Sadler said. It was so bad that "her dad was going to make the funeral arrangements, pick out a coffin. And then she woke up. She was badly scarred and she walked with a limp."[9]

The accident also left her left leg an inch shorter than her right. And she eventually went through sixteen plastic surgery procedures. She moved to Nashville the year of the accident, 1974. She married James Measles in June of 1975. They divorced two years later.

Darlene had several minor run-ins with the law in 1977 and 1978. She was arrested for driving under the influence in February and June of 1977 and for petit larceny in May of 1978—a charge that was dismissed—and had a third DUI in June. She had just taken a job as a receptionist at Heritage Realty in Fairview for three dollars an hour. She supplemented that meager salary with a moonlighting job tending bar at a Natchez Trace.

One reason Darlene moved to Nashville was to try to make it as a singer in the country music capital of the world. Not long after she arrived in town, she met Lee Emerson Bellamy, a forty-seven-year-old singer/songwriter who had a handful of decent-selling country hits in the

1950s and 1960s and later managed country music artists. In the mid-1970s he was trying to get back into the business. Bellamy's hits included "I Thought I Heard You Calling My Name" for Porter Wagoner in 1957 and "Devil Woman" and "Begging for You" for Marty Robbins in 1962 and 1963.[10]

"Darlene was a country girl just trying to make it in the music business," former Nashville homicide detective Jim Sledge said. "She liked to hang around music people or famous people. That was kind of her gig. She cut some demos for Bellamy, who was trying to push her through Waylon [Jennings] and Jessi [Colter]. But then she started playing around with Sadler and what she thought were his [music business] connections."[11]

Before Darlene met Barry she and Lee Bellamy had been an item. Darlene was smitten. "You are the closest person in *all* the world that I've let get close enough to really get to know me for what I really am and not what everyone would like to believe of me," Darlene wrote on the back of a high school yearbook photo that she gave to Lee.

"I love you even if it is hard for you to understand . . . I am your one and only—body and soul."[12]

Hooking up with Lee was not exactly the wisest choice Darlene made in her young life.

Lee Bellamy—who also went by the showbiz names of Lee Smith, Lee Emerson, and Lee Emory—was born on May 15, 1927, in Cheatham, Tennessee. He grew up in the small town of St. Paul in Southwest Virginia. Lee joined the Marine Corps on March 5, 1943, most likely lying about his age, and served in World War II in the Pacific, where he was wounded in the leg. He moved to Montana after the war and signed a pro baseball contract.

Six feet tall and thin, with thick, wavy black hair, a prominent nose, and large blue eyes, Lee was not exactly the kindest-looking man on the planet. "Though he was a friendly, soft-spoken, well-educated and artistic writer of hit country songs, he happened to look like the worst badass barroom brawler in seven states," the Nashville journalist Dennis Glaser wrote.[13]

Lee's leg wound ended his baseball career prematurely and he turned to songwriting and recording. He also started running afoul of the law.

He was arrested in January of 1948 in Bozeman, Montana, for robbery and car theft in Idaho. Tried and convicted of robbery in Boise, he was sentenced to five years in jail. Out on bail on September 7, 1949, Lee was picked up for forgery in Miles City, Montana. He broke out of jail three weeks later. Three days after that he was back in captivity and served two years of a five-year jail sentence.[14]

Lee stayed out of official trouble for a few years. Then, on the night of April 2, 1953, when he was running a nightclub in Silesia, Montana, he and Don Standish, a ranch laborer, walked into the OK Café in Billings and stole some plates and silverware. As they fled, the café's night manager, Jimmy Leung, ran after them. Lee and Standish threw the plates at Leung—along with what Leung described as a "heavy wrench." Leung pulled out a pistol and fired. He missed. The culprits were arrested, pled guilty, and were fined fifty dollars each.[15]

After that fracas Lee got serious about music and formed a country group called Lee Smith and the Western Gadabouts in Cody, Wyoming. He sang and played guitar. He met country music stars Marty Robbins and Ferlin Husky in Montana, and—with their endorsements—signed a contract with Columbia Records in the summer of 1955. He recorded his first single for Columbia, "A Pair of Broken Hearts," singing in a not-unpleasing Hank Williams–like nasal twang, in August. He followed that up with "So Little Time."

"Emerson's warble," a *Billboard* magazine reviewer wrote, "on his own material is just right."[16]

In June of 1956 Lee moved to Nashville. He and Robbins recorded "I'll Know You're Gone" (a "snappy, cleverly handled duet with a great beat and a catchy refrain") not long after that.[17] In November Lee made "I Thought I Heard You Calling My Name," his biggest hit, which has become a minor country music classic. That country weeper has been covered by many artists, including Don Gibson, Porter Wagoner, George Strait, Jessi Colter, and Rodney Crowell.

The next year he continued writing songs for Robbins and appearing in his touring show, along with recording his own tunes. Then Lee moved into music management. In 1958 he co-owned a personal management business in Nashville, the Emerson-Shucher Agency. His clients included at least one big country music star, Jim Reeves. Robbins briefly took Lee in as a partner in his Nashville music company, Marty's Music, in 1961.

Lee Emerson Bellamy's recording career came to a halt in the mid-1960s. No doubt it had to do with the fact that he had serious trouble staying out of trouble.

There was a disorderly conduct charge stemming from a bar fight in 1961; a loitering charge and conviction (with a ten-dollar fine) in 1963; an arrest for passing worthless checks in 1964; one for malicious destruction of property in 1967; an arrest for assault with a deadly weapon in 1968; one for possessing illegal drugs (barbiturates) in 1970—after which he jumped bail; a weapons charge in 1973, along with a DUI arrest and charges of burglary and receiving stolen property in 1975; and an arrest for forgery (writing country singer Webb Pierce's name on a check) in 1976.

Lee blamed his troubles on his quick temper and being in wrong places at wrong times. "I never did aim to get into trouble," he told a journalist in 1976. "I don't drink—haven't for twenty years. But I can go into a nightclub, take a table back in a corner, sit there quietly minding my own business, and some drunk will make his way through all those other people, come by my table and spill a drink on me.

"And I'll say, 'That's all right, buddy,' and he'll say, 'Whattaya mean, it's all right?' And that's when the fight starts."[18]

Lee Bellamy was deeply in debt in 1976—mainly because of a $15,000 bond that he owed after an Arkansas judge sentenced him to ten years in prison on a burglary charge. Lee said he was innocent, blaming his then girlfriend and an incompetent lawyer. It seems the woman was arrested after breaking into what she thought was the house of her ex-husband in the small town of Grady, Arkansas, near Pine Bluff. It turned out that the girlfriend, whom the police said was "high or drunk," pointed out the wrong house to Lee and another man. Then the three of them walked in and beat up a man living there.

Lee claimed he wasn't part of the misadventure. At the woman's trial, he said, "she admitted I wasn't there, but I had been picked up for not having a driver's license, and there had been a prescription bottle in my car with her name on it. When I denied knowing where she was, they charged me as an accessory after the fact."

His "jack-leg" lawyer, Lee said, advised him to turn down a one-year sentence and plead not guilty. He did, but was convicted and sent to Cummins State Prison Farm in Auburn, Arkansas, where Lee managed to get an office job. "I started singing with the prison band," he said, "and asked my lawyer about an appeal. No grounds, he said. So I paid an inmate lawyer $5 and he threw me a writ that had me back in court in ten days and I got out on a $15,000 bond appeal."[19]

Lee's friends formed the Lee Emerson Legal Defense Fund and put on a benefit concert for him at the famed Gilley's country music club in Pasadena, Texas. Willie Nelson headlined. The show sold out and Lee paid off the bond. But that did not end his legal, professional, or personal troubles.

Given Lee Bellamy's track record, it was not surprising that soon after he and Darlene got together their relationship turned volatile. In September of 1977 Darlene underwent another facial operation and lost her job. When she was unable to rent an apartment, Lee took out a lease for her in his name on a two-bedroom place at the Countrywood Apartment complex in the outer Nashville suburbs. About a week after Darlene moved in, she later said in a police statement, "he said that he was dying of cancer and needed a place to live. He said he had only two months to live, so I felt sorry for him when he asked me to make his funeral arrangements."[20]

Darlene cooked and cleaned for Lee and took a part-time job at the Roller Coaster Club. Lee did not die of cancer—in fact, he did not have cancer. The two had words after Darlene discovered that big lie. But they patched things up and Lee bought her an aquamarine ring. "That ring means the world to me," Darlene wrote to Lee, "first of all, cause you traded yours in to get me what I've always wanted in my whole life, and that was my birthstone and it means even more to know you cared that much about me."[21]

Things seemed to be going fine for Lee and Darlene. Then, one day in March of 1978, Lee hit her for the first time. Darlene had been talking to two friends in the apartment complex parking lot when Lee walked up to them. He "shoved me against the car and hit me and put me by force in my car," Darlene said.

A week later came another violent confrontation, this time inside the apartment. Lee got into a heated argument with John Harris, a physician who had come by to confront him about forging prescriptions. "Lee became very angry and picked up a piece of [fire]wood and started at Dr. John with it," Darlene said. "I took up for John, because I had seen pieces of paper where Lee had practiced John's signature. Lee hit me several times across the right thigh with the piece of wood."

In April, Lee attacked Darlene again, this time after she got home from the night shift. "Several times I would come home around 3:00 a.m. and Lee would start bouncing me off the wall," Darlene said. "He was insane when he thought that I had been out" with another man.

Darlene moved out. Lee kept going downhill. The police arrested him on May 28 for a revoked driver's license and expired license plates. The arrest report tersely referred to Lee as "a washed out songwriter who is a speed freak."

Darlene tried to get on with her life. But that would prove to be impossible. Within a few weeks Lee discovered where she lived and began stalking her there and at work. Darlene later told the police that he put sugar in her gas tank and slashed her tires.

"I was still working at the Roller Coaster and Lee would come and sit across the street and wait for me to come out and then would tell me to go straight home or I would be sorry," she said. One night, as Darlene drove home from work, Lee followed her "at a high rate of speed and [bumped] my car," she said. "I stopped and asked him what was his problem. He hit me in the stomach and said, 'This is not all that's going to happen to you.'"

More trouble came in November soon after Darlene had moved again, this time to the Knollwood Apartments, a large, well-maintained garden apartment complex on Bellevue Road not far from the Natchez Trace. Darlene's sister Wanda and her young child were visiting when Lee broke open the lock on the ground-floor apartment's sliding patio door and barged in.

"He came toward me while I was in the kitchen, and said that he was going to kill me," Darlene said. "I grabbed a knife and told him that he had hurt me for the last time. I tried to call security, but he jerked the phone cord from the wall and ran." Darlene called the police and drove into Nashville to sign a warrant against Lee. He was arrested, but soon released.

Darlene Sharpe had met Barry Sadler in the summer of 1978. In September she and her father, whom she had just picked up at the airport, were having a drink at the bar of the Hall of Fame lounge with Barry and his friend Gary Sizemore. Lee Bellamy—who had just been evicted from his apartment and was living in his beat-up 1970 Ford van—walked in. Darlene and Barry later gave slightly different versions of what happened next.

According to a statement Darlene gave to the Nashville Police, after Lee demanded that she get some demo tapes from her car, Barry told her he would go with her. "As Barry and I were walking out the front door, Lee said to Barry, 'So, you're the Green Beret. Who in the hell do you think you are?' Then Lee called Barry a son of a bitch and told Barry I didn't need a body guard. Barry said to Lee to shut his mouth and Lee said, 'What are you going to do about it?'"

What Barry did was deck Lee Bellamy with a swift karate chop out in the parking lot. "Lee got up," Darlene said, "and told Barry that he was going to get his hit man and have Barry blown away."

According to Barry's 1982 testimony in a civil suit filed against him by Bellamy's son, Lee "slapped" Darlene on the shoulder and said, "Have you got my tapes, bitch?" At which point Darlene left the Hall of Fame with Lee to retrieve the tapes from her car.

Barry "followed them to the parking lot," he said, thinking that Darlene "appeared frightened."

In the confrontation that followed, Bellamy—according to Barry—said to him, "Who the fuck do you think you are?"

"Anyone I choose to be," Barry said.

To which Lee replied, "Are you the Green Beret mother fucker?"

Lee, Barry said, then made an aggressive move, and Barry punched him, knocking him to the pavement, and telling him to leave Darlene alone.

Lee got to his feet and said, "You tough son of a bitch, I'll get you. I'll blow you away. I've got friends who will take care of you."[22]

Lee continued to harass Darlene—and Barry—for the next three months. Barry later testified that Lee made "numerous telephone calls almost daily" threatening his life. Barry asked his friend Earl Owens to tell Lee to stay away from him and Darlene.

"Barry didn't want to kill him because he knew that's probably, I guess, what was going to happen," Owens said. "Barry asked me to go and see [Waylon Jennings's] people and see if I could just talk to him because he didn't want to talk to the guy. I went up to Waylon's [office] and I didn't see Waylon there that day, but I did see some of his people. I told them to tell Lee to stay away, to just leave Barry alone."[23] If Lee got that message, he ignored it.

Not long after that, Lee barged into an office in Nashville rented by Lee Jack Powell—an office that Barry had once used. Lee threw the office door open so hard that "it was nearly ripped from the hinges," Powell said. With a cocked .38-caliber pistol in his hand, he appeared "irrational, angry, screaming obscenities and apparently drunk or on drugs."[24]

Lee accused Powell of hiding Barry and it took "quite some time" before Powell could convince Lee to leave. He drove off in his van.

Lee, Darlene, and Barry had one final confrontation. It began at the Natchez Trace on the evening of December 1, 1978, Lee Emerson Bellamy's last night on earth.

CHAPTER 15
THAT'S MURDER ONE, AIN'T IT?

"If I'd been trying to kill him, I could have put a bullet in his ear."
—BARRY SADLER, DECEMBER 2, 1978

Barry and Darlene started off the evening of Friday, December 1, 1978, drinking at the Natchez Trace with Barry's old buddy Dwight "Marty" Martz and Marty's wife, Susan. The day before, on Thursday afternoon, November 30, Barry had met Marty there and—over drinks, naturally— Barry told him that he wanted to buy a gun. Marty agreed to sell Barry a .38 revolver. They shook hands on it—and had another drink.[1]

Marty and Barry met back at the Trace late Friday afternoon and Marty brought the gun. "It was a .38 Smith & Wesson with a three-inch barrel, with rubber-type grips, a revolver," Homicide Detective Jim Sledge said. "Martz had owned it for many years. Barry paid him a hundred dollars in assorted bills for it."

Not long after the transaction, Darlene and Susie Martz showed up at the Natchez Trace. The four moved to a table near the bar and ordered drinks. Before long Darlene got tipsy and loquacious. She told several people, including Susan and Marty, that she was "carrying a piece," a gun Barry had given her. Barry also was in a boisterous mood. One Trace employee told Sledge that he received "very bad vibes" from Barry, and he was struck by his "macho image of himself" and his "loud talk" about serving in Vietnam and as a sheriff's deputy.

Not long after the couples sat down, the phone rang behind the bar. The bartender that night, Allana Zamboni-Ashley, took the call. It was Lee.

"Me and some friends want to come down there and drink," Lee said, "but I don't want to see her." Meaning Darlene. Allana hung up on him. But Lee called back—three more times.

Each time he said he wanted to speak to Darlene. Each time Allana said no. On the fourth call Barry walked up to the bar, jerked the phone out of the bartender's hand, and said, "C'mon down here and I'll blow your ass away." Allana, the Trace's manager, Shirley Legate, and a waitress, Connie Stacey, heard Barry shouting into the phone.

Barry slammed the phone down and asked Shirley Legate to call the police. She did, asking the dispatcher to have a patrol car stay in the area, but not to come inside. Then, fearing a violent confrontation, she asked Barry and company to leave.

"Don't worry," Barry said, "I'm a Nam vet, a black belt in karate and a lieutenant with the sheriff's department. If there's any shooting, I know how to make it look like self-defense where nothing can be done about it."

The four left anyway, driving in two cars to Darlene's apartment a few miles away. The men repaired to the living room, where they sat down with a bottle of booze. Darlene and Susan Martz cooked dinner in the kitchen. Susan Martz later said that she saw two guns in the apartment: the .38 Barry had just bought from Marty and a .32-caliber Mauser automatic pistol that Barry had legally purchased some time before.

The Martzes went home after that late dinner. It was around ten thirty. A few minutes later Darlene and Barry heard the doorbell ring.[2] At first Darlene thought the Martzes had forgotten something. She peered through the peephole, turned to Barry with a start, and said, "My god, it's Lee." She didn't open the door. Barry, meanwhile, got dressed and slid out the sliding patio door—armed with his newly purchased .38 and a police nightstick.

Barry and Darlene had every reason to believe Lee was there to make good on his promise to kill them. But that wasn't the case. Lee tried to barge in on Darlene that night because he wanted to retrieve a tape deck and several other pieces of recording equipment he had stored there. He was going to deliver the stuff to Waylon Jennings's new recording studio in Colorado. Detective Sledge later confirmed that with a call to Jennings.

When Darlene didn't answer, Lee went back to the parking lot and headed for his domicile—a grimy, once-white 1970 Ford cargo van with two front bucket seats. He had a makeshift curtain hanging from the roof to wall off the carpeted rear of the van. It was strewn with food—cans of chili, a loaf of bread—and clothes, suitcases, sheet music, bottles of prescription drugs, and doctors' prescriptions.[3] Sledge later discovered that "one very big rat" had taken up residence in the van.

When Lee saw Barry, he ran toward the vehicle. Barry caught up to him and hit him with the nightstick. Lee jumped into the van. He pulled his car keys out of his pocket. But Lee dropped the keys, and for some reason turned his head to look out the window. When he did, Barry shot him with the .38 through the window. The bullet hit Lee Bellamy between the eyes.

Barry, two eyewitnesses later told Sledge, then walked around to the passenger side of the van, rolled the sliding door open, and climbed in. Both witnesses said they saw the van rocking. That's because Barry beat the barely conscious Bellamy about the head and shoulders with the police baton. He also dropped the murder weapon—the .38—at Lee's feet.

Darlene came running out of the apartment after she heard the shot. She later told the police that she feared Lee had shot Barry. She looked inside the van, screamed, then huddled with Barry and ran back inside. She came out in a few minutes with Barry's .32. Barry jerked the slide back on the gun and put in a fresh round to make it appear as though it had been fired.

At 11:14 p.m. Darlene went back to her bedroom and called 911. The first police officer on the scene, Johnny Lucas, arrived a few minutes later. An ambulance was right behind him, and the EMTs spirited Lee off to the hospital. Lucas questioned Barry and Darlene in his cruiser. First Darlene, then Barry. That's when the lies started.

Barry and Darlene told Lucas—and, later, Homicide Detective Jim Sledge and at least three newspaper reporters the next day—a string of false statements. To wit:

- that when Barry confronted Lee in the parking lot, Bellamy pulled out what looked like a gun
- that Barry warned Lee not to use it, but Lee turned toward him and Barry fired his .32—but not to kill
- that somehow Lee shot himself with his own gun (actually Barry's newly purchased .38) or that Barry's bullet ricocheted into Lee's forehead

- that Lee had a gun, the .38 that Barry "saw" on the floor of Lee's van
- that Darlene heard two shots and then ran outside
- that Darlene saw Barry with the .32 in his hand when he was standing outside Lee's van (when, in fact, she brought the gun to him)

Not to mention two big lies of omission. Neither Barry nor Darlene even hinted that Barry beat Lee with the police nightstick or that Barry planted his .38 on the floor of the van—and then made it look as though he had fired his gun, the .32.

Homicide Detective Jim Sledge, working the midnight shift, pulled into the Knollwood Apartments parking lot soon after Barry gave his first statement to Officer Lucas. Sledge then took over the investigation.

Jim Sledge, age thirty-one, was born and brought up in Nashville. He joined the Marine Corps the day after turning eighteen in March of 1965. After his four-year hitch, Sledge came home and in July of 1969 joined the Metropolitan Nashville Police Department. For the next seven years, he drove a patrol car, worked on the Robbery-In-Progress Squad, and put time in with the Identification division—today known as Crime Scene Investigation (CSI). Sledge also worked juvenile street crime, mainly dealing with illegal drugs. He moved up to become a Personal Crimes Detective late in 1976.

In two years in his job on the midnight shift as what a friend called a BCHD ("Big City Homicide Detective"), Sledge had personally investigated twenty-two murders. The majority were more or less open-and-shut cases. "They were what we called 'killings,' where the suspect was either standing there waiting on you [when you arrived on the scene] or witnesses knew who did it," Sledge said. "A lot of drug deals, drunken card games, and what we now call domestics."

But the BCHD still put in plenty of time on those cases, as well as on the more vexing whodunits. He wound up spending the better part of five months investigating Lee Emerson Bellamy's violent demise.

Sledge began suspecting something fishy minutes after he went over the crime scene. As he put it: "It stunk from high heaven."

Since Barry said he fired at Lee, the first thing Sledge did was look for the spent shell casing from Barry's gun, the .32—the one he said he fired to miss. Sledge, Johnny Lucas, and two other uniformed police officers—along with Dan Miller, a local TV reporter who lived in the apartments and arrived on the scene (wearing shorts and flip-flops) after hearing the commotion—scoured the parking lot looking for it. Nothing. They also carefully went over the grassy yard in front of the van. They couldn't find any casing there either. That raised a red flag.

Sledge then drove to a nearby Pizza Hut—but not for a post-midnight snack. He was after an empty pizza box. "I was looking for something as sterile as I could find," he said. "I came back and me and the patrol officers got down on our hands and knees and wetted our fingers and picked up all the shards of [van window] glass we could and put 'em in the pizza box." He later delivered the pizza box of glass shards to the Tennessee Bureau of Investigation. The TBI lab painstakingly put the driver's window back together. The restored window showed that the bullet that killed Lee Bellamy came from outside the car and entered at the level of his head.

"The only bullet that went through that window was from outside in," Sledge said, "and Barry actually shot right at his head because that's where it entered and fractured the glass. The bullet went through the window leaving a spherical-type cone of fractured glass."

Sledge would not learn that fact, though, for several weeks. On the early morning in question, he left the Knollwood Apartments parking lot at around one o'clock and drove to nearby St. Thomas Hospital, where Lee Bellamy was about to expire. Darlene and Barry had been taken there by the uniformed officers. Sledge interviewed them both, then took them to police headquarters, which was then located in the Metropolitan Police Safety Building two blocks from the Tennessee State Capitol in downtown Nashville, for their formal statements.

This is what Barry told Sledge at two thirty that morning:

"I saw him get into the passenger side of the van. I was coming up on him and I said, 'Stop.' Then he came up with what looked like a piece. I got mine out and I again said, 'Stop.' Then he began to turn. I'm an expert marksman but I aimed in front of him so as to hit the glass. I shot one time and the glass exploded and he lurched backwards. I went over and climbed inside with him and I saw blood but I thought it was where the glass had hit him. I told Miss Sharpe to call the police, which she did."

Barry said he tried to "assist" Lee since "his breathing was raspy." When Barry got in the van, he said, "I saw a piece on the floor which I left there until the police arrived."

Lee Bellamy made it through the night. But he died at 6:55 a.m. on Saturday, December 2, 1978.

"Sadler Involved in Songwriter's Death." That was the big, bold head-line in Saturday afternoon's Nashville *Banner*. The article opened with: "A transient songwriter 'shot right between the eyes' apparently by Barry Sadler, who recoded the hit song 'The Ballad of the Green Berets,' died today at St. Thomas Hospital, authorities said."

The article identified the decedent as Lee Emerson Emory, one of Lee Bellamy's aliases. Barry was not charged in the shooting, the article said, as he "apparently was acting in self-defense." Barry told *Banner* reporter Hunt Helm that Lee had been "hounding" Darlene for more than a year, including that night, and showed up at her door unannounced.

Barry repeated the story he concocted, that Lee "pulled a piece" on him, and that Barry told him to stop. When he didn't, Barry said, he shot at him—to miss. "I'm a weapons expert," Barry said, "and there's no way my little .32 [Mauser automatic pistol] could have made the kind of wound they're talking about. I fired to miss him by two feet and I'm a damn good shot. If I'd been trying to kill him, I could have put a bullet in his ear. But I shot to miss."

Barry said Lee must have shot himself accidently with the .38. "I guess either his gun was cocked and went off or my bullet ricocheted off the glass," Barry outright lied. "Bullets," Jim Sledge later explained, "don't ricochet off glass—and they don't go around corners."

Barry said he looked inside the van, saw Lee bleeding from the head, and "immediately" called the police. "Emory's pistol," the article said, was found under the seat.

Darlene left police headquarters with a female police officer who drove her back to the apartment. Barry went home to Lavona and the children. The next day Barry called Darlene at the Natchez Trace. The conversation, Jim Sledge said, "went something like, '. . . Hi, Darling . . . I know you talked to the cops last night at the hospital, but it's all over with now. Don't tell 'em anything more. Everything will be okay. I can't see you for a while, but I'll call you as soon as I can.'"

Barry told Lavona the whole story when he came home. "Was I angry?" Lavona said after she learned the details. "Of course. Was I disgusted? Yes." Barry, she said, "told me exactly what he did. What I said to him was, 'Why would you involve someone else in a crime? You always told me that that would get you caught because somebody's going to talk.' And then he said, 'I took it like a true soldier.'"[4]

Newspaper wire services spread the tale nationwide the next day.[5] The tenor of the articles was the same as the *Banner*'s: that Barry apparently shot Lee in self-defense because he was going for a gun.

"It appears that Mr. Bellamy over the last two years has been harassing a young female," Jim Sledge was quoted as saying in an Associated Press story that went out December 2. "It appears he may have gone to the apartment complex to continue the harassment. It appears self-defense."[6]

Sledge carefully used the words "it appears." He was becoming convinced that Barry and Darlene were not telling him the truth. The day after the shooting, he started his investigation in depth. A few days later Sledge examined Lee's van at the impoundment lot. There, on the floor in the front, he found a police nightstick. It had blood on it. It was engraved with the words "To Staff Sergeant Barry Sadler from the Chicago Police Department, 1967."[7]

Barry "left that nightstick in the van and commented to Dwight Martz later that he couldn't find it," Sledge said. "I kept thinking how stupid he was to leave it in the van. And he never did tell me about it." The lab results showed human blood on the nightstick—Lee Bellamy's blood.

The autopsy results came in. They showed that Lee was shot with the .38, the one Barry planted on the floor of Lee's van. Sledge interviewed the medical examiner, Dr. T. E. Simpkins. He told Sledge that the fatal bullet entered Lee's forehead at a thirty-five-degree angle. Then Sledge interviewed Susie and Marty Martz. There was a possibility that Marty had shot Lee, as he had been the owner of record of the .38, the murder weapon.

"They were helpful," Sledge said. Marty told Sledge that right after the shooting—most likely at the hospital—Barry said to him that he shot Lee Bellamy "right between the fuckin' eyes, Marty, right between the eyes." Marty later agreed to meet with Barry and wear a recording device.

Sledge canvassed the apartment complex and found two witnesses who had looked out their windows after hearing the shot. He interviewed everyone at the Natchez Trace. He spoke several times to Darlene, who couldn't seem to avoid trouble. On Monday, two days after the shooting, she paid a visit to her ex-husband, Jim Measles. While they were in his living room, he accidently shot himself in the stomach with a small pistol. He told the police that he was trying to eject a shell when the gun went off. No one was charged in the incident.[8]

On March 8 Sledge learned that the Phoenix FBI office had conducted an investigation of Barry in 1977. It seems that an unidentified federal prisoner had told the FBI that Barry was a hit man. FBI agents found no evidence linking Barry to any hit-man activities and dropped the investigation.

But then agents from the Arizona Department of Safety's Criminal Intelligence Division (CID) in Phoenix looked into the allegation. An officer with the CID told Sledge that "information kept coming in that Sadler, 'a far right winger,' was stock-piling firearms and that he 'ran with known Minutemen,'" a militant anti-communist group. The CID determined that Barry did "associate with known Minutemen." But the firearms allegations never were proven, and the investigation ended when Barry moved to Nashville.

It's likely that the firearm "stockpiling" was merely Barry's personal collection of weapons he kept in his house near the desert. But it's also likely that Barry ran into Minutemen and other "far right wingers" during his years in Tucson. "There were a lot of survivalist types around," Bill Parrish said. "Barry was affiliated somehow with them. He told me that there were weapons' caches throughout the country [put together] by SFers anticipating a war of some type."

Was Barry stretching the truth with those tales of weapons caches? Parrish didn't think so. "Barry shot pretty damned straight with me," he said.[9]

On March 9 Sledge received a collect call from someone who identified himself as Army Capt. Drew Williams. He said he served with Barry in Vietnam, had heard about the shooting, and wanted to know about the case. He told Sledge that "calls had been pouring in from all over the country" from other former Special Forces men asking for details of the case. Sledge found one statement Williams told him particularly telling:

"Whatever is needed for Barry will be done 'cause our little group sticks together."

On March 11 Darlene sat down with Sledge and another Nashville Police detective, Shirley Davis, at police headquarters. The detectives asked pointed questions about the night in question. Darlene obfuscated. And she outright lied again, saying she'd never seen the .38 (the murder weapon) in her apartment. By the end of the interview, though, it started dawning on her that Sledge was making a strong case against Barry—and her.

"You must think Barry shot Lee and planted the gun," Darlene said. "That's murder one, ain't it?"

Darlene agreed to take a polygraph test but did not show up for the appointment. She told Sledge on March 20 that she was sick that day. She also said she had contacted a lawyer who told her that taking a polygraph "would not be in her best interest."

On March 14 Sledge and a Nashville Police lieutenant met Marty Martz at 7:30 a.m. at police headquarters and fitted him with a wireless transmitter and tape recorder. Marty then drove his gray 1976 Cadillac to the Hall of Fame. At around 9:15 he sat down at a table with Barry, who was wearing a brown leather jacket and a cowboy hat. The two men spoke for about twenty-five minutes.

"I'm glad you said nothing to the cops," Barry said. "I think I'm happy. . . . They have circumstantial evidence. . . . They'll never make a murder case. . . . They're not going to indict me without her [Darlene]. . . . I don't think they will ever make a murder case. I have heard that [they] will probably want me to cop a plea, plea bargain. . . . I just don't think they have got enough facts."

Barry and Lavona had argued about the lawyer they would hire to defend him. Barry "wanted to get some fly-by-night attorney," Lavona said. She insisted on Joe Binkley Sr., the top criminal defense lawyer in Nashville—and one of the best who ever practiced in the city.[10] Lavona prevailed. It would turn out to be a very good decision.

By early May Sledge had amassed enough evidence to convince Assistant District Attorney Victor S. (Torry) Johnson III to convene a grand jury. "We are in a position where we have completed our investigation where we stand on the case," Johnson said on May 4.[11]

At two o'clock in the afternoon on Wednesday, May 30, 1979, Jim Sledge appeared before the grand jury with an indictment charging Barry Sadler with second-degree murder and Darlene Sharpe with accessory after the fact of second-degree murder. At nine o'clock the next morning, the grand jury returned a sealed indictment against Barry and Darlene. Nashville Criminal Court judge Raymond H. Leathers told Sledge to arrest Barry and Darlene and pre-set bond at $10,000 for him and $2,500 for her.

At around twelve thirty on Friday afternoon, June 1, exactly six months after Lee Bellamy's death, Sledge spotted Barry's and Darlene's cars (a Cadillac and a Mercury) in the parking lot of the Vanderbilt Holiday Inn, where Darlene was working behind the bar at the Commodore Lounge. Two Nashville plainclothes detectives, Joe Blakely and Dennis Birdwell, met Sledge in the parking lot.

Sledge walked into the Commodore Lounge alone. Blakely and Birdwell came in a few minutes behind him and quietly sat at a table.

Sledge walked up to Barry, who was at the bar "telling war stories," Sledge said. "I said, 'Sit down, I'll buy you a beer.' So we sat down at a table. And he kept wanting to talk about Vietnam and all that.

"So I sat there and drank a beer. I drank that beer as a way of diffusing what could have been a violent situation. Barry could have kicked my ass. I figured if I bought him a beer, he'd mellow out. I didn't want to fight him."

Darlene came out from behind the bar and joined them. Barry soon realized that this was not a social visit.

"By the way, Barry, you're under arrest for the murder of Lee Emerson Bellamy," Sledge said.

"You can't arrest me," Barry said.

"The hell I can't," Sledge replied. "Stand around and watch 'cause you're arrested."

Barry, Sledge later said, "kind of got the drift when [Detectives Blakely and Birdwell] stood up."[12]

"I'm glad that it's finally over," Barry said. "I shouldn't have lied about it but I could see them blowing the [love] triangle bit up in the press."

He told Sledge he would fully cooperate and that he would "tell the truth." Sledge allowed Barry and Darlene to make several phone calls. Then he arrested them.

"We didn't handcuff them," Sledge said. "That was part of the diffusing. I walked out of the place with Barry. He sat next to me in the front seat of my car and I drove to [police headquarters] to book him." The other detectives followed with Darlene.

CHAPTER 16
A TOTAL TENNESSEE REDNECK

"The hardest thing to do is to live up to the illusion of those who want me to be a hero."

— BARRY SADLER, OCTOBER 1979

On Friday, December 1—the day that Barry killed Lee Bellamy—Barry's publisher, Ace/Charter Books, convened a sales meeting in Miami to map out publicity and marketing for the first *Casca* book, which was due to be published in July.

"Mike Seidman told Barry and me to get some publicity," Robbie Robison said. "I called Mike [the next day] at the sales meeting and said, 'I think I better tell you before you hear it on the news: Barry shot and killed a guy last night.'

"Mike said, 'We asked you and Barry to get some publicity, but this is not what Tom [Doherty, the publisher] had in mind.'"[1]

The "publicity" continued with the lurid local newspaper and TV stories about the arrests of Barry and Darlene. The wire services then spread the news nationwide. A typical headline: "Barry Sadler Charged in Killing."[2]

The Nashville DA's office held a press conference on June 1, the day of the arrests. "The published reports" that Barry fired in self-defense "were not correct," Nashville district attorney Tom Shriver said. Assistant DA Torry Johnson—who would be prosecuting—added that Sledge's investigation determined "that it was not a case of self-defense." Darlene was charged as an accessory, Shriver said, because "she has allegedly undertaken to give police false information in order to protect" Barry.[3]

On June 25 Barry pleaded innocent to the second-degree murder charge; so did Darlene to accessory after the fact. "There's a very, very long story behind this. A situation existed between Sadler and this man [Bellamy] for some time," Joe Binkley Sr. told the press that day, planting a seed for how he would defend Barry. "The man had an extensive record. He was a violent individual."

Binkley went on to say that Barry "very well might plead self-defense."[4]

Casca: The Eternal Mercenary—the first of what would be twenty-two Sadler books in that series—came out as a 246-page mass market paperback retailing for $2.50 in July. The pot-boiling, action adventure opens in Nha Trang (a city Barry knew well) in South Vietnam in 1970 at the Eighth Field Hospital, which Barry also knew very well as he had been treated there twice. Maj. Julius Goldman, a Jewish army doctor—named in honor of Barry's Fort Bragg SF friend Gerry Gitell—is attending to "a stocky, powerfully built man" with "a shiny sliver of Russian steel about a quarter of an inch in diameter" embedded in his exposed brain, the result of a "Chinese-made 60-mm mortar firing Russian ammo."

As Goldman and another doc are about to fold the soldier up in a rubber sheet, a miracle happens. "Slowly, but surely," Barry wrote, "as the two surgeons watched in disbelief, the open wound was taking steps to protect itself." The soldier, identified on his dog tag as "Casey Romain," was healing himself.

More miracles ensue. Goldman, whose hobby is studying ancient history, pulls a metal arrowhead out of the wounded man's thigh. He identifies it as dating from 300 BC to AD 400. When Romain comes out of anesthesia, he is mumbling—in Latin, "Not the Latin of the textbooks. Casey was speaking the Latin of the Caesars. Perfectly. Fluently."

And so we are introduced to Casca, who is "doomed by Jesus to an endless life as a soldier." Goldman figures out who Casca is. In his pulp fiction prose, Barry tells us that Casca is a "fine figure of a man" who is popular with the ladies. We get his back story: the business about Christ on the cross, along with Casca's violence and sex-filled years as a slave, a gladiator in Rome, and a Roman warrior. Along the way Barry provides many intimately sketched descriptions (using his medic's knowledge) of horrendous wounds and deaths. In the gladiatorial arena, for example, Casca decapitates a Greek opponent. "There was a whishing sound followed by a thunk! And the Greek's head was off. Arterial blood spurted on the much-stained sand."

Barry "could make it rain on the page," Robbie Robison said, "and he could make it rain blood. He told me once, 'No one writes slaughter like Sadler.'"[5]

Few book reviewers took notice of *Casca*. One who did was Joe White of the Gannett News Service, who wrote a generally positive review. White said that Casca using "contemporary slang" was "a little disconcerting at first." But, he opined, Barry used his "knowledge of battlefield psychology to raise the story near the level of science fiction." Barry's "knowledge of ancient warfare and battle styles," White said, "is also good."

His conclusion: "If the story is something less than classic, still it is something more than a standard pot-boiler based on bloodshed and violence."[6]

The book's cover features a realistic drawing of a Roman based on a head shot photo of Barry wearing a Nazi field cap, a cigarette dangling from his lips. The picture was taken in 1971 by the photographer David Lee Guss in Tucson for one of Robert Powers's magazine articles. It's the same photo Barry used on the back of the dust jacket of his first book, *The Moi*.[7]

A version of that photo would be used on the covers of most of the *Casca* books. In 1987 Barry's editors wanted a change and decided to use an image of the famed male model Fabio. Barry hated the idea. He sent Robbie Robison to New York City to argue against it.

"I went and jumped up and down on the editor's desk and everything, told them how dissatisfied we were," Robison said. But the editors prevailed and Fabio's image—bare-chested, naturally—graced both *Casca* No. 17, *The Warrior*, and No. 18, *The Cursed*.

"It turned out that [*Casca* 17] sold quicker than any book we'd had," Robison said. "Fabio didn't hurt us. I didn't tell [Barry] that."[8]

In the fall of 1979, while Joe Binkley Sr. continued to work his legal magic in Nashville, Barry went on the road to promote the fledgling *Casca* franchise. For an interview at a Dallas hotel in mid-October, Barry showed up wearing a cowboy hat pulled down low, a blue jean suit with an open-collar print shirt, and cowboy boots. He posed for a photo for the *Dallas Morning News* with a sly smile on his face. He smoked a cigarette during the interview.

A few weeks before his thirty-ninth birthday, Barry "no longer has that rugged military look," *Dallas Morning News* reporter Skip Hollandsworth wrote. "His stomach hangs over his belt and his gung-ho attitude only occasionally surfaces."[9]

"There's two things about me," Barry told Hollandsworth. "I'm a total Tennessee redneck and I've always wanted to be a writer. So I quit the road and the music three years ago to learn the writer's craft." Both statements contained some elements of the truth. Barry did, indeed, want to write for a good number of years. But he wasn't exactly on "the road" when he decided to do so.

Barry went on to say that he developed the Casca idea from his frequent reading of the Bible, which he called "a great book." He said Casca's endless mercenary existence would let him "run these books on and on and never have them end until I get sick of them. It's a good trick, I think."

The plan, he said, was to put Casca in "every war that fascinates me. One of my hobbies has always been reading about the great wars in history."

The talk then turned to the Vietnam War. When Hollandsworth brought it up, Barry fixed him with a stare and clenched his fists. Barry said he "believed in that war and still do. There's always going to be trouble from those [communist] people. The only thing we ever got from turning the other cheek is to be slapped twice. We've gotten rid of the draft [in 1973], and look: the American army is at its lowest point ever."

He then spoke about what it's like to fight in a war. Those who haven't been in combat, he said, "miss a great deal of self-testing. It was a tremendous experience for me. I miss it every day."

Barry never mentioned the fact that he had been indicted for murder. He may have been alluding to it, though, when he ended the interview by reflecting on the fame that followed "The Ballad."

"The hardest thing to do," he said, has been "to live up to the illusion of those who wanted me to be a hero."

On November 13, 1979, Barry showed up on a panel in a seminar called the Writing to Sell workshop in Nashville. Barry offered his thoughts on breaking into the music business at the event. It took place at—of all places—the Hall of Fame Motor Inn.[10]

On November 28, 1979, Lee Emerson Bellamy's son Rodney Wayne Bellamy Sr., the administrator of his father's estate, filed a $1.2 million civil suit against Barry and Darlene. "Before his demise, the decedent, Emerson Lee Bellamy [sic] suffered great pain and anguish of body and mind," the suit, filed in the Circuit Court for Davidson County in Nashville, said. Rodney Bellamy asked for $400,000 in compensatory damages and $800,000 in punitive damages.[11]

A few weeks later, in December, Charter published the second book in the *Casca* series, *God of Death*. This time Casca is incarnated as a Viking warrior in the third century. He travels to Mexico, where he is captured by the Teotecs (imprisonment of the hero is a theme in the books, as it is in Ian Fleming's James Bond thrillers), who later change their mind about him and anoint Casca a god. Dr. Julius Goldman makes an appearance, visiting the Boston Museum of History, boning up on "Mesoamerican art from Mexico."

There are racy sexual encounters ("she begged him to enter her deep and tear her apart with his manhood") and much blood spilling, intimately described. That includes Casca having his heart pulled out of his body. And one of his lady loves—Lida, a daughter of Ragnar the Brutal One—unhappily experiences her father living up to his name as he blinds her with a torch after she makes the mistake of saying, "I have eyes only for Casca."

On February 5, 1980, Torry Johnson announced an upcoming hearing in Criminal Court that would set a date for Barry and Darlene's trial. "Lawyers on both sides have met," Johnson said, "and discussed the pros and cons of the case, but there has been no plea bargain." That's because, he said, "there was some sort of cover-up. Some things were told to the police [by Barry and Darlene] that weren't correct."[12]

Barry spoke to reporters following the February 8 hearing, which did not set a trial date; the only thing that was decided was to postpone the hearing until February 29. "I feel like a fictional character in a bad novel," Barry said. "I wish I could tell you the whole story, because it's one good story. I'll say everything when this is over. It's hard to believe what's going on."

Johnson also told reporters that it was "a very unusual case with a lot of facts to be considered. I think we have strong evidence to show that Sadler did shoot the victim."[13]

Barry took the February 8 courthouse opportunity to speak at length about his next, non-*Casca*, novel, *Nashville with a Bullet*, which his buddy Billy Arr was writing with him. Barry said the book—for which he received a hefty $7,500 advance against royalties—would be a violence-filled "cops and robbers story" set in the world of Nashville's country music scene.

"It's kind of a country-styled version of *The Godfather*," Barry said. "We just finished negotiating the movie rights for the book. The movie will be shot in Nashville and I understand it will be a big-budget operation." No movie ever came out of the book.

Oddly enough, Barry and Billy contacted Jim Sledge several times in late 1979 and early 1980 to talk to him about the book. Sledge was not exactly thrilled about it.

"One night I'm working midnight homicide, and I get a call from Billy Arr, who says he's Barry's publicist and Barry's writing a book called *Nashville with a Bullet*," Sledge said. "I was hoping he was calling to say Barry would confess, but he didn't. Instead, he said, 'Barry wants to dedicate the book to you.' I said, 'Barry just don't get this, does he? I'm the good guy. He's the bad guy. I arrested him. He better not dedicate the damn book to me.'"

Billy Arr shrugged that off and asked Sledge to help him with Nashville police radio codes. Sledge refused. "I told him Radio Shack published the code," he said. "Or to buy a scanner and listen to it."

Barry and Billy Arr did not dedicate the book, which came out in December of 1981, to Sledge—or to anyone else. However, the book's hero is John Sherman, a hard-bitten Nashville detective who works the midnight shift. Was John Sherman based on Jim Sledge? Almost certainly, as they both are Nashville homicide detectives with the same initials. Barry and Billy Arr called Sherman a "damn good cop" who "knew the inner workings of music row like the back of his scarred hands." Those words fit Jim Sledge quite well.[14]

During the long months of legal wrangling, Sledge—who began working as an investigator for the Nashville District Attorney's Career Criminal Unit in February 1980—ran into Barry several times at the courthouse. "He would always come up to me in the hallway and want to talk," Sledge said. "I'd say, 'Get away, Barry, leave me alone.'"

Casca No. 3, *The War Lord*, burst into print in April of 1980. The book opens with Casca knocking on the door of Dr. Julius Goldman's Boston town house. The housekeeper takes one look at "the steel" between his eyes, and "ice water raced through her bowels."

Goldman and Casca sit down and the Roman soldier spills out more of his saga. Most of the rest of the book is set in Byzantium and China in the third century. Naturally, there are battle scenes and lots of blood flows. Plus, Casca becomes a warlord—and is buried alive by a vengeful Chinese emperor's concubine. Casca later reflects that he is "shocked at the depths of her cruelty. . . . Not since Salome had he known a woman as evil as this."

Casca No. 4, *Panzer Soldier*, would come out in early September. As the title indicates, Casca turns up in a German uniform during World War II. The book opens in Berlin where Dr. Goldman is attending a medical seminar. He runs into Casca, who speaks German. Casca then tells Goldman his Nazi war story. It ends in May of 1945 with Casca in the bunker with Adolf Hitler and a who's who of other Nazi bigwigs. Hitler susses out Casca's identity and, not long before his demise, says: "Casca Rufio Longinus, soldier of Imperial Rome, gladiator and mercenary. It's somewhat ironic that you have ended up fighting for the Brotherhood."

In early May of 1980, nearly a year after Jim Sledge arrested Barry and Darlene, Joe Binkley Sr. and Torry Johnson agreed on a plea bargain. Barry would plead guilty to voluntary manslaughter and Johnson would recommend a light sentence. Darlene, who had hired one of Nashville's most colorful and controversial attorneys, Charles Galbreath, would plead guilty to her charge, accessary after the fact, and get off with little jail time.

So there was no trial in the murder of Lee Emerson Bellamy. Instead, on May 8, 1980, Barry Sadler and Darlene Sharpe appeared before Judge Leathers and pleaded guilty. The judge sentenced Barry to four-to-five years in jail and Darlene to one year. Jim Sledge also appeared before the judge. He testified that Barry had apologized "for lying to me." Barry said he pleaded guilty "in order to expedite things and to avoid the embarrassment of a trial."

Barry's service in the Vietnam War—which was widely viewed in Nashville as heroic—his reputation as the patriotic singer of "The Ballad of the Green Berets," and his "All-American" good looks[15] played a large part in the prosecution's decision to overlook the fact that, as Sledge said, "Barry flat-ass killed Bellamy."

Lee Bellamy, "on paper, was a thug," Sledge said in 2015, "but that don't mean he deserved to die like that. Hell, Barry wouldn't deserve to die like that. But he didn't deserve to be shot by Sadler and have a gun planted on him."

In an official document Barry submitted to the court prior to the trial, he said nothing about beating Lee with the police baton on the night in question. And he continued to maintain that he warned Lee in the parking lot and that he thought Lee pulled a gun—and that he shot to miss. In his words: "His hand came up, I saw a flash in it, thought it was a gun . . . I drew my gun and fired, aiming in front of him. The bullet broke up on impact with the glass and a fragment hit him in the head."

Barry did admit to throwing down the .38 to make it appear Lee shot himself. "When I saw he was shot, I panicked and took a gun I had given Miss Sharpe earlier and put it in his hand," he said. (He actually planted the gun he had fired, the .38—not the .32 Darlene handed him.) "It was stupid. But, as I said, I panicked. I saw the destruction of my career and my family."[16]

Barry and Darlene did not go to jail in May. They remained free on bond as Joe Binkley Sr. worked to get Barry an even lighter sentence. That work paid off on September 26 when Judge Leathers ruled on a defense motion to suspend Barry's sentence. Leathers didn't go that far, but he drastically reduced Barry's sentence to thirty days in the county work-house—and Darlene's to one year of probation.

In his testimony at the hearing, Barry offered a new version of why he pulled the trigger on December 1, 1978. He said that the "flash" he saw when he confronted Lee Bellamy in the parking lot was probably, he later realized, from light reflecting on Lee's car keys.

"It was reflex," Barry told the judge. "I thought he was going to kill me."

Lee, Barry added, "was a sick, evil man who lived on fear. If I hadn't killed him, someone else would." Barry said he wasn't sorry he killed Lee, but he did regret planting the murder weapon on him and lying to the cops about it.

"I saw a whole world of trouble coming down on me and I didn't know what to do," Barry said. "What I have been through since then was the worst experience of my life. I'd rather go back to Vietnam for two years than to go through that again."[17]

Darlene testified, in tears, that when she heard the shot in the parking lot, she thought Lee shot Barry, which is why she ran outside with the .32. When she saw Lee bleeding, she agreed to "stick by" Barry's story. She also gave lurid testimony detailing the times Lee lied to her, threatened her, and physically attacked her. Among other things, she testified, Lee "took a piece of firewood and busted my leg muscle, and told me he was going to poke my other eye out so that I would be blind."

Three years later Barry said he had no regrets about shooting Lee, who "deserved to die." But, he said, "I don't know whether I actually intended to kill the guy or what." Still, he said, he did the deed "and the judge did have to give me some kind of sentence. But I never apologized for anything [he did apologize to Sledge for lying to him] and nobody in Nashville condemned me for it. I didn't even have a moving violation on my record."[18]

Barry began serving his thirty-day sentence in the Nashville Metro Workhouse on South 5th Street in downtown Nashville on October 3. The facility was used primarily to house those convicted of misdemeanors such as drunk driving and those serving work-release sentences. Even though the building was surrounded by chain-link fences topped with razor wire, serving in the workhouse wasn't exactly hard time.

The first time Barry's literary agent, Robbie Robison, came for a visit, he was struck by how lax things were. "I took a portable typewriter and two cartons of cigarettes to the work jail," Robison said. "There wasn't anyone on guard. You just walked in. [Barry] was back there sitting on a bunk. I walked in, and he said, 'How did you get here?' I said, 'There wasn't anyone on the door; I just walked in.' He could have walked out any time."

The workhouse, John Ed Bradley wrote in 1990, "reminded Barry of his days back in the Army. It was barracks life. . . . Some of his drinking buddies came by to visit, and they howled with laughter telling jokes. Everyone ate steak, green salad, and pork and beans."[19]

During his visit Robbie Robison said to Barry, "You know, I was just thinking on the way in here, you just got thirty days. But if you got a year or so, just think about how many books we could have turned out?"

Barry did, in fact, write a book during his brief time in jail. He "took the typewriter," Robison said, and "finished the book he was working on. He was late on it as usual"[20]

CHAPTER 17
THE SLOW DESCENT

"He's the closest friend I have in the world. We've whored together and drank together and soldiered together."
—DUKE FAGLIER, 1989

Barry walked out of the workhouse a little more than three weeks after he checked in, an early good-behavior release, a free man, albeit with a felony conviction. But being a convicted felon did not seem to hamper him during his remaining years. Barry spent most of the next three-plus years plying the writer's trade in Nashville. In that time he churned out eight books: three stand-alone mass market paperback action adventure novels and five in the *Casca* series.

He needed the book advances and royalties because income in the form of royalties from "The Ballad" had long since slowed to a trickle. Lavona worked at a local convenience store, but her salary hardly covered the grocery bills for the family of five. Barry had no other income, except for the occasional low-paying singing gig. "He had pretty well given up on his musical career," Bill Parrish said. But he did some shows "for the money."

One day in the early 1980s, for example, Barry, Bill Arr, and Parrish piled into Barry's Winnebago and drove out to the now-closed Richards-Gebaur Air Force Base near Kansas City. "Barry did a set there with a house band and a little comedy routine," Parrish said. "He did a few other military bases, too. He got paid for the gigs, but it wasn't all that much."[1]

In 1980 Barry told the Nashville District Court that he made about $20,000 a year from his books. He also said he had just $200 in savings, $1,500 in his checking account, and owed the Third National Bank of

Nashville $2,000. He was paying $400 a month on the house he and Lavona rented in Hendersonville.

It didn't help his bottom line that Barry liked to spend money. He "could go through money quicker than anyone I have ever seen," Bill Parrish said, "and he did it when he was reasonably sober, too."[2] Barry, Billy Arr said, "would buy fun before he would buy bread, and when he was having fun he wanted everyone to have fun."[3]

The felony conviction didn't stop Barry from continuing his heavy drinking and carrying on affairs with women he met at the Hall of Fame and the other bars and clubs where he hung out with his buddies, all of whom were involved one way or another in the country music business. That crew included Parrish, Billy Arr, John Buchan (who had a marketing company), Gary Sizemore (a sometime music producer), Earl Owens, Hurshel Wiginton (a regular on *Hee Haw*), and Harvey "Duke" Faglier.

"I always told Barry that he drew to him comic-type people," Lavona said. "They were over the top, and not in a good way."[4]

Harvey Larry "Duke" Faglier certainly fit the "over the top" category. Known as "Duke Danger," "Duke Paris," and "Crocodile Duke," Faglier, who died of cancer in 2015 at age sixty-seven, was a handsome, muscular, gun-toting, hard-living guitarist and singer from Georgia who wore a large diamond stud in one ear. He had played in Jerry Lee Lewis's touring band for a dozen years and on several of Jerry Lee's albums. Duke talked tough and drank hard. He spent plenty of time hanging out in bars, topless joints, and gentlemen's clubs.[5]

Faglier "was kinda like Rambo," Earl Owens said. "You've got bad asses, and then you've got Duke. Duke never threatened anybody—he promised them."[6]

Duke "was a real character," John Buchan said, "a very robust, dark-haired guy who wore a cowboy hat. He reminded me a bit of a young Paladin [the actor Richard Boone] from [the TV western] *Have Gun Will Travel*, only without the wrinkles."[7]

Barry included a character named "Duke Falger" in *Razor*, his last non-*Casca* adventure tale, which came out in February of 1988. The fictional Duke served on a Long Range Reconnaissance Patrol (LRRP) team in Vietnam and "spent some time with the Berets" and at Fort Bragg.

"Duke [the character] was a good, stable man," Barry wrote. "He'd be where he was supposed to be when he was supposed to be. Steady, he taught the course in quick-kill shooting technique—rifle, pistol, shotgun—and was a damned good hand-to-hand combat instructor as well. If he had any bad qualities it was that he didn't *have* any really bad qualities—other than being a semi-health nut and cunt junkie. But that didn't make him all bad."[8]

The real Duke Faglier, in fact, had some not-good qualities.

There was "definitely that bullshitter element" with him, said Bob Sipchen, who interviewed Duke at length for an article in the *Los Angeles Times* in 1989.[9] John Ed Bradley, who also spent a good deal of time with him for his 1990 article on Barry in *GQ*, found Duke "especially twisted."[10]

Duke, Bill Parrish said, "was not one of my favorite people. I used to work out with him in the mid-eighties until he found steroids. He was just kind of a hanger-on with Barry. He was out of touch with reality."[11]

"I didn't care for him," Lavona Sadler said. "He was one of those people on the edge, and not in a good way. I didn't like my daughter around him."[12]

By the early 1980s Barry and Duke had become close. They practiced karate together; they drank together; they partied together. They had a short-lived business called "The Sadler System of Self Defense" or "SSS," offering five-week courses for men and women at the Nautilus Gym in Madison, Tennessee, north of Nashville. SSS ads noted that the system was "not a karate course," and that it was taught by "Barry Sadler, Sr. Training Instructor, Special Forces, Ft. Bragg, NC and Duke Faglier, 1st Degree Black Belt, Special Forces Protege of Barry Sadler."[13]

They stayed friends after Duke was arrested and charged with assault with intent to commit murder in January 1981. At 5:30 p.m. on January 22, Duke was standing in the front yard of the Paris, Tennessee, home of Jack Weaver, a bank executive. When Weaver came home from work, Duke asked him about a house for sale next door. They spoke briefly. Then, when Weaver turned to go into his house, Duke attacked him from behind with a nightstick. He broke Weaver's arm and left a bleeding gash on his head. Duke pleaded not guilty to the charge.

Duke's uncle, Gene Faglier, testified in court that a former business partner of Weaver's paid him $3,000 to hire someone to tell Weaver "to mind his own business" about a pending investigation into the partner's business practices. Gene Faglier said he hired Duke and another man, Hal Vest, to do the deed.[14] Both Vest and Duke had been honorary Davidson County Sheriff's deputies—as Barry had. Vest, who also was charged in the crime, waited in his car while Duke did the dirty work.

In December of 1982 both men pleaded guilty after the charges were reduced to aggravated assault. Vest received one year of probation. Duke got two years of probation.[15]

"I love this man," Duke said of Barry in 1989. "He's the closest friend I have in the world. We've whored together and drank together and soldiered together. I guess we're as close as two men can be who aren't queer."[16]

There's little doubt about the whoring and drinking. As far as soldiering, Duke had a way of stretching the truth. He told people he had been a mercenary and that—as the SSS ads suggested—he had served in the army with Barry. Harvey L. Faglier may have been a mercenary, but it's extremely doubtful. There's little doubt, though, that he ever served in the U.S. Army, much less with Barry in the Green Berets.

According to his official military records, Duke joined the Air Force Reserve at the height of the Vietnam War on February 21, 1968. He reported for USAF Basic Training at Lackland Air Force Base on April 11. Fifteen days later, on April 26, 1968, Duke Faglier received his honorable discharge due to what the military classified as a physical disability.[17] That, according to the Pentagon, was the extent of Duke's military service.

Duke wasn't the only guy Barry went "whoring" with in the early 1980s. Bill Parrish said that on several occasions Barry would drag him to topless bars, including one called the Classic Cat. "Barry carried a stack of [*The Moi*] books, which had his picture on the back where he had a cigarette hanging out of his mouth and his German Afrika Corps hat on, his most Hemingway-looking pose," Parrish said. "He would hand those damn books out to these dancers just like they were business cards and leave these hundred-dollar tips. 'Yeah, they'll remember me,' he said."[18]

Anybody can get laid, Barry told Parrish, "but to be able to talk a dancer into some hooker action for nothing, you've really accomplished something."

Barry's books sold well. Ace/Charter wanted more. "They asked me, 'Do you have anything else?'" Robbie Robison said. "So we signed a six-book contract in '81. Then Barry and Mike [Seidman] became real good friends. One time Mike was getting on Barry about not using commas or semicolons or something like that. Barry said, 'Dammit, you can get a monkey to do that—I'm a writer.'"

Casca No. 5, *The Barbarian*, appeared in July of 1981. Barry's stylized image graces the cover with a second-century Germanic warrior's helmet perched on his Prince Valiant–haired head. In another fast-moving action adventure, Casca deserts the Roman Legion after seeing too much death on the Parthian Plains in Persia. Naturally, he moves on to even more battle action as an official Barbarian fighting with the Vikings in Scandinavia.

"It's what you call a 'male romance' novel," said Hank Schlesinger, who edited several of the *Casca* books. "You get laid, you get a gun [or a sword or a battle axe], you beat the bad guy."

Barry, Schlesinger said, "was a storyteller who came from an oral tradition. His mother, Bebe, and his father were storytellers. I suspect that he was telling himself stories and translating the stories in his head into the writing." With Barry's books, Schlesinger said, "you're not going to look for literature. You're going to look for an entertaining read . . . Indiana Jones kind of stuff. I think [the *Casca* books] were the kind of books Barry read growing up—those off-the-wire-rack books. He wasn't in the Iowa Writing School reading John Barth. He was reading Max Brand; he was reading Louis L'Amour."[19]

Barry "showed an extraordinary grasp of history," said Eliza Shallcross, who edited three of the *Casca* books. "There was nothing about his writing that looked like somebody who hadn't finished high school. It wasn't polished, but it wasn't a mess. His writing was okay . . . basically storytelling."[20]

"The guy had his [writing] chops down," said Jim Morris, who edited the last two *Casca* books. "You had to edit [the books]; you didn't have to rewrite them." And the main *Casca* plot, he said, "was a clever idea . . . perpetually chained to the wheel of war."[21]

Nashville with a Bullet arrived in December of 1981. After it came out Barry told a Nashville reporter that a movie treatment Billy Arr had shown him inspired the book—and their collaboration. "I was convinced he could handle dialogue and scene setups," Barry said. "He didn't want to do it—'I ain't no novelist,' he said—but I walked him through it. After three weeks he took to it like duck to water." Barry also gave Billy Arr credit for adding "some insight into some parts of the music business."[22]

Barry made a few appearances on local radio and TV talk shows in Nashville to talk about his books. That included *Wraparound* with Rita Whitfield on Channel 17 on September 17; Laura Hill's *Livewire* talk show on WSIX-FM on December 13, with Bill Arr; and Channel 8's *A Word on Words* on December 27.

He pumped out two more *Casca* books in May and October 1982—*The Persian*, in which our hero fights the Romans for fourth-century King Shapur the Great; and *The Damned*, in which Casca fights for the Romans against Attilla the Hun in the fifth century—along with a stand-alone mass market novel for Tom Doherty's Tor Books called *Morituri*. It was a Casca-like, blood-drenched tale told in the first person by Lucanas, the "premiere gladiator of Rome," who interacts with—among others—three Roman emperors: Nero, Claudius, and Tiberius.

Barry found a way to get rid of a giant stockpile of *The Moi* books in 1982. He volunteered to donate his time—and 2,500 copies of the book—to a Tennessee Special Olympics fund-raiser on February 12 as part of a Central Hockey League game between the Nashville South Stars and Wichita Winds. Barry autographed copies of the book for $5 that night at the Nashville Municipal Auditorium arena and turned the proceeds over to Special Olympics.[23]

When not doing the occasional altruistic act, knocking out his books, and knocking back beers and booze in Nashville saloons, Barry took a few road trips in the early 1980s. More often than not they involved visits to former military men of action who were involved one way or another with weapons. Several times Barry and Bill Parrish drove down to Powder Springs, Georgia, outside Atlanta to hang out with Mitchell WebBell, a colorful former OSS World War II operative, and a well-known arms dealer and weapons manufacturer.

WerBell "had a training camp there," Bill Parrish said. "He had a collection of every kind of weapon imaginable and a [sixty-acre] compound in Powder Springs. It was quite a place, with some interesting people. There was a Chinese guy who was about six-five who taught martial arts. There was a Marine sniper from Vietnam there, Burt Waldron."

Barry and Parrish met retired army colonel Lew Millett, a Korean War Medal of Honor recipient who also fought in World War II and the Vietnam War, at WebBell's training camp. And Ben Rosson, who claimed to have done mercenary work in Angola, Rhodesia (Zimbabwe), Afghanistan, and other places. Rosson also claimed to be a bounty hunter and sniper with more than a hundred confirmed kills in the Vietnam War and a Green Beret who met Barry in Vietnam.[24]

Ben Rosson—a thin man with dark hair and eyes whom Bill Parrish described as "country boy wiry"—soon would go into the arms business with Barry and become a very close friend.[25] But it's all but certain that Rosson—at best—greatly exaggerated his military background. In response to a Freedom of Information Act request in 1990, the Department of the Army reported that Ben Rosson's military occupational specialty (MOS) was 91B, Wheeled Vehicle Mechanic. Army snipers held an infantryman's MOS, 11B-4. So it's likely Rosson spent his time in Vietnam—if he served there—fixing army trucks and jeeps.

What's more, Benjamin Rosson is not listed as having served with the Special Forces in Vietnam in the unofficial, but comprehensive Vietnam War Special Forces database maintained by Stephen Sherman of RADIX

Press. And a search by a longtime Vietnam War military records specialist could find no evidence that Rosson served in country during the war.

Whether or not Ben Rosson was a Green Beret sniper, he certainly knew a good deal about weapons. The next time Barry ran into Rosson, he was an instructor at Colonel Millet's short-lived Mercenary School in the rugged San Jacinto Mountains outside Idyllwild, California, along with Burt Waldron, former army infantryman John S. Arvidson, and several other men described as "professional killers."[26]

The $1.2 million wrongful death lawsuit that Rodney Wayne Bellamy filed against Barry and Darlene had been winding its way through the courts since November of 1979. Along the way Darlene was dropped from the litigation. After that Barry's lawyer, Joe Binkley Sr., convinced a local court judge to lower the damages considerably: to a total of $10,000. Rodney Bellamy's attorney, John D. Kitch, tried to appeal that ruling to the Tennessee Supreme Court. But on October 4, 1982, the Court of Appeals of Tennessee in Nashville denied Kitch's application to appeal.[27]

The appeals court judges wrote that they upheld the greatly lowered amount mainly because of Lee Bellamy's character. They pointed to evidence that Lee "was on drugs," that he was "a violent, dangerous person," and that his repeated threats to Barry and Darlene made "a considerable contribution to his own demise." Lee "clearly asked for trouble" by trying to barge in on Darlene at her apartment on the night he died, the judges said.

"No one's life should be taken," the appeals court ruling noted, "and when a wrongful death is caused, the party responsible must pay. However, in determining that amount all surrounding circumstances should be considered."

When Barry "pled guilty in the criminal case, that was an admission that established liability, and so the only question was the amount of damages," John Kitch said in 2015. "Unfortunately, the trial judge did not believe the decedent's life was worth all that much."[28]

Barry accepted the verdict, but then decided that he would make it difficult for Rodney Bellamy to get his $10,000. Although Barry was "calm and quiet," Patricia R. Young, an attorney who worked on the case with Joe Binkley Sr., said, "the biggest thing I remember was that he said he was going to pay that judgment in pennies."[29]

Barry didn't pay the $10,000 in pennies. But neither did he pay it voluntarily, John Kitch said. "The way we collected it was that he had written a series of books [and] his agent [Robbie Robison] was collecting the royalties. I found that out and was able to run a garnishment and collect it out of the royalties. We garnished the money that came in to the agent that would have been dispersed to Sadler."

Barry pumped out three more books in 1983. *Casca* No. 8, *Soldier of Fortune in Cambodia*, appeared in April. In this one Barry took his eternal mercenary to 1976 in the aftermath of the Vietnam War when the Khmer Rouge communists took over Cambodia and carried out a holocaust against their own people. Casca's dangerous, sex-and-violence-filled task in this tale was to smuggle a family of Chinese refugees out of the hell of Khmer Rouge Cambodia.

Cry Havoc, a non-*Casca* adventure, arrived in June. This one was set in Vietnam in Ple Jrgon, a Special Forces camp in the Central Highlands that resembled Barry's former unit at Ple Do Lim. The words to "The Ballad" introduce the blood-soaked tale, in which Barry resurrects the sadistic enemy Captain Lim and the Green Beret Sergeant Reider from *The Moi*.

The unlucky Reider once again falls into Lim's clutches as a POW and suffers at the hands of his "taunting, sadistic master." Barry named a few characters in the book after people he knew: senior medic Mac Rigsby (for Billy Arr, nee Rigsby), Master Sgt. Sizemore (for his pal Gary Sizemore), and Capt. Chandler (after his real-life commanding officer at Ple Do Lim, Chandler P. Robbins III).

Casca No. 9, *The Sentinel*, came out in December. Set in the fifth and sixth centuries, in this tale the eternal mercenary fights off marauders in the Alps only to get entombed in an ice cave where he languishes for a few decades until a beautiful woman comes to his rescue. The pair move on to Constantinople, where Casca joins yet another army. This time he's fighting against a group of warriors so vicious and bloodthirsty that their name became synonymous with barbarity: the East Germanic Vandals. No surprise: Much blood is shed. The ending is not a happy one.

In early July Barry had driven to Cocoa Beach, Florida, to try to set up a gig at a place called D.J.'s Lounge located in a one-time steakhouse. While in town Barry dropped in at the annual National Green Beret Convention at the Holiday Inn on July 5. He had a few drinks and a few laughs and the guys gave him a stuffed bear dressed in fatigues. But not all went smoothly.

Not for the first time, a tipsy former Green Beret lit into Barry. "This guy I never met before comes over to me and goes, 'I don't like you,'" Barry told a local reporter, "and he doesn't say why, but I know why. He resents the success I had, that I made money off the song."

"Look man," Barry said to the guy, "I didn't cut that thing to get rich. All the money I made while I was in uniform went back into the armed services and I established a scholarship fund for the children of men who were killed in action. What did you do?" (Barry did start the foundation, but he kept the royalty money he earned from the song when he was in uniform.)

Then Barry said, "Would you turn down one million dollars if somebody offered it to you?" After which the guy, Barry said, "just kinda mumbled something and didn't answer."[30]

Barry then talked to the reporter about the Vietnam War, his role in it, his decidedly bad feelings about how his military career ended, and the state of his emotional well-being. He said he came under fire in Vietnam "about forty times," which likely was an exaggeration. "It was exciting back then," he said. "It was a good little war. It was like everything you'd ever read in books, living with savages with their teeth filed down to the bone, living on the edge. It was a tremendous experience."

He called his Vietnam War tour of duty "a romantic thing." Most "professional soldiers," he said, "are incurable romantics. It's the most intense experience you'll ever have. You maybe spend only thirty minutes in combat, but it'll be the realest thirty minutes of your life."

When the talk got around to killing, Barry did not glorify it. Nobody, he said, "cries more than a soldier, for themselves, for their buddies that die, and for their buddies . . . somewhere in the VA hospital that nobody'll ever see." Still, he said, "I'd go back again. Man is aggressive by nature, and everybody wants a high adventure in their life, and most adventures are dangerous. It's a testing ground."

Barry ended the interview reflecting—bitterly—about the fame that came his way with "The Ballad."

"I wasn't a hero," he said. "I was a manufactured hero by the media. I'm the best known soldier of the Vietnam War and that's wrong. The people who were writing all those things back then couldn't even name one Medal of Honor winner."

Barry said he volunteered to go back to Vietnam in 1966, but the army didn't want to risk the life of its most effective recruiting tool. Which is why, he said, he decided to get out.

"I could've been another figurehead" by staying in, Barry said, "but that's not what I was trained to do. It's being with the men, out there in the field. Me having to leave the service at that time was like being kicked out of your own house by your father.

"I knew nothing about being a civilian. The military was the only place I ever felt really comfortable. I'm not comfortable at all now. I probably never will be."

By the end of 1983, Barry's discomfort extended to the Sadler home front. He and Lavona fought bitterly over his womanizing and drinking. So bitterly that Barry stormed out of the house one day, threw his belongings (including his new Apple 2E personal computer) into his car, and took off. "He just kind of blew up and moved out," Bill Parrish said, "and into a trailer with a bartender who worked downtown."[31] Lavona called it a "dump."[32] Barry stayed there a short while, then found his own small apartment on Murfreesboro Road.

He had contemplated leaving the country several times in the late 1970s and early 1980s. That included "serious plans about moving to Ireland," John Buchan said, after the Irish government enacted a law exempting writers, musicians, and artists from paying income taxes on their earnings. But because of his arrest and the legal wrangling following the Bellamy killing, Buchan said, "Barry said he couldn't leave."[33]

In 1982 or 1983 Bill Parrish introduced him to an old friend, Bill Thomerson, a former Kentucky Air National Guard pilot who was involved in arms sales in Central America. After a brush with the law prevented him from leaving the country, Thomerson asked Parrish to go to Guatemala City to finish an arms deal for him. Parrish declined, but after Thomerson and Barry became friends, Parrish said, Barry said he'd do the deal.

"Sadler ended up going down there and, according to Thomerson, screwed up whatever the deal was," Parrish said. "But Barry liked it there. There were a lot of expatriates there, a lot of military types."[34]

Barry liked it so much that he decided to leave Nashville and move to Guatemala. He told some people he was going there to get into the arms business; he told others that he needed a place to write his books in peace and quiet.

"Oh, hell, I can't write around here, there's too much interference," he said to John Furgess, a Nashville Vietnam War veteran friend. "There's too much going on. I'm gonna go down there and write."[35]

Robbie Robison said Barry made the move for one simple reason. "He'd been down there a time or two and just really liked the place," Robison said. "He loved bars where a lot of guys hung out and all talked together—[whether it was] the music business or selling guns or the mercenary business. So he leased a place and came back and said, 'I'm going.'"[36]

Bill Parrish had another explanation for the move. "The simple truth is, Barry went to Guatemala to escape his failures and his rejection from the music business," Parrish said. "He had lost his sense of direction. The alcoholism, I could see it happening to him, the slow descent."[37]

CHAPTER 18

LIFE OUT ON THE EDGE

"I do exactly as I please and I get paid for it."
—BARRY SADLER, 1988

On Sunday, January 22, 1984, the phone range at Robbie Robison's house. It was Barry. He was at Nashville International Airport, on the way to open what would be the last chapter of his life, the move to Guatemala. Barry had money on his mind.

"He said, 'Let's draw up something so if I'm out of pocket, you can sign,'" Robison said. "So we did about a three-line contract." When Barry called, Robbie was heading for an appointment with country music singer Marty Stuart. "Marty never met Barry and wanted to meet him," Robbie said. So the two men drove out to the airport, where they sat down and signed the contract. Marty Stuart signed as the witness.[1]

The contract contained one typed sentence and two handwritten ones. To wit:

"I Barry Sadler, authorize my agent Rob Robison to act on my behalf in any way in all matters concerning literary properties past present and in the future. Starting on this date January 22, 1984."

Below that typewritten portion, Barry wrote in long hand: "Lavona half of all: Send her all of $4,000 Cry Havoc. I'm to keep $750 of same. Mike Clarke . . . I owe him $2,000.00. Pay out of Cry Havoc & spend the rest!"[2]

In early 1984 the Central American Republic of Guatemala was in the twenty-fourth year of what would be a thirty-six-year civil war. Leftist rebels (included many Mayan people) battled it out against a military-dominated central government headed by Gen. Óscar Humberto Mejía Víctores. A similar situation existed in neighboring El Salvador, where an insurgency led by left-wing rebels called the Farabundo Martí National Liberation Front (FMLN) carried on guerrilla actions against the military-led Salvadoran government of José Napoleón Duarte. In nearby Nicaragua the situation was reversed: The leftist Sandinista government under Daniel Ortega, which had been in power since 1979, faced a guerrilla-style revolt from a right-wing movement known as the Contras, which was supported by the United States.

Barry Sadler fit in well in this boiling cauldron of Central American armed insurrection. He either strongly hinted or stated outright to friends, strangers, and the occasional inquiring journalist that he was a player in the macho world of borderline-legal military activity. He told people he was a working mercenary; that he was an international arms dealer; that he worked as a "technical adviser" for the Guatemalan military; and that he trained Contras in counterinsurgency techniques.

Was Barry being honest or was he burnishing his image by doing what he often did—telling people what they wanted to hear? "It was very hard with Barry sometimes to tell where truth ended and the legend that Barry was creating around himself began," said Eliza Shallcross, one of his *Casca* editors.

This much is true: Barry did interact with Honduran soldiers and Contra fighters (there are photos of him with both). But most of his close friends believe that Barry was doing little more than posing for pictures while doing on-site research for his books (which he pumped out roughly every six weeks), rather than taking any active soldierly role with the Honduran military or the Nicaraguan Contras.

"From 4:00 to midnight, he drank. Midnight to 5:00 he wrote. Five to noon, he slept with women," Billy Arr, who spent time with Barry in Guatemala, said. "You tell me where he found time to be a mercenary."[3]

Barry and Ben Rosson "didn't train mercenaries or anything like that," Barry's son Thor said, calling the mercenary tales "one of the bullshit stories I've heard."[4]

Bob Brown, the founder and publisher of *Soldier of Fortune*, who knew Barry, scoffed at the idea of him as a 1980s soldier of fortune. "With my contacts," he said in 1988, "I never had his name come up" as a mercenary.[5]

Lew Millet agreed with Billy Arr, Thor, and Bob Brown. "I don't think Barry was directly involved as a soldier of fortune," Millet said in 1989. "It keeps you young to stay in touch with your old profession, and that was Barry's interest" in Guatemala.[6]

Barry "talked about Hemingway more than any other writer," his Nashville buddy Gary Sizemore said. "He admired his lifestyle. I think the mercenary stuff was all crap."[7]

As he had done virtually all his life, Barry surrounded himself with plenty of weapons in Guatemala. And he and Ben Rosson also operated some kind of arms-selling business. When *Soldier of Fortune* magazine writer Lance Motley asked Rosson in 1988 what kind of business they ran, the reply was: "We do some buyin' and some sellin'." What Rosson didn't say, Motley wrote, "is that they buy and sell everything from uniform material to heavy weapons."[8]

Barry and Rosson did some of that business in the Guatemala City equivalent of the Hall of Fame in Nashville, the Don Quixote bar in the Hotel Europa. The Don Quixote "was a bar where a lot of mercenaries who came in to do a gun deal or something along those lines, hung out," Robbie Robison, who visited Barry several times in Guatemala, said. "Barry was sort of a hero to them."[9]

Soldier of Fortune magazine portrayed the Don Quixote as a hangout for special forces veterans from all over the world, including Green Berets, SEALs, and French Legionnaires, some of whom had permanent rooms at the Europa. A good percentage were Vietnam War veterans. Nearly all were fervent anti-communists. Some of the men, the magazine said, fought with the Contras or for the military governments of El Salvador and Guatemala. Some were "retired bullfighters and some present-day ones, merchant seamen, pilots, traders, manufacturers and money changers."[10]

Two men who drank there ran a Special Assault commando school in Orangevale, California. One guy billed himself as National Director of

Air Operations for a group called Civilian Military Assistance in Memphis, which actively recruited American veterans to train and fight with the Contras. Two members of the group died in September of 1984 when the helicopter they were riding in was shot down in Nicaragua.[11] A former U.S. Army lieutenant who hung out there specialized in selling "survival tools" and "special weapons" from his Island Lake, Illinois–based business. The owner of an outfit called Base Operation School in Mesa, Arizona, offered guerrilla training, survival medicine, and seminars, all "given by Green Berets."[12]

Some of the denizens of the Don Quixote were always armed; that included Rosson, who sometimes carried a hand grenade. Duke Faglier (described by *Soldier of Fortune* as "a long-time veteran and old friend of Barry's, now a security consultant in Europe but a frequent visitor to the bar") called the scene, "life out at the edge."

Barry rented a large hacienda on two acres outside Guatemala City, complete with a gardener and a cook, for $300 a month. "He also had Maritza, his aide-de-camp," Robbie said. The place "was surrounded by a seven-or-eight-foot-tall fence. You had an opening [in the fence] coming in from the road with two pretty large gates and you could lock them. There was a courtyard in front of the house. There were three or four bedrooms. And the house had a big living room with a fireplace."[13]

Barry, who spoke Spanish, named the place Rancho Barracho, "Drunkard's Ranch." Barry more than lived up to that name there and at the Don Quixote. He worked and partied "with an intensity that might have crippled a man half his age," John Ed Bradley wrote.

"Don't tell anybody what a great deal I've got here," he told Billy Arr on the phone one day, "because they'll all want to come down."[14]

Barry, Duke Faglier said in 1989, "lived like a king. Long-necked beers are thirty cents. The best-looking hooker in Guatemala City costs thirty dollars." In Guatemala, a Nashville friend said, Barry "had like fifteen different girlfriends. I'd get envelopes full of snapshots. Barry with his arms around all these women, all looking up to him adoringly."[15]

Motley's *Soldier of Fortune* article referred to "Maggie, Barry's pretty Guatemalan girlfriend." It included a posed photo of the young woman sitting next to Barry at the Don Quixote, with her long black curly hair cascading below her shoulders, her arm around him. A salt-and-pepper-bearded Barry, a half grin on his face, a lit cigarette in his hand, sits in front of a giant Jack Daniel's bottle on a table, along with a hand grenade and what appears to be an Uzi submachine gun.

Barry professed contentment with his life in Guatemala. "Hell," he told *Soldier of Fortune*, "I was raised in a little Colorado mining town. Never in my wildest dreams did I ever think I would have the life that I've had. I have been almost everywhere and have done almost everything. Even now I do exactly as I please and I get paid for it. I even have a beautiful, 21-year-old woman that thinks a fat old man [Barry was forty-eight] like me is sexy. What more can a man ask?"[16]

For the next four and a half years, Barry held court among the men of action who came to Guatemala at his rancho ("He always had company," Robison said) and at the Don Quixote. During that time Barry also pumped out eighteen books, thirteen in the *Casca* series and five stand-alone action adventure novels. The first, *Casca 10, The Conquistador*, in which the mercenary fights with Cortez in sixteenth-century Mexico (which Barry had written in Nashville), came out in February of 1984. The last one, *Casca 22, The Mongol*, was published on January 1, 1990, two months after Barry's death.

It wasn't all drinking and carousing in Guatemala. Barry accumulated a large closetful of rudimentary medical supplies at the rancho. He treated his neighbors, most of whom could not afford to pay a doctor, for free, and paid medical visits to Mayan villages, where many Indians lived subsistence lives. "He did lots for people down there," Robbie said.[17] Barry reveled in the fact that some Indians called him by the Hemingway-esque name "Papa Gringo."

Several times a month Barry "drives his battered Honda Civic into isolated Indian villages," *People* magazine's Deirdre Donohue wrote in the summer of 1986. "Armed with drugs and his Special Forces medical handbook," Barry "treats everything from TB to parasites. 'It's only what I did in Vietnam,' says Sadler, 'meatball medicine.'"[18]

A "Green Beret is not always a killer. He is a teacher. He is there to help," a veteran told journalist Cynthia Cotts, who wrote a long article about Barry in the *Village Voice* in 1989.[19]

When "a prostitute picked up the clap, she went to Papa Gringo for a shot of penicillin," John Ed Bradley wrote. "When an Indian kid broke an arm, Mama hauled him off to the white man who liked to wear a T-shirt that said, in Spanish, 'SANDINISTAS AND COMMUNISTS ARE THE SAME THING.'"[20]

The other positive thing Barry did in Guatemala for nearly four years was research and write the *Casca* books and the stand-alone action adventure novels. He banged them out on a Zenith Data Systems computer (which replaced the Apple 2e) and mailed the pages to his editors in New York City. Robbie took care of the business details.

And it was a business. Barry needed income and the books provided it; they sold extremely well, pushing his advances for each new book into the $15,000 to $20,000 range—a not insignificant sum for a mass market paperback in the mid-1980s. Barry occasionally called his editors with updates and questions, but he never showed up at their offices in New York City.

"We spoke on the phone and we communicated by letter," Hank Schlesinger said. "He didn't come up here." Barry "called me, usually. When I called him, I would get his housekeeper and I'd have a woman in the office talk to her because I don't speak Spanish."[21]

"We didn't call him; he called us," Eliza Shallcross said. "He was impossible to get hold of. And he didn't call very often. Pretty much he just sent the manuscripts in. But the books were good enough that we were willing to keep on doing them." On the other hand, she said, the "books were always late and I think he was getting bored with the series. He was sort of running out of ideas. There were other things in his life that were more interesting. But the money was nice."

Still, Shallcross said, "Barry wasn't a troublemaker. He was a nice guy and he was really funny. When he said he'd write something, he did deliver. Even though he was erratic, the manuscripts did come in and they were good."

"We got the manuscripts in a box," Jim Morris, who edited the last two *Casca* books, said, "usually one that would hold a ream of paper. Because those books weren't a ream worth of paper, usually there'd be a little crumpled stuff to fill it out." Barry, Morris said, was a "guy who had his [writing] chops down. You had to edit them; you didn't have to re-write them."[22]

Schleshinger said he edited each book "to be a fun read. I knew I wasn't editing Faulkner. You want to keep the story moving. . . . You moved it along."

Basically, "the way we dealt with the *Casca* books was that we really didn't," Shallcross said. "Technically, I was his editor, but it was only just kind of shuffling them through. He had his vision for the series. He knew his market. He was doing a good job with it. It was a bit like he would turn in a manuscript when he felt like it and he needed the money. And then he'd go off [somewhere] and life would go on in New York. We'd publish the book and then Barry would turn up again and send us a new proposal."

Barry was coming close to running out of *Casca* story lines, though, because by 1988 he had had his eternal mercenary fight in a high percentage of the best-known wars in history. The books he wrote in Guatemala alone had Casca in World Wars I and II, the French Indochina War, the Vietnam War, the 1954–1962 Algerian War, the Boxer Rebellion, the Yom Kippur War, and rebellions and other military machinations across the centuries in Africa, the Middle East, and Asia.

Barry also appeared to be wearying of life in Guatemala. He told friends he didn't want to write any more *Casca* books. He told *Soldier of Fortune* magazine that he and Rosson planned to "take an around-the-world business trip selling weapons."[23] He said he wanted to write a literary novel called *One More Time* that he hoped would be a best seller.

"It would be a Vietnam War novel featuring the lives of the dead as well as of the living," John Ed Bradley wrote. "There would be ghosts galore, legions and legions of killed American soldiers returned to fight and win a war that had been lost some twenty years ago."[24] No such book saw the light of day.

Barry made a few short trips to the United States during his time in Guatemala. He flew to New Orleans early in July of 1985 to make an appearance at the annual Special Forces Association Convention. Sometime in 1986 he turned up at Fort Benning in Georgia where—acting out a line from "The Ballad"—he literally pinned the silver jump wings on his son Thor's chest after the young man had finished Army Airborne training.

In July of 1988 Barry showed up at a fund-raising event in Jerome, Pennsylvania, for the newly formed Johnstown, Pennsylvania, Vietnam Veterans of America chapter. Barry sang "The Ballad" and several other tunes at two shows.

"Both shows were absolutely packed," said Tom Haberkorn, a founding member of the chapter. "I said to him, 'We served in Vietnam together at different times,'" Haberkorn joked. "But he wasn't a real sociable type of guy. He kind of gave me a surly look."[25]

Back in Guatemala in September, Barry called Lavona and told her that he wanted to come home so—among other things—he could get to know his ten-year-old daughter, Brooke. During the call Lavona thanked Barry for the last check he'd sent her, adding that she hadn't asked for it.

"You're the only one who never has," Barry said.

"Barry," Lavona replied, "you sound so remote."

"What do you expect?" he said. "I'm two thousand miles away." And then he told Lavona he wanted to come home.

"You're not lying to make me feel good, are you?" she asked.

"I was afraid to approach you about coming back," Barry said, "because I was afraid you'd say no."[26]

CHAPTER 19
THE CONSTITUTION OF AN ELEPHANT

"Sadler had a reputation of playing with loaded guns and even pulling the trigger when he was drinking."
—Bob Brown, publisher,
Soldier of Fortune magazine, 1990

Late on Friday night, September 7, 1988, Barry poured himself into a taxi cab in Guatemala City after yet another day (and night) of heavy drinking. According to Ben Rosson, he and Barry had spent most of the day "horsing around town," drinking and waiting for two friends to fly into Guatemala City.[1]

That night Rosson and Barry had just finished an alcohol-fueled dinner at a restaurant, after which Rosson left with a friend and Barry stayed behind to have a nightcap or two.[2] When he was ready to go home, Barry made his way onto the street, where he flagged down a cabbie he knew. He asked the guy to take him to Rancho Barracho and hopped into the passenger seat in the front. Before long Barry spotted a young woman of his acquaintance, had the driver stop the cab, and offered her a ride. The woman accepted. She plopped down in the back.

As usual, Barry was armed. That night he carried a small, but deadly, steel-and-chrome .38 Beretta semi-automatic pistol, a Cheetah 84, a weapon that Israeli police officers, among others, favored. Barry was in a good mood, expansive and joking in the front seat—and waving the Beretta around. The cab driver got nervous, Rosson said, and asked Barry to put the gun away. He didn't. Then, according to Rosson, the pistol went off. A .38 round blew into Barry's head at his upper right temple next to his ear. The bullet went clean through his skull, exiting at the hairline on the other side of his head. It ended up embedded in the taxi's headliner.

Ironically—and eerily—Barry very nearly described his own horrific condition in the first few pages of the first *Casca* book, *The Eternal Mercenary*, which he wrote nine years earlier. Casca, in the guise of an American soldier, Sgt. Casey Romain, is on a stretcher in an army hospital in Nha Trang after being shot in the head. The "stocky, powerfully built man," Barry wrote in 1979, had an "exposed brain." The "open area of the brain was about four inches long and three inches wide and ran up to where the part in a man's hair would normally be. This section of the skull had been just simply blown away; an adjoining section was held on by a flap of skin."[3]

The cab driver sped off to the hospital. The Guatemalan police, according to Rosson, questioned the driver and the female passenger "extensively." The police concluded—based on physical evidence, including finding the bullet in the headliner and the cartridge case on the floor of the cab—that the shooting was accidental.

Soldier of Fortune publisher Bob Brown, who met Barry at several 1980s *Soldier of Fortune* conventions where he performed "The Ballad," believed the Guatemalan police got it right. "Sadler had a reputation for playing with loaded guns and even pulling the trigger when he was drinking," Brown said in 1990. "There were holes in his house from when these situations had occurred. So I tend to think he just had an accident."[4]

But few of Barry's friends and family members believed that he shot himself. Rumors flew that he was the victim of a robbery, or a hit ordered by a rival arms dealer or by the CIA or the KGB, or that a disgruntled former girlfriend shot him. Or that he took a bullet ordered by a Guatemalan government official because Barry was having an affair with his wife. Or that Ben Rosson himself did the deed.

Barry shooting himself accidentally was "the biggest horse manure I ever heard," Robbie Robison said, "because there's one thing about Barry: He knew weapons, drunk or sober. Besides, there's no one who liked money better than him, and he knew I had [just made a book] deal for us to make some more money."[5]

Duke Faglier had little doubt what happened. "Rosson shot Barry with one of my guns," he told John Ed Bradley. "It's a .223 Heckler and Koch [semi-automatic] rifle that I'd left down there at the ranch."[6] A bullet from a Beretta .38 pistol would have made a much larger entry wound in Barry's head than the bullet that hit him did, Duke said. Plus, "if someone's shot at close range, it leaves powder burns," and Duke claimed that he did not see any evidence of powder burns at the entry wound.[7]

Duke said that Rosson killed Barry for two reasons. "One was jealousy, the other greed," he said. "He was jealous because Barry was fucking his girlfriend, and he was greedy because they were selling helicopters to the Guatemalan army and Rosson wanted to cut Barry out of the deal."

Ben Rosson vehemently denied the allegation. It's "the dumbest fucking thing I ever heard in my life," he told Bradley in 1990. "If you ask me, Duke is jealous of the relationship I had with Barry. He liked to pass himself off as a big professional hired gun when all he knows how to do is play guitar. . . . Last I heard, he was selling 'em—guitars—somewhere in Georgia and lying to everyone about what a big hero he was. . . . Duke's a fucking liar."[8]

When Cynthia Cotts asked Rosson in Guatemala City why he thought Duke and other people accused him of shooting Barry, Rosson replied: "I don't know why but I'd like for the sons of bitches to come down here and say it to my face."[9]

Barry Sadler did not die in Guatemala. "He suffered a very traumatic injury. As described to me, half his head had been blown away," Hal Hardin, Lavona Sadler's Nashville attorney, said. "Hell, any mortal man would have died sustaining a blow like that."[10]

If Barry had remained in the hospital in Guatemala City, he probably would have died. That's the conclusion his friends came to when they learned he had taken a bullet in the head and was in critical condition. Three days after Barry was shot, on September 10, 1988, Robbie Robison and Duke Faglier—with crucial financial help from Bob Brown—arranged to fly Barry to Nashville in a private jet.

"I got a phone call from Guatemala from Ben Rosson from the Don Quixote," Robbie said. "And he said, 'Barry's been shot and they say he's got a ten percent chance of living and is on life support in a local hospital.'"[11] Robbie sprang into action. He put in a call to Barry's ranch. "He had a family staying there. I called them and said, 'Don't touch anything. Don't let anybody in and don't let anybody take anything out of there until you hear from me.'"

Robbie then called Duke in Atlanta, and they figured out the best way to get Barry out of Guatemala City. "Duke and I started making calls," Robbie said. "In two hours we put together a plan. We decided that [Duke] would go to Guatemala to see if Barry could be moved. I would stay here and arrange for ambulances, hospitals and doctors, etc. We got a Lear jet, two pilots, two battlefield nurses and a neurosurgeon to fly to Guatemala. And Duke went to meet them. Then they went to the hospital—Duke and the nurses—to see if Barry could be moved."

The money for the jet came from a $9,050 loan from Bob Brown, who paid for the plane (owned by Ambassador Airways of Naples, Florida) using his company's American Express Platinum credit card. Brown said he put the money up after Duke called him and said Barry would not survive in the Guatemalan hospital, that Duke didn't have enough money to pay for a plane, and that the operators of air ambulances "would not fly without payment in advance." Brown agreed to cover the cost after Duke assured him that he would be reimbursed "as soon as the immediate emergency had passed."[12]

When he arrived at the hospital in Guatemala City, Duke immediately saw that Barry was in bad shape. "His eyes," Duke said, "were thin needle squints, black and glassy. . . . Blisters had formed on the heels of his feet because he hadn't been turned much since the shooting. . . . His lips were white and bloodless, his ears sort of blue."[13]

Duke and the medical team, Robbie said, "figured he could be [moved] so they got him on a gurney, took him out to the plane, and put him in a body bag to get him on the plane. The nurses were fabulous. The plane was getting ready to take off and the tower said to hold the plane for a minute. Duke pulled out his .45 and said, 'Put us in the air, we're going home.'"

Duke told Bradley that the plane dodged a hurricane in the Caribbean and refueled at Key West. Barry at that point "was fleshy, bloated," Duke said. "You never would have known what an athlete he once was. A stubble had grown on his face; his hair was plastered to his scalp. He looked dead already."

The plane, Robbie said, "landed [in Key West] and we got another plane to come in and they transferred Barry. Myself and two ambulance guys and the guy from [the local] ABC [television station] waited and waited" at the Nashville airport. "Then, about seven hours later . . . in the evening—it had just gotten dark—here it comes. As the plane got close to Nashville, [we] heard a radio from the plane saying that the nurses were losing Barry."

They didn't lose him. The plane landed and taxied over to where the two Nashville EMTs and Robbie were waiting on the tarmac. The nurses, dressed in scrubs, and a bearded Duke, wearing a tight turquoise polo shirt and blue jeans, emerged from the plane. They needed help to get Barry out the door. It took seven people to manage it. One nurse held an IV bag, one held the ventilator mask pressed over Barry's mouth and nose. White-shirted EMTs slowly helped maneuver the awkward blue body bag they used as a sling out the jet's door and down the few steps onto the tarmac. The group then positioned Barry on a gurney and strapped him in tightly.

Duke turned to Robbie and said, "He's stable. He's got a fifty-fifty chance. . . . We had a little problem in Key West . . . another plane had to come and get us. . . . These ladies were saints."

As the ambulance drove off the tarmac, the driver shouted out the window: "Vanderbilt or the VA? Is it the VA?"[14]

It was both. A team of neurosurgeons from Vanderbilt University Medical Center operated on Barry at the adjacent Nashville VA Medical Center. Lavona had rushed to the hospital and signed the required permission forms. The operation began at 1:40 on the afternoon of September 13. It took nearly seven hours.

The doctors performed a tracheostomy—cutting a hole through Barry's neck into his windpipe to help him breath. They then began the main operation, a frontal craniotomy, in which the surgeons removed a piece of bone from Barry's skull in order to get to the dead and damaged blood, tissue, and bullet residue and clean out the wound around the two frontal lobes of his brain. The operation also included what's known as elevation of depressed skull fracture; that is, removing the parts of Barry's skull bone that were broken by the bullet and reassembling them with metallic plates and screws.

Barry was then taken to intensive care. The doctors listed him in critical condition. He fell into a coma. "His chances of survival were ten percent in Guatemala and they are fifty percent here," Duke told reporters in Nashville that day. "They just had no facilities to treat him there. I knew we had to get him out of there."

Duke went on to say that he believed Barry had been murdered. "He had death threats written on the walls [of his ranch] saying 'Die Gringo.' Gunshots had been fired into his building."[15] Duke also said that he and Barry were training Contras in Honduras.

The truth is that Barry may have had death threats, but no one else reported that anyone fired into Barry's ranch house. And it's all but certain Barry was not training the Contras.

Robbie and Lavona visited Barry in the VA hospital the next day. Robbie told reporters that "from what we know, it was an attempted robbery. He was on his way home in a cab. He's been living down there. He writes down there and lives temporarily on a ranch outside of Guatemala [City]."[16] The next day Robbie reported that it was "nip and tuck on whether [Barry] pulls through. The biggest thing was getting him out of Guatemala."[17] The operation "was successful," Robbie added. "The doctor told us to maintain hope. With these things, it takes time to see how the brain will heal."[18]

Barry's "head was huge with all the blood in his brain," Lavona said. "And he had a tube going into his brain." As a former nurse, she said, "that didn't bother me, but it's not pleasant to look at. The doctor was trying to warn me, but I knew it wasn't going to be pretty."[19]

Following the surgery, Lavona met with one of the neurosurgeons in the VA hospital waiting room. The doctor told her that Barry had lost about a third of his brain mass and that his chances for surviving were bleak. He also said that it appeared that Barry had been shot—not with a pistol—but with a "high-powered rifle."[20]

Bill Parrish also had a talk with the surgeon. "He said that he had seen a lot of gunshot wounds, and that [Barry was hit with] a .223 rifle. . . . [The bullet] exited through the opposite side of his forehead. He doubled his fist and showed me where it had exited."[21]

Barry remained in a coma for more than a month. But within a week after the operation, doctors began issuing cautiously optimistic reports about his recovery prospects. "He's got the constitution of an elephant," Bebe Sadler told a newspaper reporter in Denver (where she lived) on September 15 after speaking to his doctor in Nashville. "Even in a coma, he responds to pain. They say his prospects look really good."[22]

On September 23 Robbie announced that Barry was "improving every day. They are not saying if he will come out of the coma, they are saying 'when.' The doctors feel he will come out of it very soon."[23] Three weeks later, on October 15, came more encouraging news. "He is doing much better," Robbie said. "He moves sometimes and he opens his eyes some, but we can't make a real prognosis until he comes out of the coma."[24]

Robbie visited Barry nearly every day. "He was out," Robbie said. "They had him all covered up. They finally took the bandages off and he had a concave on one side. He didn't open his eyes. One day I visited him and the doctor said, 'Talk to him, talk to him, talk to him.'" So Robbie—who is no slouch in the talking department—started talking to his old friend and business partner.

Barry, Robbie said, "opened his eyes. The nurse said, 'Robbie, walk around the bed.' And I did and Barry followed me. He couldn't move his head, but he followed me with his eyes. That went on for—I don't know—two weeks or so. He never said anything."

Then, in late October, Robbie said, "They were feeding him some ice. I'm in there and talking to him and I'm getting ready to leave and I get to the door and there's a word come out, 'Robbie.'

"Man, the hair came out on the back of my neck. It was Barry."[25]

CHAPTER 20
THE LAST BATTLE OF THE VIETNAM WAR

"I hate her guts, and if I could, I would kill her."
—BEBE SADLER ON LAVONA SADLER, NOVEMBER 1988

The good news: Barry came out of the coma. The not-so-good news: The operation left him all but paraplegic (he had very limited movement in his right arm) and with severely limited cognitive ability. The tracheostomy the doctors performed when they operated on him affected his speech; he could barely speak above a whisper.

Barry could speak, though, and "was well aware of what was going on around him," Lavona Sadler said in 2015, "but he was not always cohesive. I remember when Thor came by with his eventual wife, Dare, when Thor introduced him to Dare, he said, 'Oh, Dare to be great.' And when Baron came in uniform to see him, he kept calling Baron 'Thor' because he had a uniform on. He didn't think Baron would ever go into the military."[1]

Lavona said she "was glad that he had his faculties." One day Barry "tried to bite me on my finger. He used to do that [playfully] before he was shot, way back when. But in the hospital, I [let him do] it because he wanted to and he bit me. That scared me."[2]

When Bill Parrish came to visit, one of the VA nurses told him that Barry "probably wouldn't recognize me," Parrish said. "When I went in, [the nurse] said, 'Do you know who this is?' And Sadler said, 'Bill.'" On the other hand, Parrish said, Barry soon became deadly serious. "Just about all he would say was 'help me,' because I know he wouldn't have wanted to live in that condition."[3]

Earl Owens, who spoke to Barry on the phone during his hospital stay, never made an appearance at the VA. That's because when he spoke to Barry, Owens said, he "didn't sound good at all. He said, 'You don't want to see me like this, Earl.'"[4]

One person who did want to see Barry: his mother, Bebe, who showed up at the hospital not long after he came out of the coma. When Barry heard that his mother was in the building, he was not happy.

"I remember Barry saying, 'Put sentries at the door,'" Lavona said.[5] Although Barry may have been joking, given Bebe's track record as a disruptive influence in his life, there's little doubt that he was not happy to see her.

Bebe—whom Barry and Lavona hadn't seen or spoken to in about ten years— had written a letter to Barry from Denver on October 17. In it she made no mention of their long estrangement. Instead she expressed her deep love for him and Lavona and their children, along with her fervent wish that he get well soon.

"To my angel," the letter begins. "Remember when you were small I always called you my 'Angel Baby.' Now you are my dearest and favorite archangel. . . . I truly believe as you always said you are indestructible . . . I know that with all your knowledge of the power of the mind, you can heal yourself as before. Hippocrates said, remember, physician heal yourself.

"Think of the lost time as if you're taking a long deserved rest, practice meditation & relax & rest your poor overworked mind.

"I pray daily to 'mother Earth,' our creator. I feel she has her strong arms around you, giving you strength from the earth & Soon you will be filled with an abundance of adrenaline.

"I know you are a loving father & that your children love you dearly, and your strength & wisdom & your great love will make fine men & a wonderful lovely lady of your intelligent little daughter.

"I'll be back allways [sic] as often as you need me. I'm all ways as close as the phone.

"I have almost completely defeated my arthritis. So don't worry about me. I really [am] quite fit. I have a new ski exercising machine. . . .

"I can't tell you how sorry I am that you are suffering as I don't know enough descriptive adjectives to even express or explain how terribly I am hurting & my heart is broken again for you. (How many times I can't count.)

"I want to congratulate you & Lavona on the excellent job you have done rearing your beautiful daughter & handsome sons.

"I close as I don't want to tire or bore you. You never liked long letters.

"Rest my beloved Angel.

"Much, much Love, Bebe

"P.S. I see a lot of Delfino. [He] is a great comfort to me & grieves for you. He sends all his love & will be there when you want him. —Mom"[6]

Early in November, a few weeks after he came out of the coma, the VA doctors decided to move Barry temporarily to a specialized rehabilitation treatment center, the Wade Park Unit, at the VA hospital in Cleveland, Ohio. He would be returned to Nashville for extended care on January 9, 1989, after completing the two-month program. Although Lavona agreed to the transfer to Cleveland, she was not thrilled about it.

"I have no idea why he was sent up to Ohio," Lavona said in 2015. "That never made sense to me—never, never, never."[7]

Nevertheless, the move came on November 8, 1988. Except for being more than 500 miles from his family, all went reasonably well for nearly two months. Then all hell broke loose.

It started when Bebe Sadler, who was seventy-one, moved from Denver into an apartment in Cleveland sometime early in December and hooked up with two former Green Berets, Paul Hill and Stephen Somers, the latter a Cleveland-area attorney.[8] "She basically showed up out of nowhere," Hal Hardin, the prominent Nashville attorney Lavona hired to represent her and the children in the ensuing legal battle over Barry's treatment, said. "She lived in Denver, flew into Cleveland, and moved into the apartment—it appears—of one of the other lawyers."[9]

Bebe, Hill, and Somers—along with a few other Special Forces veterans and Hill's wife, Phyllis, and daughter Dianna—made frequent visits to Barry in the hospital. They found, they said, that Barry was being treated abysmally. "They left Barry Sadler lying in his own [excrement]," Hill later said. "His urine bag was so full, it pulled the catheter out" and the "nurses wouldn't get him up and take him to therapy like they were supposed to."[10]

While there were problems at the Cleveland VA hospital, it's difficult to believe that those serious charges about Barry's care were true.[11] For one thing Barry Sadler was a famous patient and it's almost certain that if he had received any ill treatment, the Cleveland (and national) media would have found out and reported it. Second, except for Hill and Somers, no one who visited Barry reported anything out of the ordinary about his care and treatment. Plus, hospital officials denied that there was mistreatment.

Whether or not the VA mistreated Barry, his mother, Hill, and Somers also came to believe that Lavona and the children were doing little more than waiting for him to die. They soon took it upon themselves to be Barry's protectors.

In doing so they all but excluded people they viewed as not on their team from talking to Barry in his hospital room. Barry "had these self-appointed guardians . . . who were telling me I couldn't visit him and couldn't even look at him," said Bob Sipchen, a *Los Angeles Times* reporter who flew to Cleveland to write a feature article about Barry. "Somehow, I was able to b.s. my way in [to his room] with them. We got to his bedside and these guys who thought they were his bodyguards were with me."[12]

During his short visit Sipchen found Barry sitting in a wheelchair, "his toes sticking out from blue hospital slippers, a panther tattoo on his thick arm partly concealed in light-blue hospital pajamas." Barry looked "strong as a bull," Sipchen wrote in 1989. "A corduroy Giants [baseball] cap is pulled down over his head, almost concealing the fact that one side of his head is caved in."[13]

Sipchen handed Barry his business card. Barry read his name out loud, "quivering slightly." Sipchen then asked him a few questions. Barry answered "direct questions with brief phrases," Sipchen reported. "More complicated questions leave him silent; his eyes flicker and roll up as if the answer might be printed on the red brim of his cap."

"Who would you like to have custody of you?" Sipchen asked.

"My wife," Barry whispered.

"Where would you like to stay while you're being treated?"

"Nashville."

Sipchen said that Bebe, Hill, and Somers later told him that was the first time Barry "had answered those questions this way."

Then Sipchen asked Barry what he wanted to tell people who cared about him about his condition.

"Leave me alone," Barry replied.

Did he want to talk about how he was shot?

"No."

Are there people out to hurt him?

"Yes."

When Sipchen asked who those enemies were, Barry didn't respond.

"He just chews his gum and gives his famous killer stare."

Bebe soon instigated what Cleveland *Plain Dealer* reporter Karen Farkas called a "public feud" with Lavona over who should direct Barry's medical care. She lashed out at her daughter-in-law, claiming, for one thing, that Lavona (whom she just had congratulated in the October 17 letter for doing a great job raising her kids) maliciously had told her children that she was dead. Barry, Bebe also said, "knows what people are talking about, and all he wants is peace and quiet. His wife is a witch and wants to put him in a nursing home to deteriorate and die."[14] She wants "Barry to stay a vegetable."[15]

"I hate her guts," Bebe told another reporter. "And if I could, I would kill her."[16]

"It was high drama," Hal Hardin said. Bebe "thought this was some giant conspiracy with unknown people and the government, etc., to kill Barry."[17]

In addition to the encouragement from Somers and Hill, Bebe had support in her vitriolic attack on Lavona from other SF veterans. That included James M. Perry, a former Green Beret lieutenant who claimed that he had served with Barry at Fort Bragg in 1966 and said that he was "a close, personal friend."

Perry wrote a letter to Paul Hill—in care of the local Special Forces Association Chapter XLV—saying he was concerned about Barry's welfare. An "injured man in Barry's condition needs the love and attention of his mother," Perry wrote, "rather than the discompassionate personal-desire-for-gain attitudes of an estranged wife with a well-versed reputation for promiscuity. Will she be willing to sit beside him hourly and hold his hand as a mother will, if need be?"[18]

If "you listened to them, you'd think I was a whore," Lavona said. "I don't care about the money. I just want Barry to get better."[19]

Bebe, Hill, Somers, Perry, and others "thought that we were part of a conspiracy to take Barry back [to Nashville] or we really wanted to kill him," Hal Hardin said in 2015. "There were all kinds of crazy allegations being made. And all we were doing was—as a family, we [said we] would just like to have him back home in a hospital. It was that simple."[20]

Lavona later told a reporter that she "didn't even want custody" of Barry and that she "was concerned about his welfare. Period."[21]

Thor Sadler, age twenty-four, said that Bebe and her former Green Beret allies were acting out of financial greed, trying to gain control of Barry's medical care only to get their hands on his money. "If money is my grandmother's motivation for keeping my father up there," Thor said, "then she's in for a surprise. My dad is broke."[22]

Not just broke. Thor said that Barry owed more than $100,000 in back taxes and penalties to the IRS; an additional $50,000 to the hospital in Guatemala City; and $3,000 in legal fees. Thor spoke disparagingly of his grandmother, saying, "She and the so-called friends of my father's in Cleveland believe there is a pot of gold hidden somewhere."

Somers and Hill showed up at the VA hospital on Christmas day 1988—not to bring Barry holiday greetings, but to remove him from the hospital. But security personnel stopped them because the men had no legal authority to do so. So, on January 5, 1989, Somers filed a petition in Cuyahoga County Probate Court to have Bebe named Barry's legal guardian. On January 8, 1989, before any legal ruling came down—and just hours before Barry was to be moved back to Nashville—Somers and Hill returned to the hospital with Bebe.

They made their way into Barry's room, where Barry told them—they said—that he wanted to leave the hospital but to stay in Cleveland. They then produced a document that Somers had drawn up appointing Bebe his legal guardian. Since Barry couldn't move his arm or hand,[23] it appears that the men held his hand and guided it on the dotted line, although all they could manage was a shaky "X" for his signature. Somers then notarized the document.

Then they packed up Barry's few belongings, placed him in a wheelchair, and took him to the lobby. A "hospital official," Somers said, tried to prevent them from taking Barry out, saying that he was brain dead.

"I told him, 'Listen . . . you go over and ask him,'" Somers later said.[24] When the man did, he looked "startled," Somers said, when Barry said he wanted to leave. Then Somers and Hill proffered the paperwork authorizing Bebe to take charge of her son.

"Barry Sadler was discharged at his request," Somers said. "The VA complied with Barry's verbal request to be discharged immediately."[25]

The men didn't tell the family—or anyone else—what they were doing or where they were taking Barry. That first night they moved Barry into an apartment in Cleveland. Then they took him to a private Cleveland-area hospital, Southwest General Hospital in Middleburg Heights.

On January 10, when Lavona found out that Barry had been taken out of the hospital, Hal Hardin filed suit on behalf of her, Thor, Baron, Brooke, and Robbie Robison in Probate Court in Nashville. "The word we had was the ex–Green Berets had come and taken" Barry, Hardin said, "and we needed to act quickly."[26]

The suit petitioned the court to appoint a guardian for Barry and to issue a temporary restraining order prohibiting Bebe, Somers, and Hill from interfering with his "safety, health, and welfare."[27]

In the suit the family claimed that Somers and Hill "interfered" with Barry's "treatment, rehabilitation, and hospitalization." The men "claim to be friends of Barry Sadler," the suit said, but "in actuality Mr. Somers and Mr. Hill are merely residents of Cleveland, Ohio, who did not even know Barry Sadler until he was sent to" Cleveland for treatment. The suit went on to allege that Somers and Hill provided Barry "with cigarettes and alcohol, which have been prohibited by his doctors."

"Why in the world would they give him alcohol?" Lavona said. "That's how crazy these people were. I just know [they] took him out of the hospital for no reason other than that maybe [Bebe] thought he had money. You have no idea what I went through. But Barry went through worse."[28]

The lawsuit noted that Barry had sustained "massive head injuries and permanent brain damage," was "unable to attend to his business affairs, make rational decisions or control all of his bodily functions." What's more, he had a "life-threatening blood clot in his left leg" and the decision to discharge himself was "not in his best medical interest." Bebe, Hill, and Somers's motives, the suit said, "may be based upon the erroneous belief that Barry Sadler has a considerable estate."

At "the present time," the suit noted, "the whereabouts of Barry Sadler is unknown."

Bebe, Somers, and Hill stuck to their story that Lavona and the VA were mistreating Barry and that he asked to get out of the hospital and into his mother's care. "All this garbage about him being abducted, etc. is pure manure," Somers said. "The person on duty simply asked him what he wanted to do. . . . They realized this man is totally coherent. He is presumed to be competent unless proved otherwise. There was no underhandedness, no collusion. It was his own request. Period."[29]

It's possible Barry was thinking clearly when he indicated that he wouldn't mind getting out of the hospital and having a drink and a smoke. Nevertheless, Thor and Lavona said that Barry was not even close to being "totally coherent" or competent to make his own health care decisions.

"Dad's like a parrot," Thor said. "You tell him one thing and he'll repeat it. His logic center is gone. I don't know what these people's motives are. They shouldn't be there in the first place."[30]

In the next few days, newspaper headlines across the country sensationalized the situation. To wit: "Songwriter Sadler Exits Hospital; Family in Dark," "Singing Soldier Disappears," "Singer Barry Sadler Vanishes," "Ailing 'Green Beret' Author Focus of Guardianship Fight," "Search for Sadler," "Writer Sadler Object of Family's Search," "Barry Sadler Checks Out . . . and Vanishes."[31]

Meanwhile, back in Nashville, Davidson County Probate Judge Jim Everett appointed Thor Sadler as his father's temporary guardian. He also named Nashville attorney Philip W. Duer, a Vietnam War veteran, as guardian ad litem. In that temporary position for the length of the litigation, Duer was given the power to protect Barry's interests and make health care and other decisions based on what he believed would be in Barry's best interest.

Then Thor, Hal Hardin, and his associate James A. Davis Jr. flew to Cleveland to argue their case—despite the fact that the family did not know Barry's whereabouts. Hill and Somers convinced attorney Joseph Patrick Meissner—a Cleveland native, Harvard Law graduate, and 5th Special Forces Vietnam War veteran—to represent Barry.

Meissner announced on January 11 that he had spoken to Barry. He said Barry told him that he didn't want to go to Tennessee. When asked about Barry's whereabouts, Meissner refused to answer, saying instead: "He does not want publicity, and I feel he has rights that people should listen to." Barry "certainly needs good medical care," Meissner added, "and I would hope that that's what everyone cooperates to see that he gets it."

When asked who was paying for Barry's stay in what was presumed to be a Cleveland-area private hospital, Meissner answered: "He doesn't have any money."[32]

"I hope," Meissner said, "this doesn't turn into the last battle of the Vietnam War."

Cuyahoga Probate Court judge John J. Donnelly—who had been a trial referee, court administrator, and judge for the Probate Court for twenty years—held a hearing in the ornate, French Classical Revival Cuyahoga County Courthouse on January 13 to consider Bebe's petition to be appointed Barry's guardian. Joseph Meissner indicated that Barry would show up at the hearing. He did not. Somers, representing Bebe; Davis, representing Lavona, the children, and Robbie Robison; and Meissner, representing Barry, appeared before Judge Donnelly.

After conferring by phone with Judge Everett in Nashville, Donnelly ordered that Barry undergo a psychiatric evaluation. He also issued a temporary restraining order prohibiting the family from moving Barry out of Southwest General Hospital. The order also urged that Thor be permitted "to visit and confer" with his father.[33]

Before the psychiatric exam the court had appointed a magistrate, Alan Shankman, to investigate Barry's competency. Shankman had examined Barry on January 10 in what he erroneously called "a home owned by an ex-military acquaintance"—that is, the apartment where Somers and Hill deposited Barry before they checked him into Southwest General. Barry and his "friends," Shankman reported, said that he "had been self-discharged, apparently against medical advice," from the VA hospital because of "fears of a transfer" back to the Nashville VA hospital. No one mentioned anything about Barry being mistreated at the Cleveland VA.

Shankman asked Barry a series of questions that centered on the fight over his medical care. Barry "was unable to speak beyond a whisper," Shankman reported. He appeared to understand what was happening, but he "did not specifically recall signing" the consent form making Bebe his legal guardian. Barry, Shankman said, "is physically incapable of signing his name." Nor was Barry willing to answer questions about "his estate or family relationships."

Shankman concluded that Barry was mentally competent because he was "sufficiently oriented as to his situation and surroundings."[34]

The next act in the Barry Sadler medical care drama took place during two days of tense, contentious hearings before Judge Donnelly on January 30 and 31. With Bebe spouting off viciously in the newspapers, and Somers hammering away menacingly at Lavona—and former Green Berets seemingly threatening to take things into their own hands—Judge Donnelly feared that tensions would erupt into violence inside his stately old courtroom. So he had conspicuously armed Cleveland police officers prominently placed throughout the room, in which a hand-carved wooden eagle perched over the judge's bench and witnesses sat in an ornate wooden chair that wouldn't have been out of place in a late–eighteenth-century European court chamber.

"It wasn't a comfortable feeling like you have in most lawsuits where you understand that people have differences of opinion but they're rational and they're calm to a degree. I was concerned that a lot of people on the other side were deranged," Hal Hardin said. "Things were tense and the judge—and I agreed with him—had made darn sure that there was a lot of security. It was kind of wall-to-wall security. I was very happy to have it."

Lavona and Thor showed up arm in arm at the hearings, carefully avoiding any contact with Bebe. Cynthia Cotts described Lavona as "tall and slender with a tumble of honeyed curls and an inch thick of mascara. . . . She kept a shimmery white raincoat tightly belted, her fine legs crossed, her lips sealed." She had "steely-eyed Thor," Cotts wrote, by her side "at all times."

The rarely silent Bebe chattered away throughout the two days of hearings in hushed tones with Somers, Hill, and his wife. Bebe, Cotts wrote, was a "tiny lady with long white hair, wearing blue jeans and a sweatshirt." She looked "to one observer like 'something out of Appalachia.'"

During breaks Bebe smoked Pall Mall cigarettes. At one point she hissed at a camera crew: "Ah, knock it off. They don't have a right to have no pictures."[35]

During the two days of hearings, the court heard from four mental health professionals (three psychologists and a psychiatrist) who interviewed Barry at Southwest General. Judge Donnelly paid Barry a visit as well.

Joel Steinberg, a Cleveland-area psychiatrist, spoke to Barry twice. Steinberg—whose fees were paid by Somers and Hill—told the court that Barry had suffered "devastating and profound neurological loss" due to the damaged tissue that had been removed from his right and left frontal lobes. Steinberg and the three psychologists testified that Barry did not initiate any conversations and that he seemed to prefer using nonverbal responses (winks, grimaces, and growls) to speaking, probably because of damage to his vocal chords from the tracheostomy.

Steinberg said he didn't expect Barry to have "much capacity," but found him to be alert and "oriented," but occasionally "unresponsive." Although he could speak Spanish, Barry couldn't count past six in that language and gave different answers when asked if he wanted to be treated in Cleveland or Nashville.[36]

Judge Donnelly reported that Barry "repeatedly" said, when asked, that the year was 1980. Barry, Donnelly said, also could name only two of his three children and believed he was in Tennessee. All in all, his responses to questions, the judge said, "were confusing," which was not a good sign that Barry was competent.

During the second day of the hearings, the lawyers met with Donnelly for three hours and hammered out an agreement that put an abrupt end to the tempestuous legal wrangling. When the meeting ended, Donnelly ruled that Barry was mentally incompetent and incapable of deciding whether or not to remain in Cleveland or go home to Nashville.

He determined that his court did not have jurisdiction in the case because Barry lived in Tennessee. Donnelly therefore ruled that Judge Everett in Nashville should appoint an independent guardian for Barry, preferably someone who had "a special concern for Viet Nam veterans," if possible, a Vietnam veteran himself.[37]

Judge Donnelly also ruled that Barry be returned to the Cleveland VA and that the guardian "give all due consideration" to moving him back to Nashville. The guardian also was ordered to consult with Bebe, Meissner, Thor, Lavona, Baron, and Robbie before making any "major decisions" about Barry's medical and financial "necessities." Finally, the court urged all parties to "attempt to cooperate" to help get Barry "the best and most appropriate medical care and therapy."

Pursuant to Judge Donnelly's order, Somers, Hill, and Bebe readmitted Barry to the Cleveland VA hospital the next day, February 1. Lavona's legal team visited him there several times in the next few weeks.

Barry "had bandages all over his" head, Hal Hardin said in 2015. "I was surprised that he was as lucid as he was, considering what he had been through and what he was going through at the time. He answered a lot of my questions like he understood what was going on. He wasn't totally in charge of his facilities, but I was surprised at how much of his brainpower that he had left."[38]

Hardin even found a bit of Barry's sly humor. When the Nashville lawyer asked him if he knew Bill Parrish, Barry answered, "Parrish the thought." When he said those words, Barry "had a whimsical look like, 'That's really cute, isn't it?'" Hardin said. "He knew he'd scored on that one."

Back in Nashville Judge Everett issued his ruling in the case on February 9. "I think," he said in an understatement, "everybody probably has the right purpose in mind, but they're not going about it in the right way."[39]

Everett then officially determined that Barry was incompetent, and he appointed Nashville attorney David Brandon, a former Marine, as his independent guardian. Everett gave Brandon the authority to determine who could visit Barry, in consultation with family members, Barry himself, and his doctors.[40] The judge also scolded Bebe, Lavona, and Thor, enjoining them from making "any derogatory remarks" about each other in Barry's presence or in front of his doctors or nurses. Judge Everett also ruled that Barry be returned to the Nashville VA or the Murfreesboro, Tennessee, VA hospital "as soon as possible."

On that same day, February 9, Philip Duer presented a detailed, seven-page report to Judge Everett. In it Duer recommended that Barry receive complete nursing care, and not be "left lying in bed in a nursing home." In addition to recommending that Barry undergo daily physical therapy, Duer also warned that he should not be "over-stimulated by visitation."

Since his doctors recommended that Barry receive long-term nursing care in a facility with a rehabilitation program, Duer suggested that the best place would be the VA hospital in Murfreesboro, Tennessee, which had such a program. The hospital also was close to where Lavona, Thor, and many of Barry's Nashville friends lived.[41] Bebe, whom Duer said "appears to be very interested in her son's welfare," should not be restricted from seeing him.

As Judge Everett did, Duer admonished the family to stop their public squabbling, warning them not to "create a media event concerning their feelings about the other party or what is best for Mr. Sadler." The "friction" between Bebe and Lavona, he said, "needs to be stopped." The "additional friction" caused by Hill and Somers in Ohio, Duer said, also needed to come to an end.

Duer addressed Barry's financial condition in the report. It was not good. Barry, Duer discovered, had no liquid assets. It appeared, he wrote, "that the only assets he does have are his books." The royalties from the twenty *Casca* books and the stand-alone adventure novels—hundreds of thousands of dollars—in other words, were gone.

As for royalties from "The Ballad," none were "known at the present time," Duer reported.

Around the time that Philip Duer prepared his report, Jove Books released the twenty-first *Casca* mass market paperback, *The Trench Soldier*, with the words "Over Two Million *Casca* Books in Print!" emblazoned on the cover. This time the Eternal Mercenary turns up in the guise of one Rufus Casterton, an American soldier in the British army in 1914.

Barry wrote the book sometime in the spring or summer of 1988. It centers on Casca as a relentless, efficient, brutal fighting machine killing scores of "Krauts" in—as the cover puts it—"the blood-soaked slaughter of World War I," including the Battles of the Marne and Verdun. He has flashbacks across centuries to other battles "in the time of the Caesars, of Charlemagne, Crecy in the fourteenth century and Agincourt during the Hundred Years' War, the campaigns of Charles in the sixteenth, the Thirty Years' War in the eighteenth."[42]

Since this is a Barry Sadler–style male romance, Casca and his mates escape the trenches for some debauchery in Paris. It culminates in the "living quarters" behind a café in Paris where Casca and one of his fellow Tommies have sexual intercourse on the dining room table with the wife and daughter of the proprietor. When the man of the house discovers them, Casca beats him up, binds and gags him, and makes him watch. After finishing Casca ties up the women with "serviettes" and gags them, too. Then he and his buddy "returned to the café, finished their drinks, paid one of the waitresses, and left quickly." [43]

Later Casca is severely wounded (his wounds heal themselves as usual), is buried alive, is taken prisoner behind German lines, where he encounters Herman Goering and Baron Von Richtofen, escapes, and fights—and fights and fights.

Near the end he is engulfed by a German flamethrower, turning his skin to "charcoal." He is placed on a ship with other severely wounded and dead men. On its way across the English Channel, the ship is sunk by a German U-boat. Casca floats to the surface, along with several dead British troops. Another British ship discovers the floating bodies. They are recovered and the captain orders the dead men to be buried at sea.

Just as Casca is about to be thrown overboard, the burial detail is startled to see that he is alive. Casca is saved once again to fight another day in another war—in *Casca* No. 22, *The Mongol*, the last of Barry Sadler's *Casca* books.

It came out on January 1, 1990, two months after Barry died.

CHAPTER 21

A MAN'S MAN

"He was never happy. He would have been happier if he'd never writ-ten that song."
  —GARY SIZEMORE ON BARRY SADLER, DECEMBER 1989

The VA moved Barry back to Tennessee in late February, into the Alvin C. York Medical Center in Murfreesboro, about thirty-five miles south-east of downtown Nashville.[1] From all accounts he received excellent care there. "From what I have seen at the VA in Murfreesboro, it appears that they are very much interested in Barry and are attempting to do the best they can," Philip Duer said in late May.[2]

The care was good. On the other hand, Barry was not improving. "He still does not initiate conversation," Duer said. As for his physical therapy, Barry "especially does not like the wheelchair," Duer reported, "as it puts pressure on his spine and rear. . . . [He] tries not to cooperate."

Although Barry had several seizures, he showed some improvement during the summer and fall of 1989. "He was a man of few words before, and he still is to some degree," Duer told a reporter in October. "But he's not a vegetable. He's not a potted plant. He's fairly lucid most of the time. Of course, he'd like to get out [of the hospital]. Anybody would."[3]

Lavona and the children, including thirteen-year-old Brooke, visited him often. Lavona reported some good news about his condition in mid-September. Barry liked to watch soap operas on TV, she said, and make sarcastic comments while doing so.[4]

"He's much improved," Lavona told a reporter in mid-October. "He talks and writes his name. He's starting to remember the past. The things they told me he may not be able to do, he can."[5]

Bebe made her way to Nashville and visited on occasion. While there were no huge blowups, she and Lavona did not exactly forget the brouhaha in Cleveland. Barry picked up on the iciness between the two when they visited at the same time. He was not thrilled about it.

"It upset him, the way his mother was acting around him," Lavona said.[6]

Around that time Lavona and Barry discussed spiritual matters. Barry, Lavona said, "always said he was agnostic but he admired my faith." Lavona asked her husband if he would accept Jesus "as his true savior." Barry said yes, Lavona said.

"I just wanted his soul to be free," she said.[7]

Barry Sadler turned forty-nine on November 1. Sometime between six and seven o'clock on Sunday morning, November 5, he died in his hospital bed of cardiac arrest. The doctors believed he had had a stroke, most likely due to the damage in the centers of the brain that control the heart.

"When they checked him, he had been asleep and then someone on the ward found him in that way," a hospital spokesman said in announcing the death.[8]

"We thought his medical condition had been fine," Phil Duer said. "It was somewhat unexpected." Barry "looked good," Robbie Robison added, "but with the type of injury he had, he was susceptible to a lot of things."[9]

Doctors performed an autopsy. The state medical examiner's preliminary finding, announced November 8, was that Barry died of cardiac arrhythmia, and that neither foul play nor suicide was suspected. Barry's body was then moved to Cole & Garrett Funeral Home in Hendersonville. Lavona said that she and Barry had discussed what would happen next and both agreed that he would be cremated.

Then came one last bit of drama. The funeral director somehow heard that Bebe and Steve Somers might try to steal Barry's remains, so, Lavona said, "he took them home and locked them up."[10]

There was no theft, and the funeral took place at the Nashville National Cemetery in South Madison on November 10, a day before Veterans Day. A few days before that, Lavona had had a call from Darlene Sharpe's sister. Darlene, she said, asked if it would be okay if she came to the funeral. Lavona didn't have a problem with that.

"I said, 'Why not?'" Lavona said in 2015. "We sat together [at the funeral]. We talked. I didn't hold any animosity toward her."[11]

Barry received full military honors at the National Cemetery on that nippy, overcast November morning. A contingent of active-duty Green Berets from the 5th Special Forces Group made the trip from Fort Bragg, as did many other active-duty Green Berets and SF veterans.

"I was amazed at the number of Special Forces guys who showed up. A lot of guys from all over the country came in," Bill Parrish said. "One Medal of Honor [recipient] gave Lavona a Silver Star off of his array of badges. And he gave her a rose and one spent cartridge. That was a tradition."[12]

The official ceremony conducted by Chaplain Christen Anderson in Section NN, Site 64 included six Green Berets folding an American flag over the small box that housed Barry's remains, a three-volley gun salute from a seven-man SF rifle squad, and a lone bugler playing "Taps" on a nearby hill. Thor and Baron, both in their U.S. Army uniforms, sat with Lavona and Brooke—and with their grandmother Bebe.

The family keep things simple. The tombstone was the standard National Cemetery model with a cross and the words:

BARRY A
SADLER
S SGT
US ARMY
VIETNAM
NOV 1 1940
NOV 5 1989

Before the graveside service ended, Bebe moved away from her daughter-in-law and grandchildren. "I saw her . . . off in the distance,"

Bill Parrish said. "She had on a khaki raincoat and she wouldn't join the crowd. It was really weird."[13]

The mourners included a group of people in the country music business—along with Fate Thomas, the Nashville sheriff. "He was a man's man," Thomas told a Nashville reporter. "We would have some trouble in the cell block" when Barry was a deputy, "and Barry would get in there and beat on a few of 'em. We wouldn't have no more trouble out of that cell block."[14]

Barry "beating on" bad guys. Barry being a "man's man." Barry as the "tough guy." That certainly was the public image Barry Sadler projected from his teenaged years to the second a bullet tore through his skull in Guatemala City. And, most of the time, Barry lived up to that macho posturing.

There was another Barry Sadler, of course—a smart, knowledge-hungry, charming, funny, and sometimes gentle husband, father, and friend. A man who overcame a rough childhood, served his country in peace and war, and gained national fame and admiration.

But all too often the tough guy took over. The tough guy who drank too much, who was quick to anger, who killed a man for no good reason, who spouted ultra-right-wing political tropes, who surrounded himself with weapons, whose tragic, violent death at age forty-nine surprised few who knew him.

For those who didn't know him, the image of the tough, resolute, patriotic Green Beret sergeant endures. As does only one fact: Barry Sadler was the man who wrote and recorded the mega 1966 hit "The Ballad of the Green Berets."

That song all but perfectly fit in the early 1966 American zeitgeist. It captured the national imagination when the Vietnam War was widely seen as a necessary step in the American-led fight against a worldwide communist insurgency. But as American involvement in the Vietnam War steeply escalated, as American casualties mounted, and as little progress seemed to be made, more Americans turned against the war and society and culture underwent a huge change. As for Barry's "Ballad," if it had come out a year later, it could not have become a showbiz phenomenon and Barry Sadler never would have had his hour strutting on the national stage.

"You talk about the right place at the right time," Barry's old Green Beret medic-training-buddy Steve Bruno said. In January of 1966 "there was a war raging over there. Guys were getting killed. The country hadn't turned against it yet. And here is this Green Beret, the symbol of America's strength and courage, and he became a rock star."[15]

But not for long—and not without disastrous consequences. Born in 1940, Barry Sadler was not a part of the Baby Boom generation that was about to change virtually everything in American culture and society. Barry Sadler was part of the older half of the generation gap that split American society in the late 1960s and early 1970s. Simply put: His tough guy brand did not sell as the nation went through the political, social, and cultural upheaval of the Sixties.

His second, commercially successful act as a pulp novelist notwithstanding, Barry Sadler was a victim of his meteoric success, of his unhappy childhood, and of the times in which he lived. Very likely the most famous Vietnam veteran of his time—and perhaps of all time—Barry Sadler also was one of countless victims of that tragic conflict, which provided the fertile ground for the song that made him famous and helped contribute to the disastrous downward spiral that ended in his violent early death.

ACKNOWLEDGMENTS

I wish to thank my friend and fellow Vietnam War veteran, the journalist and author John Mort, who started a never-completed biography of Barry Sadler, and who generously sent me the material he had acquired and encouraged me to take up the task. Thanks, too, to my literary agent and friend Joseph Brendan Vallely, another American veteran of the Vietnam War, for believing in this book and selling it.

I am extremely grateful to my editor Dave Reisch, and to Alexandra Singer, Stephanie Otto, and the rest of the team at Stackpole Books and Rowman and Littlefield for their great work and encouragement. Thanks, too, to Kate Hertzog for doing a terrific copy-editing job, and Galen Schroeder for the excellent index.

As I mention in the bibliographic note, I relied heavily on interviews with people who knew Barry Sadler, as well as those who served in the Special Forces during the Vietnam War and others who had special insights into his life and times. The complete list of the seventy-one people I interviewed is in that section. I'd like to give extra acknowledgment to the following, who were especially helpful.

In Nashville: Lavona Sadler answered all of my questions thoughtfully and sometimes painfully. Bill Parrish spent hours with me going over Barry's life and turbulent times when they were close friends from the mid-1970s until Barry's death. Robbie Robison, Barry's close friend and literary agent, welcomed me into his home, talked with me for hours, answered many e-mails, and graciously allowed me the use of personal letters and photographs and other materials. Hal Hardin, the Sadler family's lawyer, gave me full access to the mountain of paperwork involving the legal fight over Barry's medical care—and answered many questions during two interviews and lots of e-mails and phone calls. Hal's assistant, Tammy Williams, graciously did a ton of photocopying for me.

A special thanks to former homicide detective Jim Sledge, who recently retired from the Nashville District Attorney's Office. Jim took me step by step through his investigation of the murder of Lee Bellamy, allowing me full access to all the police files. He also graciously let me pick his brain about the case in several long telephone interviews and in his office. And he took me to the scene of the crime and to the Commodore Lounge, where he arrested Barry.

Bob Barkwill, Barry's friend and agent in the late 1960s and early 1970s, was extremely helpful. He told great tales of adventures with Barry in Tucson and Hollywood in our many phone conversations and e-mails. Bob Powers, who knew Barry well (and wrote three feature articles about him) during his time in Tucson, shared his research and his personal memories of Barry. Seth Gitell, the son of the late Green Beret lieutenant Gerry Gitell, generously provided memories of his father, along with letters and other documents I never would have found without his help.

Thanks also to the following veterans who served with Barry and who shared their memories:

Air Force: Paul Alford and H. D. Graham

Special Forces training: John Gissell (who started the ball rolling), Steve Bruno, Larry Emons, Joe Ewald, Frank Graham, Joe Hannon, Rich Sirois, and Al Weed

Vietnam War: Vernon Gillespie Jr., John Opshinsky, Jimmy Walker, and Al Wilhelm

Thanks, too, to three of Barry's editors of the *Casca* series: Jim Morris, Hank Schlesinger, and Eliza Shallcross, and to Bob Brown, the publisher of *Soldier of Fortune* magazine; to Rich Kolb, the publisher and editor in chief of *VFW* magazine, who generously shared a large amount of information he had in his files, as well as to Steve Sherman, who keeps a massive database on the Green Berets who served in Vietnam; and to my old friend Bill Fogarty, who helped me unravel legal complexities.

Janice Fox, the local history coordinator at Lake County Library in Leadville, Colorado, very kindly shared her extensive knowledge of the town where Barry grew up and provided several images as well as contact information for others in town. Through her help I was able to interview Loretta Sparkman, Thomas "Tommy" Gomez, Howard Tritz, and Suzy Kelly. Bunny Taylor of the Lake County School District filled me in on Barry's academic record at Leadville Senior High.

Thanks to Debbie May in the Special Collections Department of the Nashville Public Library, who graciously photocopied some three dozen newspaper articles from the Nashville *Banner* and *The Tennessean* from her Barry Sadler clipping file and sent them to me. And to my friends at the Middleburg branch of the Loudoun County (Virginia) Library, especially Branch Manager Sheila Whetzel. And to interlibrary loan wizard Anita Barrett.

My good friend and colleague David Willson sent me copies of articles from his voluminous Vietnam War files I never would have found on my own. Elizabeth Tremblay of the Mine Run, Virginia, DAR Chapter kindly compiled Barry's genealogical chart for this book. Psychology professor Justin Ramsdell of George Mason University expertly guided me through the intricacies of mental incompetency and the law.

I am very grateful for the unstinting support of my longtime friend and colleague Michael Keating, the editor of *The VVA Veteran* magazine at Vietnam Veterans of America. And to Xande Anderer, the magazine's art director, my web designer, and good friend. I couldn't have written this book without their help and encouragement.

Lastly, I greatly appreciate the support and encouragement from friends and family: Bud Alley, Walter Anderson, Chip Bishop, Cliff Boyle, Lin and Bernie Brien, Barbara Burkhardt, Bob Carolla, Denis Cotter, Elizabeth Cromwell, Cathy Curtis, Larry Cushman, John Czeplewski, Patrick Sheane Duncan, Russell Duncan, Dale Dye, Bill and Sue Ferster, Joe Galloway, Gail Guttman, Brian Jay Jones, Evan Leepson, Ellen and Peter Leepson, Treavor Lord, Hunt Lyman, Sandra and Joe Markus, Bobbie Ann Mason, Greg McNamee, John Metz, Mike Morency, Josh Muss, Ann and Tom Northrup, Ron Osgood, Angus Paul, Margie and Dan Radvosky, Barbara and Pat Rhodes, Len Shapiro, and Walter Woodson.

Special thanks to my biography widow, Janna, for putting up with the long hours, days, weeks, and months that I spent barricaded in my office working on this book.

ENDNOTES

PROLOGUE – A SOLDIER AT HEART
1 Author interview, June 16, 2015. Longtime Nashville public relations man Earl Owens has represented many country music business performers, including Jerry Lee Lewis and Charlie Louvin.
2 Author interview, September 29, 2015.
3 "Voluntary Statement of Barry Allen Sadler," Metropolitan Police Department, Nashville, Tennessee, 2:30 a.m., December 2, 1978.
4 E-mail to author, February 3, 2016.
5 Author interview, August 10, 2015.
6 Quoted in Mike Sante, "'Ballad of the Green Berets' Ruined Barry Sadler's Life, Friends Say," KRTN news service, in, for example, the Baton Rouge, Louisiana, *State-Times Advocate*, November 1, 1990, p. 45.
7 Author interview, October 1, 2015.
8 Quoted in Mark Wolf, "Barry Sadler, 'A Soldier at Heart,' Fights for His Life," *Rocky Mountain News*, September 16, 1988.
9 Author interview, September 14, 2015.
10 Quoted in Drew Jubera, "Requiem for a Green Beret," *Atlanta Journal-Constitution*, December 31, 1989, p. M3.
11 Author interview, December 29, 2015.

CHAPTER ONE – TOUGH GUY
1 "Double Killing Motive Not Yet Told to Public," *Waxahachie Daily Light*, April 19, 1928. Texas State Board of Health, Bureau of Vital Statistics, Standard Certificate of Death No. 15099, April 19, 1928.
2 A Sadler family tree compiled by Elizabeth Tremblay shows that John Bright Sadler was born on March 5, 1911, in Cleburne, Texas, and married Blanche (Bebe) Handsford Littlefield, probably in 1935. Bebe Littlefield was born September 5, 1917, in Jefferson, Arizona.
3 *I'm A Lucky One*, p. 24. Barry Sadler more or less dictated the book to the Texas journalist Tom Mahoney during the height of his fame in 1966. The book was released in March 1967.
4 Author interviews, May 23, 2014, and June 8, 2015.
5 Author interview, October 19, 2015.
6 "No Time for Sergeanting," *Time*, April 15, 1966, p. 85.
7 The census contained information gathered as of April 1, 1940. Giving Barry Sadler's version the benefit of the doubt, it is possible (but unlikely) that John Sadler graduated from plumber's helper in a shop to owning his own successful plumbing and electrical business before he and Bebe divorced in 1945.
8 The Dogwood Festival, where Barry appeared in Charlottesville, Virginia. Dogwood Festival officials Jim Schisler and Al Maracaibo heard Sadler utter those words. Author interviews, June 4 and June 23, 2015.

9 Author interview, September 3, 2015.

10 Author interview, November 25, 2015. The friend asked that her name not be used in this book.

11 Author interview, June 11, 2015.

12 Author interview, September 14, 2015.

13 Gillian Klucas, *Leadville: The Struggle to Rebuild an American Town* (Island Press, 2004), p. 46.

14 Author interview, December 17, 2015.

15 See Jan MacKell, *Brothels, Bordellos & Bad Girls: Prostitution in Colorado, 1860–1930* (University of New Mexico Press, 2004), pp. 260–61. In February 1976 the Pioneer's two bars and glassware cabinet were dismantled and shipped to a restaurant owner in Sacramento, California. Today they are a prominent feature of Fat City Bar and Café on Front Street in Sacramento.

16 Author interview, December 2, 2015.

17 Author interview, November 3, 2015.

18 *I'm A Lucky One*, p. 28.

19 Quoted in David Martin, "'Play That Song You Made Up,'" *Life* magazine, March 4, 1966, p. 96.

20 Author interview, October 1, 2015.

21 Barry also listed Gouch Firestone and Dunne's Men's Store in Marysville, California, as credit references. His five character references included two U.S. Air Force officers and a U.S. Air Force staff sergeant he served with, as well as Joe Plute of the Leadville Police Department and Richard Maestas of the Vendome Hotel in Leadville.

22 Author interview, November 23, 2015.

23 Author interview, December 17, 2015.

24 Author interview, November 25, 2015.

25 "Green Berets' Balladeer Has Much to Remember," *Tucson Daily Citizen*, August 10, 1972, p. 3.

26 *Chicago Sun-Times* article, reprinted in *Evansville* (Indiana) *Courier and Press*, July 7, 1966.

27 *L.A. Times*, Powers, p. Z-19.

28 Author interview, June 16, 2015.

CHAPTER TWO – AN EXTREME BEGINNER

1 *I'm A Lucky One*, pp. 33, 34. The bulk of the information on Sadler's air force career in this chapter is from his autobiography.

2 In his book Sadler says he and the other trainees were pulled out of basic "with three weeks of training to go," and sent to Keesler. Sadler's official U.S. Air Force records were destroyed in a disastrous July 1973 fire at the National Archives' National Military Personnel Records Center in St. Louis, which incinerated some sixteen million personnel files. However, the basic details of Sadler's air force service are included in his official U.S. Army records (which were not destroyed in the fire). According to those records, Sadler trained at Keesler from July to September of 1958.

3 Author interview, February 7, 2016. Barry and H. D. Graham did not serve together in the air force. The two young airmen bonded while waiting for a long-delayed USAF flight at Travis Air Force Base in May of 1962, and they remained pen pals for nearly two decades into the early 1980s.
4 Author interview, October 1, 2015.
5 Author interview, June 11, 2015.
6 The Madera USAF station opened in 1950 as the cold war heated up; it was deactivated in 1966.
7 Author interview, April 15, 2016.
8 Division of Probation and Paroles, Nashville, Tennessee, "Barry Allen Sadler, Social History," 1980.
9 Quoted by David Martin, "Hail to 'Green Berets,'" *Life* magazine, March 6, 1966, p. 96.
10 Ibid.
11 See, for example, *GQ*, p. 246.

CHAPTER THREE – WHY DON'T YOU WRITE A SONG ABOUT US?
1 See *Vietnam Studies: U.S. Army Special Forces, 1961–1971* (Center of Military History, Department of the Army, 1973), pp. 3–5.
2 "Green Berets," John F. Kennedy Presidential Library and Museum, www.jfklibrary.org/JFK/JFK-in-History/Green-Berets.aspx.
3 Ibid. After President Kennedy was assassinated on November 22, 1963, his family asked that Special Forces members join the Honor Guard for his funeral. Forty-six Green Berets from Fort Bragg did so. The SF training center at Fort Bragg was renamed the John F. Kennedy Special Warfare Center and School.
4 "Green Berets 'Top' Special Service Men," Van Nuys, California, *Valley News*, November 9, 1961, p. 30.
5 "Green Beret to Distinguish Guerrilla GIs," *Oregon Statesman*, December 10, 1961, p. 20.
6 The army's first Parachute Badge was designed by then captain William P. Yarborough of the 501st Parachute Battalion in 1941—the same William Yarborough who twenty years later pushed JFK to adopt the green beret as part of the SF official uniform.
7 Quoted in Gene Scroft, "Eternal Mercenary," *Soldier of Fortune*, February 1989, p. 89.
8 *Village Voice*, p. 18.
9 Author interview, July 28, 2015.
10 Author interview, July 14, 2015.
11 Author interview, July 1, 2015.
12 Author interview, August 1, 2015.
13 *I'm A Lucky One*, p. 79.
14 Quoted in *Soldier of Fortune*, February 1989, p. 35.
15 In an interview in the Washington, DC, *Evening Star*, February 19, 1966, and the Boston *Record American*, February 27, 1966.
16 "'Green Beret' Composer Surprised by Success," *Tucson Daily Citizen*, March 1, 1966.
17 David Martin, "Hail to 'The Green Berets.'" *Life* magazine, March 4, 1966, p. 98.
18 Author interview, December 29, 2015.

19 Author interview, June 28, 2015. The former Special Forces medic asked that his name not be used in this book. He trained with Barry Sadler at jump school at Fort Benning, medic training at Fort Sam Houston, on-the-job training at Fort Jackson, and SF advanced medic training at Fort Bragg.
20 E-mail to author, June 24, 2015.
21 Author interviews, May 23, 2014, and September 14, 2015.
22 Author interview, November 5, 2015.
23 Mary A. Casserly, Major AMC, Chief Nursing Service to Commanding Officer, Special Forces Training Group (Abn. 8220), U.S. Army Special Warfare Center, Fort Bragg, North Carolina, September 18, 1963.
24 Author interview, September 14, 2015.
25 *I'm A Lucky One*, p. 89.

CHAPTER FOUR – BY AN UNKNOWN SOLDIER

1 Gerald Gitell resume, 1968. Copy provided to the author by Seth Gitell.
2 Author interview, September 5, 2015.
3 *I'm A Lucky One*, p. 89.
4 The Singing Nun, also known as *Soeur Sourire* ("Sister Smile" in French), was the stage name of Jeanne Deckers, a member of the Dominican Order in Belgium.
5 Quoted in John Crosby, "Army Special Forces Singer Scores with Hit Recording," NEA [Newspaper Enterprise Association syndicate], *Cumberland* (Maryland) *News*, February 12, 1966, p. 1.
6 At Gerry Gitell's funeral in November of 2010, a group of former Special Forces soldiers sang "The Ballad of the Green Berets."
7 See Harry G. Summers Jr., *Vietnam War Almanac* (Facts on File, 1985), pp. 30–33.
8 The House of Representatives passed the Tonkin Gulf Resolution unanimously, even though President Johnson hadn't told Congress the circumstances of the incidents or the ships' covert missions. Only two senators voted against the resolution, Wayne Morse of Oregon and Ernest Gruening of Alaska. In 1970, after it was determined that no second attack took place and that the *Maddox* more or less provoked the first one by approaching too close to the North Vietnamese coastal defense forces, both Houses repealed the resolution. See Edwin E. Moise, "Tonkin Gulf Resolution," in Spencer C. Tucker, ed., *Encyclopedia of the Vietnam War* (ABC-CLIO, 1998), Vol. II, p. 695.
9 Lyndon B. Johnson, "Radio and Television Report to the American People Following Renewed Aggression in the Gulf of Tonkin," August 4, 1964. Online by Gerhard Peters and John T. Woolley, *The American Presidency Project*, presidency.ucsb.edu/ws/?pid=26418. Also see William Conrad Gibbons, *The U.S. Government and the Vietnam War: Executive and Legislative Roles and Relationships, Part II, 1961–1964* (Princeton University Press, 1986), p. 342.
10 See John Prados, *The Hidden History of the Vietnam War* (Ivan R. Dee, 1995), pp. 72–78.
11 See Col. Francis J. Kelly, *Vietnam Studies: U.S. Army Special Forces, 1961–1971* (U.S. Army Center of Military History, 1989), pp. 3–18. Also see Shelby L. Stanton, *Green Berets at War: U.S. Army Special Forces in Southeast Asia, 1956–1975* (Presidio, 1985).
12 *I'm A Lucky One*, p. 92.

CHAPTER FIVE – A LUCKY ONE

1 Author interview, November 6, 2015.

2 *I'm A Lucky One*, p. 99.

3 "Montagnards" is the name the former French colonizers of Vietnam gave to thirty-three tribes, numbering nearly a million people, who lived in the Central Highlands. Ethnically and culturally different from the Vietnamese, the Montagnards never considered themselves part of Vietnamese society and rejected the authority of the South Vietnamese government. For their part the Vietnamese looked upon the Montagnards as inferior, forcing them to live in the remote Central Highlands. Thousands of Montagnards left Vietnam after the end of the war in 1975 and settled in the United States, many of them in North Carolina, the home of Fort Bragg and the U.S. Army Special Forces.

4 *I'm A Lucky One*, p. 123.

5 Ibid., p. 130.

6 Author interview, August 21, 2015.

7 *Life* magazine, March 4, 1966, p. 96.

8 *I'm A Lucky One*, p. 106.

9 National Archives, *5th Special Forces Group (Airborne) Records of A Detachments, 1962–1970*, Box 186, "Monthly Medical Training Report," 1 March–31 March 1965.

10 *I'm A Lucky One*, p. 133.

11 E-mail correspondence with author, January 16, 2016.

12 "Viet Nurse Now Knows Feeling," New Orleans *Times-Picayune*, August 4, 1966, p. 55.

13 *I'm A Lucky One*, p. 134.

14 Author interview, November 5, 2015.

15 Recreated dialogue in *I'm A Lucky One*, p. 147.

16 Author interview, November 5, 2015.

17 The song, one of a dozen Sadler tunes on his best-selling 1966 album, "The Ballads of the Green Berets," pays tribute to two other Green Berets who died in Vietnam. Staff Sgt. Horace Earle Young was killed in action on May 11, 1965. Sgt. Emmett Harvey Horn died on December 23, 1964.

18 *I'm A Lucky One*, p. 9.

19 Author interview, October 27, 2015.

20 *I'm A Lucky One*, p. 9.

21 See, for example, "GIs in Viet Nam Have Song; It's 'Ballad of Green Berets,'" Richmond *Times-Dispatch*, February 27, 1966, p. 107.

22 *Life* magazine, March 4, 1966, p. 96.

23 *I'm A Lucky One*, p. 17.

24 U.S. military lore also had it that 33 Biere was made with formaldehyde.

25 *I'm A Lucky One*, p. 170.

26 Author interviews, September 14 and 22, 2015.

CHAPTER SIX – THE RIGHT MAN WITH THE RIGHT SONG

1 Author interview, September 14, 2015.

2 *I'm A Lucky One*, p. 171.

3 Robin Moore, *The Green Berets* (Crown Publishers, 1965), p. 11.
4 Christian Appy, *American Reckoning: The Vietnam War and Our National Identity* (Viking, 2015), p. 126.
5 Alice Payne Hackett and James Henry Burke, *80 Years of Best Sellers: 1897–1975* (R. R. Bowker, 1977, p. 196). Moore went on to write two other bestsellers, *The French Connection* in 1969 and *The Happy Hooker* in 1972. Also see John Hellmann, *American Myth and the Legacy of the Vietnam War* (Columbia University Press, 1986), p. 53.
6 Phyllis Fairbanks to Herbert Gitell (Gerry Gitell's brother), August 2, 1965. From the private collection of Seth Gitell.
7 *I'm A Lucky One*, p. 172.
8 Bob Ellison, "He Wore Green Beret," *Chicago Sun-Times*, reprinted in the Lincoln, Nebraska, *Sunday Journal and Star*, March 13, 1966, p. 6.
9 See, for example, the Bryan, Texas, *Eagle*, August 5, 1965, p. 1.
10 *I'm A Lucky One*, p. 174.
11 Joseph Galloway, "Ia Drang: The Battle That Convinced Ho Chi Minh That He Could Win," *Vietnam* magazine, October 2010. *We Were Soldiers Once . . . And Young* (1992), Galloway and Hal Moore's book on the Battle of the Ia Drang Valley and its impact on the course of the Vietnam War, is widely considered among the best accounts of the war.
12 Quoted in John Crosby, "Army Special Forces Singer Scores with Hit Recording," *Cumberland* (Maryland) *News*, February 12, 1966, p. 1.
13 *I'm A Lucky One*, p. 176.
14 In the music business Artist and Repertoire (A&R) people are responsible for scouting new talent, overseeing an artist's recording process, and then helping market and promote the record.
15 Whitney Bolton, "Glancing Sideways," *Cumberland* (Maryland) *Evening Times*, February 14, 1966.

CHAPTER SEVEN – A HOT NEW SINGLE WITH A READY-MADE MARKET

1 A Gallup Poll taken in March 1966, for example, reported that just 26 percent of Americans believed that this country made a mistake sending troops to fight in Vietnam. That same poll found that 54 percent approved of President Johnson's handling of the war.
2 For a thorough history of the anti–Vietnam War movement, see Nancy Zaroulis and Gerald Sullivan, *Who Spoke Up? American Protest against the War in Vietnam, 1963–1975* (Doubleday, 1984). The chapter on the year 1966 is entitled "Becalmed in a Sea of Uncertainty."
3 Government Printing Office, *Public Papers of the Presidents of the United States: Lyndon B. Johnson, 1966.* Volume I, entry 6, p. 3.
4 Quoted by syndicated columnist Bob Greene, in June 1977. See, for example, "Clancy—the Walking Exclamation Point," Freeport, Illinois, *Journal-Standard*, July 26, 1977, p. 12.
5 "RCA Dressing Up 'Berets.'" *Billboard*, January 22, 1966, p. 4.

6 Author interview, April 21, 2015.

7 Author interview, December 12, 2015.

8 Author interview, January 15, 2016.

9 Author interview, January 20, 2016. For a good look at the parodies of "The Ballad," see Doug Bradley and Craig Werner, *We Gotta Get Out of This Place: The Soundtrack of the Vietnam War* (University of Massachusetts Press, 2015), pp. 35–37.

10 Quoted in Richard Stacewicz, *Winter Soldiers: An Oral History of the Vietnam Veterans Against the War* (Twayne, 1997), p. 49.

11 Quoted in Doug Bradley and Craig Werner, *We Gotta Get Out of This Place*, p. 35. Jim Kurtz later changed his mind about the Vietnam War and the song, saying that "rather than ringing true, the song rings hollow. . . . 'The Ballad of the Green Berets' is a bunch of nonsense, especially the end of the song where the father dies and asks his wife to put the silver wings on his son's chest. It's nonsense."

12 Author interview, July 1, 2015.

13 Louis Calta, "Wounded Veteran Writes Song on Vietnam War," *New York Times*, February 1, 1966, p. 27.

14 "Vietnam Blues," *Newsweek*, February 21, 1966, p. 91.

15 David Martin, "Hail to 'Green Berets,'" *Life* magazine, March 4, 1966, pp. 93, 97.

16 See, for example, "Writer of Hit, 'Green Berets,' Fights Cong, Composes Songs," Long Beach, California, *Independent*, February 11, 1966, p. 4.

17 John Crosby, "Army Special Forces Singer Scores with Hit Recording," NEA [Newspaper Enterprise Association syndicate], *Cumberland* (Maryland) *News*, February 12, 1966, p. 1.

18 "Barry Sadler, Western Style Singer, Honors Green Berets and Leadville," Leadville, Colorado, *Herald Democrat*, February 11, 1966.

19 See, for example, "'Green Beret' Money Rolls In," *Greensboro* (North Carolina) *Daily News*, February 14, 1966, p. 5.

20 Evelyn Piano, "The Sound Track" column, *Fitchburg* (Massachusetts) *Sentinel*, February 8, 1966.

21 Brenda Kollar, "Browsing . . . with Brenda," Dover, Ohio, *Daily Reporter*, March 9, 1966, p. 1.

22 "America's Best,'" *Augusta* (Georgia) *Chronicle*, February 12, 1966, p. 3.

23 *The Daily Standard*, of Sikeston, Missouri, March 8, 1966.

24 Un-bylined column in the *Springfield* (Massachusetts) *Union*, March 6, 1966, p. 65.

25 Drew Jubera, "Requiem for a Green Beret," *Atlanta Journal-Constitution*, December 31, 1989.

26 "No Time for Sergeanting," *Time* magazine, April 15, 1966, pp. 84–85.

27 Timothy S. Mayer, "The Ballads of the Green Berets," *Harvard Crimson*, March 30, 1966.

28 Linda Mathew, "The War Goes On Without a Song of Its Own," *Los Angeles Times*, January 7, 1968.

29 George Forsythe, "War Songs Tell a Story," *Boston Herald*, February 6, 1966, p. 22.

30 Author interview, June 11, 2015. Bishop, the author of *Quentin and Flora: A Roosevelt and a Vanderbilt in Love during the Great War* and *The Lion and the Journalist: The Unlikely Friendship of Theodore Roosevelt and Joseph Bucklin Bishop*, died August 5, 2016, at age 71.
31 Quoted in the Cleveland *Plain Dealer* Magazine, October 22, 1989, p. 21.
32 *I'm A Lucky One*, p. 17.
33 Statistics cited in *Billboard*, March 5, 1966. Other big-selling single records in February and March included "California Dreamin'" by the Mamas and Pappas, "Nowhere Man" by the Beatles, "19th Nervous Breakdown" by the Rolling Stones, "Daydream" by the Lovin' Spoonful, and "Homeward Bound" by Simon and Garfunkel.
34 Hugo Keesing and Wouter Keesing with C. L. Yarbrough and Justin Brummer, "Vietnam on Record: An Incomplete Discography," LaSalle University, Connelly Library, Department of Special Collections, 2015.
35 Author interview, October 1, 2015.
36 Author interview, September 14, 2015.

CHAPTER EIGHT – A DIRTY, OLD STAFF SERGEANT

1 *I'm A Lucky One*, pp. 181–82.
2 *L.A. Times*, Powers, p. Z-19.
3 Author interview, September 14, 2015.
4 See Walter Jaehnig, "Green Beret Maneuvers Outflank Sadler's Fans," *Louisville Courier-Journal*, May 5, 1966, p. 29, and the *New York Times*, February 1, 1966. Barry told Robert Powers that he was putting "10 percent of his earnings" into his foundation.
5 Author interview, June 5, 2015.
6 Author interview, September 22, 2015.
7 There were only a handful of pro-war rallies in the late sixties and early seventies, a time when massive antiwar protests took place in Washington, D.C., San Francisco, New York, Chicago, and other places around the nation.
8 AP wire service article. See, for example, "Giant Rally Backs War in Viet Nam," *Abilene Reporter News*, February 13, 1966.
9 Quoted by Ronnie Oberman, Washington, D.C., *Evening Star,* February 19, 1966, p. 33.
10 Kent Biffle, "Sadler Still Wears Green Beret," *Dallas Morning News*, February 22, 1966.
11 Writing in *Boston Traveler*, February 23, 1966, p. 3.
12 Jim O'Reilly, "A Smash Success," *The Heights*, March 4, 1966, p. 8.
13 Dorothy Madlee, "G.I. Singer Sadler Hails U.S. Loyalty," *Boston Record American*, February 27, 1966, p. 9.
14 "'Green Beret' Composer Surprised by Success," *Tucson Daily Citizen*, March 1, 1966.
15 Quoted in an AP wire service article. See, for example, "20 at U. of Minnesota Fight Broadcasting of War Song," *New York Times*, March 2, 1966, p. 47.
16 The whole quote, as reported by Maureen Cleave, in the March 4, 1966, edition of the *London Evening Standard*: "Christianity will go. It will vanish and shrink. I needn't argue about that; I'm right and I will be proved right. We're more popular than Jesus now. I don't know which will go first, rock 'n' roll or Christianity. Jesus was all right but his disciples were thick and ordinary. It's them twisting it that ruins it for me."

17 Quoted in "Japan Victor Giving 'Berets' 4-Star Pitch," *Billboard*, March 5, 1966, p. 30.

18 Quoted in Robert Powers, "The Readjustment of Barry Sadler," *Arizona Republic*, March 5, 1972, p. 241.

19 Quoted by Ruth Nathan, North American Newspaper Alliance news service. See, for example, "Barry Sadler Says Ballad Neither for Nor Against War," *Omaha World-Herald*, March 24, 1966.

20 It appears that Barry's ribbons included the blue Air Force Longevity Service Award, which he received for serving for four years in the USAF. Army regulations at the time prohibited the wearing of another service's ribbons.

21 W. T. Little, "Patrons of the Pioneer Bar Believe in 'The Green Berets,'" *Rocky Mountain News*, April 4, 1966.

CHAPTER NINE – A YOUNG, CREW-CUT TROUBADOUR

1 "'Green Beret' Composer Presented 'Key to the City,'" *Florence Morning News*, April 5, 1966.

2 Author interview, September 14, 2015.

3 "No Time for Sergeanting," *Time* magazine, April 15, 1966, p. 86.

4 See, for example, "'Long Green' for Soldier: Barry Sadler to Try Show Business," *Eureka Humboldt Standard*, April 18, 1966.

5 Author interview, March 4, 2016.

6 Facebook message to author, March 5, 2016.

7 Author interview, June 23, 2015.

8 Author interview, April 20, 2016.

9 *LA Times*, Powers, p. Z-19.

10 William A. Shires, "It Happened in North Carolina," (Burlington, North Carolina), *Daily Times-News*, April 23, 1966, p. 1.

11 Bill Schemmel, *Marietta* (Georgia) *Journal*, April 29, 1966, p. 1.

12 Quoted in Robert Powers, "The Rise and Fall of Barry Sadler," *Crawdaddy*, August 1973, p. 32.

13 *Richmond Times-Dispatch*, June 26, 1966, p. 84.

14 "The Green Beret Boom," *Newsweek*, May 2, 1966, p. 102.

15 Walter Jaehnig, "Green Beret Maneuvers Outflank Sadler Fans," Louisville *Courier-Journal*, May 5, 1966, p. 29.

16 "Sgt. Sadler Gets Job Done: In Fight, Song or Speech," *Danville* (Virginia) *Register*, May 8, 1966, p. 1.

17 Jim McAllister, "Sgt. Sadler and Randy Boone Might Form Team," *Greensboro* (North Carolina) *Daily News*, May 9, 1966, p. 11.

18 Author interview, September 14, 2015.

19 Bill Coombs, "Barry Sadler in Panama," in *Tales from the Teamhouse*, Vol. III (Old Mountain Press, 2015).

20 Author interview, June 25, 2015.

21 *Omaha World-Herald*, May 19, 1966, p. 18.

22 Considine column, for example, in the Lincoln, Nebraska, *Star*, June 13, 1966.

23 Letter from Col. Frank W. Morrow to Commanding General, U.S. Army Special Forces Training Station, June 22, 1966.

24 E-mail to author, December 19, 2015. Richter, the last survivor of Detachment 101, was ninety-nine years old in 2015.

25 Reprinted in, among other newspapers, the Evansville *Courier and Press*, July 7, 1966, p. 30.

26 John Michaels, "Barry Sadler: 'You Don't Have to Shake Dandruff,'" *KRLA Beat*, July 9, 1966, p. 2.

27 Lyndon B. Johnson, "Remarks to the Delegates to the American Legion National Convention," August 30, 1966, The American Presidency Project, University of California at Santa Barbara, "Public Papers of the Presidents."

28 Quoted in M. S. Handler, "Nixon Tells Legion Convention Vietnam War May Last 5 Years," *New York Times*, September 1, 1966, p. 6.

29 "Sgt. Sadler, Children's Parade Cheered by 10,000 at Foliage Festival Events," *Springfield* (Massachusetts) *Union*, September 21, 1966.

30 "Fitzsimmons Men Entertained by Balladeer of Green Berets," *Rocky Mountain News*, October 6, 1966, p. 20.

31 Author interview, August 10, 2015.

CHAPTER TEN – THE BEST THING THAT EVER HAPPENED TO HIM

1 *Billboard*, December 3, 1967, p. 18.

2 Whitcup, who got his start writing big band music in the 1930s, never had a hit song in his long career. He co-wrote "One Day Nearer Home" with Lucy Stokes, "Not Just Lonely" with Phyllis Fairbanks, and "A Woman Is" with Leo Corday.

3 *Billboard*, December 24, 1966. "California Dreamin'" by the Mamas and the Poppas was listed as the No. 1 Top Single of 1966, followed by "96 Tears" by Question Mark and the Mysterians and "What Becomes of the Broken Hearted" by Jimmy Ruffin. The Top LP of 1966 was "Whipped Cream and Other Delights" by Herb Alpert and the Tijuana Brass. "Cherish" by the Association came in No. 2 on the Hot Singles list, followed by "(You're My) Soul and Inspiration" by the Righteous Brothers and "Reach Out I'll Be There" by the Four Tops.

4 National Archives, "Statistical Information about Fatal Casualties in the Vietnam War," Incident or Death Date (Year), April 29, 2008.

5 Lyndon B. Johnson, "Remarks at a Reception for a Group of Veterans of the War in Vietnam," December 15, 1966, The American Presidency Project, University of California at Santa Barbara, "Public Papers of the Presidents."

6 "From the Rack," *The Age* (Melbourne, Australia), October 17, 1968.

7 Quoted in the *Washington Post*, January 14, 1967, p. 46.

8 AP article in, for example, the Greenwood, South Carolina, *Index-Journal*, February 2, 1967.

9 Evelyn M. Dent, "Hearty Time Had by All at Military's Valentine Ball," *Washington Star*, February 4, 1967, p. 11.

10 AP article in, for example, *Greensboro Daily News*, February 6, 1967, p. 16, and the *Amarillo Globe-Times*, March 8, 1967, p. 4.

11 Lila Brown, writing in the *Bemidji Daily Pioneer*, March 13, 1967.

12 Russel Kay, writing in the *Playground Daily News* of Fort Walton Beach, Florida, June 22, 1967.

13 Bobbetta Gochis, writing in the La Crosse (Wisconsin) *Tribune*, April 16, 1967.

14 Bonnie Aikman, "Troubadour of Vietnam," *Evening Star*, March 12, 1967, p. 54.

15 Clarence Doucet, "The Boy in the Green Beret," *Times-Picayune*, April 2, 1967, p. 59.

16 Linda J. Greenhouse, "Ghost of the Green Beret," *Harvard Crimson*, March 4, 1967. Greenhouse, who graduated from all-female Radcliffe College, then all-male Harvard University's "women's annex," in 1968, went on to a Pulitzer Prize–winning reporting career at the *New York Times*, where she covered the U.S. Supreme Court for three decades.

17 According to the Fort Bragg Press Center, bragg.army.mil/Pages/Museums.aspx.

18 Mike Causey, "Jokes and Songs Launch Bond Drive," *Washington Post*, April 13, 1967.

19 Author interview, December 9, 2015.

20 Robert Powers, "The Rise and Fall of Barry Sadler," *Crawdaddy* magazine, p. 33.

21 Skip Hollandsworth, "Notes on 'Only Nam Hero,'" *Dallas Morning News*, October 18, 1979, p. 6C.

CHAPTER ELEVEN – BEING A FAMILY

1 Author interview, September 14, 2015.

2 Originating as a radio show in the early 1930s, *Death Valley Days* began as a syndicated TV show in 1952 and ended its run in 1970. The half-hour westerns were shot in desert areas of California, Utah, and Arizona and sponsored by the Pacific Coast Borax Co. (maker of 20 Mule Team Borax). *Death Valley Days* TV hosts included future President Ronald Reagan.

3 Quoted in "Ballad Writer Turns Actor," Statesville, North Carolina, *Record and Landmark*, February 3, 1968, p. 2.

4 Author interview, December 24, 2015.

5 Author interview, September 14, 2015.

6 Author interview, February 7, 2016.

7 Shea worked primarily as a TV sitcom director and producer for four decades. Among many others shows, he directed 110 episodes of *The Jeffersons* in the 1970s and 92 of *Silver Spoons* in the 1980s.

8 Dan Pavillard, "Balladeer Barry Sadler Now Making Movie," *Tucson Daily Citizen*, December 4, 1967, p. 3.

9 "Sadlers Get Beachcomber Drink Permit," *Tucson Daily Citizen*, January 3, 1968.

10 Author interview, June 11, 2015.

11 Author interview, December 29, 2015.

12 E-mail to author, February 2, 2016.

13 Author interview, April 21, 2015.

14 See William Head, "The Battles for Saigon and Hue During the Tet Offensive of 1968," *Virginia Review of Asian Studies*, Vol. 27 (2015), p. 78.

15 Some 300 western movies and TV shows have been filmed and taped in Old Tucson and on its sound stages since 1939.

16 E-mail exchange with author, December 28, 2015.

17 A. H. Weiler, "Dayton's Devils," *New York Times*, October 3, 1968.

18 *L.A. Times*, Powers, p. Z-20.

19 Author interview, April 13, 2015.

20 Author interview, September 12, 2015.

21 *Village Voice*, p. 17.

22 See Blaine Taylor, *Volkswagen Military Vehicles of the Third Reich: An Illustrated History* (Da Capo, 2004), p. 95.

23 Author interview, December 29, 2015.

24 *L.A. Times*, Powers, pp. Z-19, Z-20.

25 Quoted in Robert Windeler, "Defiant Wayne Filming *Green Berets*," *New York Times*, September 27, 1967, p. 41.

26 Renata Adler, "Screen: 'Green Berets' as Viewed by John Wayne: War Movie Arrives at the Warner Theater," *New York Times*, June 20, 1968, p. 49.

27 Charles Mohr, "U.S. Special Forces: Real and on Film," *New York Times*, June 20, 1968, p. 49.

28 Gilbert Adair, *Vietnam on Film: From the Green Berets to Apocalypse Now* (Proteus, 1981), p. 51.

29 Brock Garland, *War Movies* (Facts on File Publications, 1987), p. 110.

30 *Chicago Sun-Times*, June 26, 1968. See also rogerebert.com/reviews/the-green-berets-1968

31 "The *Playboy* Interview," *Playboy* magazine, May 1971, p. 89.

32 Author interview, June 12, 2015.

CHAPTER TWELVE – A NICE GUY

1 *L.A. Times*, Sipchen.

2 Quoted by Deirdre Donahue, "The Balladeer of the Green Berets, Sgt. Barry Sadler, Now Pens Pulp Novels," *People*, July 7, 1986, p. 139.

3 National Archives, "Statistical Information about Fatal Casualties in the Vietnam War," Incident or Death Date (Year), April 29, 2008.

4 Author interview, January 13, 2016.

5 Author interview, April 28, 2015.

6 In the Abilene, Texas, *Reporter-News*, August 11, 1971, p. 52.

7 *Wichita Eagle*, May 19, 1971, p. 2. Founded in 1958 by Robert W. Welsh Jr., an executive with the James O. Welsh Company, a candy manufacturer, the John Birch Society, Thomas Mallon wrote in the January 11, 2016, *New Yorker*, "was the most robust political fringe group of its day." The group's main goals, Mallon wrote, were "thwarting any U.S.-Soviet cooperation, withdrawing America from the United Nations, exposing communists in the federal government, and impeaching Chief Justice Earl Warren."

8 E-mail exchange with author, January 5, 2016.

9 *L.A. Times*, Powers, p. Z-19.

10 Robert Powers, "The Rise and Fall of Barry Sadler," *Crawdaddy*, August 1973, p. 32.

11 R. Kent Burton, "'Green Berets' Balladeer Has Much to Remember," *Tucson Daily Citizen*, p. 3.

12 Barkwill orchestrated two publicity stunts for Montie Montana in New York City in June 1971: taking his horse, Poncho Rex, to the top of the Empire State Building and into the barbershop at the Hilton Hotel to get his whiskers cut.

13 Author interview, September 21, 2015.

14 Author interview, September 14, 2015.

CHAPTER THIRTEEN – WHERE THE MONEY IS

1 Author interview, December 29, 2015.

2 E-mail to author, January 2, 2016.

3 Author interview, April 13, 2015.

4 Author interview, June 8, 2015.

5 See *Newport Navalog*, October 25, 1974.

6 See the Lincoln, Nebraska, *Evening Journal*, May 16, 1675, p. 1.

7 Advertisement in the Mansfield, Ohio, *News-Journal*, May 23, 1975.

8 McMahon, age twenty-one, and Judge, age nineteen, were killed during a North Vietnamese army rocket attack near Tan Son Nhut on April 29, 1975, as they were protecting American diplomats about to leave South Vietnam. They had been in country for only about a week. Their bodies were, indeed, left behind, but were sent to the United States in March of 1976. McMahon was buried in Woburn, Massachusetts, his hometown; Judge in his hometown, Marshalltown, Iowa.

9 Advertisement in the Winchester, Virginia, *Evening Star*, August 20, 1976.

10 Author interview, September 14, 2015.

11 Author interview, June 11, 2015.

12 Author interview, October 19, 2015.

13 E-mail to author, February 3, 2016.

14 Fate Thomas was indicted and convicted of taking kickbacks and other corruption charges and served four years in a federal prison from 1990 to 1994.

15 Photocopy of Barry Sadler's Sheriff's Office, Davidson County ID from the files of Detective Jim Sledge, Metropolitan Police Department, Nashville, 1978.

16 Author interview, August 18, 2015.

17 *GQ*, p. 304.

18 Quoted in Stephanie Mansfield, "A Singing 'Duke' Put Patriotism on the Charts," *Washington Post*, February 5, 1978, p. K 1.

19 That allegorical movie—a surreal reworking of Joseph Conrad's novel *Heart of Darkness*—is considered a cinematic classic, earning the number thirty spot on the American Film Institute's list of the 100 best American movies.

20 *The Tennessean*, September 24, 1978, p. 108.

21 *GQ*, pp. 247, 304. Billy Arr declined to be interviewed for this book.

22 Barry Sadler, *Everything You Want to Know About the Record Industry* (Aurora Publishers, 1978), p. xii.

23 Stacy Harris, "So You Want to Break Into Music," Nashville *Banner*, August 5, 1978.

24 *The Tennessean*, July 9, 1978, p. 90.

CHAPTER FOURTEEN – THE ONLY HERO OF THE VIETNAM WAR

1 Stephanie Mansfield, "A Singing 'Duke' Put Patriotism on the Charts," *Washington Post*, February 2, 1978, p. K6. Lash Larue was a 1940s and 1950s cowboy movie star; the Cisco Kid, a 1950s TV cowboy hero.

2 Joe Edwards, "Nashville Sound," in, for example, the Childress, Texas, *Index*, March 25, 1978.

3 "Green Beret Singer Shifts Musical Image," Nashville *Banner*, November 21, 1978.

4 Author interviews, June 16, 2015, and October 28, 2016.

5 *GQ*, p. 304.

6 Author interview, September 14, 2015.

7 Author interview, June 8, 2015.

8 State of Tennessee, Division of Probate and Paroles, "Work Sheet for Pre-Sentence Report," Darlene Yvonne Sharpe, May 29, 1980, p. 3.

9 Author interview, September 14, 2015.

10 Robbins later claimed that he had written those songs. See Dennis Glaser, *Music City's Defining Decade: Stories, Stars, Songwriters & Scoundrels of the 1970s* (Xlibris, 2011), pp. 126–27.

11 Author interview, August 18, 2015.

12 Inscribed photo of Darlene Sharpe from the Nashville Metropolitan Police Department files.

13 Glaser, *Music City's Defining Decade*, p. 125.

14 FBI records of Bellamy from the Nashville Metropolitan Police Department files.

15 See "Shooting Case Taken to Court," *Billings Gazette*, April 3, 1953.

16 *Billboard*, January 28, 1956.

17 *Billboard*, June 9, 1956.

18 Dennis Glaser, "A Tough Dude with the Knack for Cranking Out Country Hits," *Country Rambler* magazine, December 2, 1976, p. 4.

19 Ibid.

20 Metropolitan Police Department, Nashville, Tennessee, "Voluntary Statement of Darlene Sharpe," December 4, 1978, p. 1.

21 Darlene Sharpe to Lee Bellamy, April 16, 1978, Metropolitan Police Department, Nashville, Tennessee.

22 According to testimony in "BELLAMY v. SADLER (640 S.W.2d 20 [1982]), Rodney Wayne BELLAMY, Sr., Plaintiff-Appellant, v. Barry SADLER, Defendant-Appellee, Application for Permission to Appeal," Court of Appeals of Tennessee, Western Section, Sitting at Nashville, October 4, 1982.

23 Author interview, June 16, 2015.

24 Testimony in BELLAMY v. SADLER (640 S.W.2d 20 1982)

CHAPTER FIFTEEN – THAT'S MURDER ONE, AIN'T IT?

1 The bulk of this account of the events of December 1, 1978, and the police and legal work that went into the murder case is based on extensive interviews, conversations, and e-mail exchanges with Jim Sledge, as well as the case's voluminous files in the Nashville District Attorney's office.

2 Barry told a friend he and Darlene were having sex on the living room couch at that moment.

3 The prescription slips (in the names of Lee Emerson, W. A. Jennings, and Darlene Sharpe) were for the stimulants Preludin, Ritalin, and Biphetmine (black beauties) and other drugs.

4 Author interview, September 14, 2015.

5 The news also went international. Jim Sledge remembers seeing a copy of the *Times of London* with a headline about the murder on the front page.

6 See, for example, "Singer Barry Sadler Slays Songwriter," Santa Cruz, California, *Sentinel*, December 3, 1978.

7 Barry received the nightstick in May of 1967 when he attended a Chicago Police Department awards ceremony in the Windy City.

8 "Sadler Case Woman on Scene during Accidental Shooting," Nashville *Banner*, December 5, 1978.

9 Author interview, October 1, 2015.

10 Joe Binkley Sr., who died in 2001, "was one of the best—if not the best—criminal defense lawyers in Nashville," his son, Davidson County Circuit Court Judge Joe Binkley Jr., said in a July 22, 2015, interview. "He worked magic in the courtroom."

11 Quoted in Mike Pigott, "Emory Death Facts Set for Grand Jury," Nashville *Banner*, May 4, 1979.

12 Author interview, August 18, 2015.

CHAPTER SIXTEEN – A TOTAL TENNESSEE REDNECK

1 E-mail to author, June 16, 2015.

2 San Bernardino County *Sun*, June 3, 1979.

3 Shriver and Johnson were quoted in *The Tennessean*, June 2, 1979.

4 Quoted in *The Tennessean*, June 27, 1979.

5 *L.A. Times*, Sipchen.

6 See, for example, "Barry Sadler Turns Novelist," Santa Fe *New Mexican*, August 5, 1979.

7 No one ever asked Guss for permission to use that image—a version of which appeared on the covers of most of the *Casca* books. "As a gesture of good will I gifted him with a master 11x14" print of the image," Guss said. "I never gave Barry permission to use reproductions of my gift in any editorial or commercial venture." When he discovered the situation, Guss said, "I let the matter pass." E-mail to author, January 5, 2016.

8 Author interview, June 16, 2015.

9 Skip Hollandsworth, "Notes on 'Only Nam Hero,'" *Dallas Morning News*, October 18, 1979, p. 1C.

10 See Grahame Browning, "Songwriters Bring Hits to Seminar," *The Tennessean*, October 18, 1979, p. 40.

11 *Rodney Wayne Bellamy, Sr., Plaintiff v. Barry Sadler and Darlene Sharpe, Defendants*, Circuit Court for Davidson County, Tennessee, Sitting at Nashville, No. C-10442, November 28, 1979.

12 Associated Press article in, for example, the Greenwood, South Carolina, *Index-Journal*, February 6, 1980.

13 Kurt Schmalz, "Case Like 'A Bad Novel' to 'Green Beret Sadler,'" Nashville *Banner*, February 9, 1980.

14 Sherman also could have been named after another Nashville police detective, Sherman Nickens.

15 In a January 25, 1980, internal memo, Torry Johnson summed up Joe Binkley's two main arguments that led to the plea deal: "They will portray Sadler as the all-American boy who served in Vietnam and was nothing but a fine, upstanding soldier, albeit that he was having some kind of an affair with Darlene Sharpe at the time of the incident. As far as Bellamy is concerned, they have lined up numerous people to come in and testify that he was without any redeeming features."

16 Nashville Probation Office, "Work Sheet for Pre-Sentence Report," May 29, 1980.

17 Quoted by Adell Crowe, "Court Slashes Sadler's Term in Gun Death," *The Tennessean*, September 27, 1980.

18 Quoted in Billy Cox, "The Ballad of Barry Sadler," *Florida Today*, July 5, 1983, p. 1C.

19 *GQ*, p. 244.

20 Author interview, August 16, 2015, and e-mail to author, January 30, 2016.

CHAPTER SEVENTEEN – THE SLOW DESCENT

1 Author interview, October 1, 2015.

2 Author interview, June 8, 2015.

3 *L.A. Times*, Sipchen.

4 Author interview, September 14, 2015.

5 In "Barry Sadler With a Bullet," John Ed Bradley said Duke Faglier described himself in 1990 "as a cop, a ballistics expert, a self-defense instructor, a martial artist, a cracker-jack rifleman, a bodyguard to the stars, a musician proficient at thirteen instruments, an ace photographer, a former mercenary who fought for Truth, Justice and the American Way, a Great White Hunter . . . , a songwriter, a diarist, an editor of several of Barry Sadler's books, the subject of a future biography, the lover of more women than you could ever hope to count . . . , and the husband of a woman who works at what he repeatedly refers to as a 'titty bar.'" (p. 244)

6 Author interview, June 15, 2015.

7 Author interview, October 19, 2015.

8 Barry Sadler, *Razor* (Charter Books, 1988), pp. 21–22.

9 Author interview, June 12, 2015.

10 E-mail to author, April 22, 2015.

11 Author interview, October 1, 2015.

12 Author interview, September 24, 2015.

13 See, for example, advertisements in *The Tennessean*, November 23, 1980, p. 69, and December 14, 1980, p. 177.

14 "Paris Businessman Sentenced, Fined in Banker Attack," *The Tennessean*, July 21, 1982.

15 "Ex-Deputy Pleads Guilty to Lesser Count in Assault," *The Tennessean*, December 3, 1982.

16 *L.A. Times*, Sipchen.

17 National Archives, National Personnel Records Center, "Information Releasable Under the Freedom of Information Act, Faglier, Harvey Larry." NA FORM 13164, July 7, 2015.

18 Author interview, October 1, 2015.

19 Author interview, July 7, 2015. Frederick Faust (1892–1944) wrote some 300 western novels, many under the pseudonym Max Brand. Louis L'Amour (1908–1988) wrote some ninety western novels.

20 Author interview, July 12, 2015.

21 Author interview, June 22, 2015.

22 Walter Carter, "'Nashville with a Bullet': Musical Murder Mystery," *The Tennessean*, January 2, 1982.

23 See Gloria Ballard, "Hockey, Fashion Team Up Friday," *The Tennessean*, February 7, 1982, p. 84.

24 Jack McGraw, in "Where the Mercs Are: Suds, Studs and Duds in Guatemala City's Bar Don Quijote," *Soldier of Fortune*, February 1989, wrote: "Rosson and Sadler first met under fire in Vietnam, 25 years ago in the U.S. Army Special Forces, and have been firm friends ever since. Between them they have fought in nine armies, rather more wars, and countless short-term assignments." Cynthia Cotts, in the *Village Voice*, wrote that Rosson "hired out to a dozen war zones. . . . Like all Green Berets trained to kill, he has no compassion and a reputation for brutality."

25 Author interview, October 1, 2015.

26 See *Special Operations Association* (Turner Publishing, 2006), p. 112.

27 Court of Appeals of Tennessee, Western Section, "Bellamy v. Sadler," 640 S.W.2d 20 (1982).

28 Author interview, August 6, 2015.

29 Author interview, July 16, 2015.

30 Quoted in Billy Cox, "The Ballad of Barry Sadler," *Florida Today*, July 5, 1983, p. 1C.

31 Author interview, October 1, 2015.

32 Author interview, September 14, 2015.

33 Author interview, October 19, 2015.

34 Author interview, June 8, 2015.

35 Author interview, June 11, 2015.

36 Author interview, June 16, 2015.

37 *GQ*, p. 305.

CHAPTER EIGHTEEN – LIFE OUT ON THE EDGE

1 Author interview, June 16, 2015.

2 Photocopy of contract, courtesy of Rob Robison.

3 Quoted in Drew Jubera, "Requiem for a Green Beret," *Atlanta Constitution*, December 31, 1989, p. M2. Jubera also quoted Lavona Sadler saying: "He wasn't a mercenary; mercenaries get paid."

4 Quoted in Mike Sante, "'Ballad of the Green Berets' Ruined Sadler's Life, Friends Say," KRTN news service, November 1, 1990. See Baton Rouge *State Times Advocate*, p. 45, for example.

5 Mark Wolf, "Barry Sadler, A 'Soldier at Heart,' Fights for His Life," *Rocky Mountain News*, September 16, 1988.
6 Quoted in Jim Molpus, "Sadler's Death Leaves Questions," Nashville *Banner*, November 6, 1989.
7 Quoted in Jubera, *Atlanta Constitution*, December 31, 1989, p. M2.
8 Writing as Gene Scroft, "Eternal Mercenary," *Soldier of Fortune*, February 1989, p. 36. Motley was killed by Karen guerrillas in Burma in May 1989 while on assignment for *Soldier of Fortune*.
9 Author interview, June 16, 2015.
10 McGraw, "Where the Mercs Are," *Soldier of Fortune*, February 1989, pp. 38–39.
11 President Ronald Reagan encouraged private groups to support the Contras, calling such efforts "quite in line with what has been a pretty well established tradition in our country." Reagan said he would "be inclined to not want to interfere with" individual Americans working with the Contras. See Philip Taubman, "Private Aid to Latin Rebels at Issue," *New York Times*, December 13, 1982.
12 Information from business cards collected by Robbie Robison at the Don Quixote.
13 Author interview, June 16, 2015.
14 *GQ*, p. 305.
15 *Village Voice*, p. 18.
16 Scroft, "Eternal Mercenary," p. 80.
17 Author interview, September 30, 2015.
18 Deirdre Donohue, "The Balladeer of the Green Berets, Sgt. Barry Sadler, Now Pens Pulp Novels," *People*, July 7, 1986, p. 143.
19 *Village Voice*, p. 19.
20 *GQ*, p. 305.
21 Author interview, July 7, 2015.
22 Author interview, June 22, 2015.
23 Scroft, "Eternal Mercenary," p. 80.
24 *GQ*, p. 306.
25 Author interview, August 17, 2015.
26 *GQ*, p. 306.

CHAPTER NINETEEN – THE CONSTITUTION OF AN ELEPHANT

1 *Village Voice*, p. 20.
2 See the sidebar, "Sadler Shooting," accompanying Lance Motley's (writing as Gene Scroft) *Soldier of Fortune* magazine article, "Eternal Mercenary," February 1989, p. 35.
3 Barry Sadler, *Casca: The Eternal Mercenary* (Charter, 1979), pp. 2–3.
4 Quoted by Mike Sante, "'Ballad of the Green Berets' Ruined Barry Sadler's Life, Friends Say," Baton Rouge *State-Times*, November 1, 1990, p. 45.
5 Author interview, September 30, 2015.
6 *GQ*, p. 245.
7 *L.A. Times*, Sipchen.
8 *GQ*, p. 247.
9 *Village Voice*, p. 20.

10 Author interview, October 21, 2015. Hal Hardin is a former U.S. attorney in Nashville, Circuit Court judge, and law professor at the Nashville School of Law.

11 Author interview, June 16, 2015.

12 "Affidavit of Claim, In re: Barry Sadler, Thor Sadler, Petitioner," Probate Court of Davidson County at Nashville, February 1, 1989. Brown was not repaid until after Barry died. "We requested payment from the estate [but] they refused, [so] we had to go legal," Brown said in a March 13, 2015, e-mail to the author, and "finally got reimbursed, but the lawyers cost me $3,000."

13 *GQ*, p. 242.

14 Local TV news raw footage provided to author by Rob Robison.

15 Quoted in Jim Molpus, "Sadler Is Critical but Stable," Nashville *Banner*, September 13, 1988.

16 Associated Press article, September 13, 1988. See, for example, "'Green Beret' Writer Critical After Being Shot in the Head," *Kokomo Tribune*, September 13, 1988, and "Balladeer of the Green Berets Badly Wounded in Guatemala," *New York Times*, September 15, 1988, p. A-8.

17 United Press International article, September 14, 1988. See, for example, "Barry Sadler, Vietnam Balladeer, Shot at Home," *Boston Herald*, September 14, 1988, p. 22.

18 Quoted by Jerry McCaskill, "Singer Reported Critical After Brain Surgery Here," *The Tennessean*, September 14, 1988.

19 Author interview, September 15, 2015.

20 Author interview, May 23, 2014.

21 Author interview, June 8, 2015.

22 Quoted by Mark Wolf, "Barry Sadler, 'A Soldier at Heart' Fights for His Life," *Rocky Mountain News*, September 16, 1988.

23 United Press International article, September 23, 1988, "Sadler, 'Green Berets' Composer, Still in Coma." See, for example, Tyrone, Pennsylvania, *Daily Herald*, September 23, 1988.

24 Quoted by Jim Molpus, "Comatose Sadler Shows Signs of Recovery," Nashville *Banner*, October 15, 1988.

25 Author interview, September 30, 2015.

CHAPTER TWENTY – THE LAST BATTLE OF THE VIETNAM WAR

1 Author interview, September 14, 2015.

2 Author interview, September 22, 2015.

3 Author interview, June 8, 2015.

4 Author interview, June 16, 2015.

5 Author interview, September 22, 2015.

6 Bebe Sadler to Barry Sadler, October 17, 1988, Barry Sadler files at the law offices of Hal Hardin, Nashville, Tennessee.

7 Author interview, September 14, 2015.

8 Somers died on April 27, 1995. Hill—who served in the army from 1962 to 1976—died January 27, 2014.

9 Author interview, October 21, 2015.

10 Quoted in Karen Henderson, "Friends Assail Care Given to Legendary Author at VA," Cleveland *Plain Dealer*, November 7, 1990, p. 31.

11 The only local media report on Barry's alleged mistreatment was the November 7, 1990, article cited above in the *Plain Dealer*. The article also mentioned "numerous complaints" about the care at the Cleveland VA, including "dirty conditions." ABC-TV's *Prime Time Live* had investigated the situation in the fall of 1990. On October 10, 1990, the *ABC Evening News* reported that the hospital's administrator, Dr. Peter Stajudhar, had been "temporarily relieved" of his position.

12 Author interview, June 12, 2015.

13 *L.A. Times*, Sipchen.

14 Quoted by Karen Farkas, "'Green Beret' Singer Faces Tests," Cleveland *Plain Dealer*, January 14, 1989.

15 *L.A. Times*, Sipchen.

16 Quoted in "Mental Testing Ordered for Sadler," Nashville *Banner*, January 14, 1989.

17 Author interview, October 21, 2015.

18 James M. Perry to Paul Hill, January 9, 1989, copy of letter in the Barry Sadler files at the law offices of Hal Hardin, Nashville, Tennessee. Perry claimed that he wrote to H. Ross Perot, asking the Texas billionaire to provide the funds for the "private physical therapy the VA wouldn't provide." Perot's sister, Perry said, called him to say that her brother didn't contribute to "individuals, only organizations." See "Ross Perot a 'Phony,'" Letter to the Editor, Mobile, Alabama, *Register*, July 29, 1992, p. 5.

19 *Village Voice*, p. 21.

20 Author interview, September 14, 2015.

21 Quoted in the Cleveland *Plain Dealer Magazine*, October 22, 1989, p. 20.

22 Quoted by Jose Lambiet, "Barry Sadler Legal Battle Shifts to Ohio Courtroom," Nashville *Banner*, January 13, 1989.

23 Barry was able to shave, brush his teeth, and eat, but only with the use of a ball bearing feeding orthosis, also known as a mobile arm support, a mechanical metal armlike device that is attached to a wheelchair. For every other bodily function, including urinating and defecating, he depended on help from the nursing staff. He also suffered from chronic anemia.

24 Quoted in Karen Henderson, "Friends Assail Care Given to Legendary Author at VA," Cleveland *Plain Dealer*, November 7, 1990, p. 31.

25 Quoted in John Griffith, "Ailing 'Green Beret' Author Focus of Guardianship Fight," Cleveland *Plain Dealer*, January 12, 1989, p. 16-A.

26 Author interview, September 14, 2015.

27 Probate Court for Davidson County, Tennessee, "In Re: Lavona Ruth Sadler . . . Petitioners. Petition for Appointment of Guardian and Entry of a Temporary Restraining Order," Civil Action 92032, January 10, 1989.

28 Author interviews, September 15 and September 22, 2015.

29 *L.A. Times*, Sipchen.

30 Ibid.

31 Headlines in *The Tennessean*, January 11, 1989; Nashville *Banner*, January 11; *Los Angeles Times*, January 11; Cleveland *Plain Dealer*, January 12; Macon, Missouri, *Chronicle Herald*, January 12; Associated Press, January 12; *Seattle Times*, January 12.
32 Quoted by Kirk Logan, "Sadler Said Unwilling to Return to Nashville," *The Tennessean*, January 12, 1989. Joseph Meissner practices law in Cleveland. He did not return several voice mail messages from the author.
33 Court of the Common Pleas, Probate Division, Cuyahoga County, Ohio, "In the Matter of Barry Allan Sadler," Temporary Restraining Order and Judgment Entry, Docket 1026, Case No. 1027942C, January 13, 1989.
34 Probate Court of Cuyahoga County, Ohio, "In Re: Barry Sadler, Alleged Incompetent," Report of Investigator, Docket 1026, Case No. 1027942, January 9, 1989.
35 *Village Voice*, p. 20.
36 Quoted in "Judge Describes Sadler as Alert but Disoriented," Nashville *Banner*, January 31, 1989, and Karen Farkas, "Singer to Get Independent Guardian," Cleveland *Plain Dealer*, February 1, 1989, p. 12.
37 Probate Court of Cuyahoga County, Division of the Court of Common Pleas, "In Re: Barry Allan Sadler, Alleged Incompetent," Judgement Entry, Docket 1026, Case No. 1027842, January 31, 1989.
38 Author interview, October 21, 2015.
39 Quoted in Jim Molpus, "Local Lawyer to Handle Sadler Affairs," Nashville *Banner*, February 10, 1989.
40 Probate Court for Davidson County, Tennessee, "In Re: Lavona Ruth Salder . . . Petitioners. Order of Appointment of Guardian," Civil Action 92032, February 9, 1989.
41 Probate Court for Davidson County, Tennessee, "In Re: Lavona Ruth Salder . . . Petitioners. Report of Guardian Ad Litem," Civil Action 92032, February 9, 1989.
42 Barry Sadler, *Casca: The Trench Soldier* (Jove Books, 1989), p. 153.
43 Ibid., p. 98.

CHAPTER TWENTY-ONE – A MAN'S MAN

1 Named in honor of Tennessee native army sargeant Alvin Cullum York (1887–1964), one of the most decorated soldiers of World War I.
2 In a letter to Hal Hardin, Steve Somers, Joe Meissner, Bebe, Lavona, and Robbie Robison, May 26, 1989. In the Barry Sadler files in the law offices of Hal Hardin in Nashville.
3 Quoted in the Cleveland *Plain Dealer Magazine*, October 22, 1989, p. 20.
4 Author interview, September 15, 2015.
5 Ibid.
6 Author interview, September 22, 2015.
7 Author interview, November 5, 2015.
8 Quoted in Todd Eisenstadt, "Singer, Novelist Barry Sadler Dies in Murfreesboro Hospital," *The Tennessean*, November 6, 1989.
9 Quoted in Jim Molpus, "Sadler's Death Leaves Questions," Nashville *Banner*, November 6, 1989. The famed pianist Vladimir Horowitz died the same day at age eighty-seven in New York City.

10 Author interview, September 14, 2015.
11 Ibid.
12 Author interview, June 11, 2015.
13 Author interview, October 1, 2015.
14 Quoted in Jim Molpus, "Sadler Saluted by Elite Army Corps," Nashville *Banner*, November 10, 1989.
15 Author interview, August 10, 2016.

A NOTE ON SOURCES

I interviewed more than seventy people for this book, some of them—including Lavona Sadler, Bill Parrish, Bob Barkwill, Jim Sledge, Bob Powers, Robbie Robison, Hal Hardin, Steve Sherman, and Steve Bruno—extensively. All quotes from interviews and e-mails are footnoted. Barry Sadler's children—Thor, Baron, and Brooke—chose not to contribute to the book.

I made extensive use of Barry Sadler's official U.S. Air Force and U.S. Army records, which are publicly available—since he is a celebrity—from the National Archives Military Personnel Records section in St. Louis. I found the official records of Barry's main unit in Vietnam, Special Forces Detachment A-216 at Camp Hardy, at the National Archives in College Park, Maryland.

Barry Sadler's 1967 memoir, *I'm A Lucky One*, which essentially he dictated to the writer Tim Mahoney, served as a roadmap for the first few chapters of this book. I tried to corroborate what I used from the book with primary sources.

I searched through thousands of newspapers using several online newspaper archives. Newspapers.com, genaologybank.com, and news paperarchive.com specialize in small and medium-size newspapers, many of which covered Barry Sadler in 1966 and 1967 when "The Ballad" was popular. Google Books was a main source for secondary material, as well as for virtually all the back issues of *Billboard* magazine.

Former Nashville Police Detective Jim Sledge allowed me unlimited access to all of his files from the Lee Bellamy murder case, scores of documents that are stored at the U.S. Attorney's Office in Nashville. Sadler family attorney Hal Hardin helped me go through a mountain of legal documents, letters, and other materials related to the legal wrangling over Barry's medical care after he was shot in Guatemala in 1988.

Four journalists—John Ed Bradley, Cynthia Cotts, Bob Sipchen, and Robert M. (Bob) Powers—wrote extensively researched articles on Barry. The late Lance Motley—writing under the pseudonym Gene Scroft—also interviewed Barry and his friends in Guatemala for his article "Eternal Mercenary" in the February 1989 issue of *Soldier of Fortune* magazine.

Those journalists interviewed many people, including several key players in Barry's life who have since died. A good number of quotes from their articles play an important part in this book. I am grateful for their work and for Bradley, Cotts, Sipchen, and Powers's help in 2015 and 2016 when I was writing this book.

Here are the citations and the abbreviations I used for those articles in the endnotes.
Bradley, John Ed, "Barry Sadler with a Bullet," *GQ*, April 1990—*GQ*
Cotts, Cynthia, "Veteran Blues," *Village Voice*, April 4, 1989—*Village Voice*
Powers, Robert M., "Ain't Gonna Sing About War No More," *Los Angeles Times, West Magazine*, November 28, 1971—*L.A. Times*, Powers
Staff/Sgt. Barry Sadler with Tom Mahoney, *I'm A Lucky One* (Macmillan, 1967)—*I'm A Lucky One*
Sipchen, Bob, "The Ballad of Barry Sadler: The War-Glory World of an Acclaimed Soldier of Song Has Shrunk to a Hospital Bed, and a Bitter Family Battle, *Los Angeles Times*, January 27, 1989—*L.A. Times*, Sipchen

What follows is an alphabetical list of those I interviewed for this book.
Paul Alford, Walter Anderson, Bob Barkwill, Joe Binkley Jr., Chip Bishop, John Ed Bradley, Ferrel Broslawsky, Bob Brown, Steve Bruno, John Buchan, Cynthia Cotts, Nelson DeMille, Jay Diamond, Philip Duer, Pat Duncan, Dale Dye, Ron Edwards, Larry Emons, Joe Ewald, Bill Fogarty, Janice Fox, John Furgess, Vernon Gillespie Jr., John Gissell, Seth Gitell, Tommy Gomez, Frank Graham, H. D. Graham, David Lee Guss, Tom Haberkorn, Joe Hannon, Hal Hardin, Jim Hasse, Richard Jenkins, Hugo Keesing, Suzy Kelly, John Kitch, Bruce Love, Al Maracaibo, Frank McAdams, William McManus Sr., Greg McNamee, Phil Milio, Jim Morris, John Opshinsky, Earl Owens, Philip Page, Bill Parrish, Doug Peacock, Felix "Pete" Peterson, Robert Powers, Jane Rager, Justin Ramsdell, Art Reed, Allen Richter, Rob Robison, Lavona Sadler, Hank Schlesinger, Ray Severn, Eliza Shallcross, Steve Sherman, Jim Schisler, Bob Sipchen, Rich Sirois, Jim Sledge, Loretta Sparkman, Howard Tritz, Jimmy Walker, Al Weed, Al Wilhelm, David Willson, and Patricia R. Young.

INDEX